AN INTRODUCTION TO
ROMAN LEGAL AND
CONSTITUTIONAL
HISTORY

AN INTRODUCTION TO
ROMAN LEGAL AND CONSTITUTIONAL HISTORY

SECOND EDITION
based on the sixth German edition
of *Römische Rechtsgeschichte*

WOLFGANG KUNKEL

*Emeritus Professor of Roman Law at the
University of Munich*

TRANSLATED BY J. M. KELLY

*Professor of Jurisprudence and Roman Law
University College, Dublin*

OXFORD
AT THE CLARENDON PRESS

Oxford University Press, Ely House, London W. 1

GLASGOW NEW YORK TORONTO MELBOURNE WELLINGTON
CAPE TOWN IBADAN NAIROBI DAR ES SALAAM LUSAKA ADDIS ABABA
DELHI BOMBAY CALCUTTA MADRAS KARACHI LAHORE DACCA
KUALA LUMPUR SINGAPORE HONG KONG TOKYO

ISBN 0 19 825317 6

© *Oxford University Press 1966, 1972*

First edition 1966
Second edition 1973
Reprinted 1975

(*Sixth German edition 1971:*
Böhlau-Verlag, Köln and Graz)

Printed in Great Britain
at the University Press, Oxford
by Vivian Ridler
Printer to the University

CONTENTS

FOREWORD

THIS short introduction to the history of the Roman state and of Roman law corresponds in its scope and arrangement with the lecture-courses in Roman legal history customarily taken by law-students at the German universities. Naturally, the most important thing for a young law-student is to gain some knowledge of the factors which determined the growth of Roman *private* law; and for this reason I have limited my treatment of constitutional history to a simple outline, and have dealt, in connection with criminal law, more with procedure than with the substantive rules, and discussed civil procedure only in so far as I thought this indispensable for an understanding of praetorian legislation. In general, I have acted in the belief that it was more important to provide a clear historical picture than to offer detailed information on individual points.

The bibliographical appendix is not intended to provide support for the conclusions in the main body of the work, but rather to afford the reader some idea of the basis of our knowledge and of the development of research. In accordance with this purpose I have not merely given a list of sources and book titles, but have attempted to make the appendix into a readable text with a short description of at least the most important works. The fact that the book was originally intended for German students explains the preponderance in the appendix of books and articles in German; though the translator has added some additional references to important works in English.

The English version is based on the text of the fourth German edition. I am most grateful to my friend Professor Kelly for undertaking the work of translation.

W. K.

Munich, November 1965

FOREWORD TO THE
SECOND EDITION

THIS second English edition incorporates changes and additions made in the fifth and sixth German editions. My thanks are due once more to Professor Kelly for undertaking this substantial work of revision, and I am grateful also to the Clarendon Press for agreeing to reset the entire work.

W. K.

Munich, July 1972

Part One

THE EARLY PERIOD: TO THE MID THIRD CENTURY B.C.

1

THE EARLY CITY STATE AS THE STARTING-POINT OF ROMAN LEGAL DEVELOPMENT

1. *Area and population*

THE history of Roman law, the law destined ultimately to dominate the civilized world, began in a community the modesty of whose circumstances it would be difficult to exaggerate. The early Roman state was one of those numerous city states of antiquity which were built around a fortified settlement, the scene of commercial traffic and of all political life; around it stretched a countryside on which nothing stood but isolated farmsteads and open hamlets. An impression of the smallness of this hinterland—the entire area of the Roman community's state—may be gained from the *ambarvalia*, a solemn procession around the fields in which sacrifices were offered at various erstwhile boundary-points, which took place each year in May and continued into Christian times; it took in an area which could be comfortably crossed on foot in any direction in three hours. In the economic conditions of the early Roman period this area, perhaps about fifty-eight square miles, can have sustained only about 10,000 or 12,000 persons.

In the first dim centuries of Roman history both area and population increased considerably. At the beginning of the fourth century B.C., at a time when the city was already playing an important part in the political life of central Italy, and when its sack by the Celts attracted attention as far away as Greece, the Roman state occupied about 600 square miles, many times its original area, but still not more than half the area of modern Luxembourg. Not until the fourth and third centuries B.C. did Rome develop into a state which might be called large by modern standards and which eventually came to dominate all Italy. This development into a large state was, however, also significant in the history of Roman law, for it brought with it fundamental economic changes which imposed entirely new tasks on the legal system.

The population of Rome was basically of Latin race. It was connected with other Latin communities, its neighbours to the east and south, by a common language, a similar culture (and legal system), and also by the immemorial tribal cult of Jupiter Latiaris which had its seat on the *mons Albanus*, three hours south-east of Rome. The speech of the Latins, destined through the political rise of Rome to become a world language, is one of the Indo-European group of languages and is thus related in origin to Greek, Celtic, Germanic, and Indo-Iranian. Of these the most closely related to Latin was Celtic, while the speech of the Umbro-Sabellian and Samnite tribes bordering on the Latins to the north-east, east, and south-east shows a closer relationship with Greek. Like these neighbouring peoples, the Latins must have immigrated into Italy in prehistoric times, probably in the later second millennium B.C. Whence and how they came is disputed; but archaeological finds seem to indicate that their ancestors had once been settled in the Danubian lands of southern Hungary and Serbia. It is likely that in the course of their migration and later in Italy itself they absorbed other racial elements as well as foreign cultural influences; at any rate, the earliest recognizable form of Latin-Roman culture already exhibits basic features which must be regarded as 'Mediterranean' and indeed partly as specifically 'Italic'.[1]

The nature and extent of these foreign cultural influences becomes more clearly discernible in the age of early Roman history, i.e. from the sixth century B.C. onwards. They came in this era principally from two culturally superior peoples, the Etruscans and the Greeks.

The Etruscans lived directly to the north of the Roman state. This people, organized in numerous city states, speaking a non-Indo-European language, and with a culturally predominant stratum which seems to have originated in the north-west of Asia Minor, exerted at the zenith of its power what was to be a more or less enduring influence over the whole of Italy. Etruscan art, great quantities of which have been revealed by archaeology, followed Greek originals so far as form was concerned, but transformed these originals with its own very characteristic spirit. In other cultural areas as well, notably that of religion, the Etruscans developed in

---

[1] This fact must throw doubt on the attempts frequently made by scholars of the older generation to explain the beginnings of the Roman legal and social system by reference to Indo-European peoples, in particular the Germanic race.

their own way ideas which came from Greece. Particularly in the second half of the sixth century B.C., Rome was intensely affected by its Etruscan neighbour, who at that time had gained a foothold also in the south of Latium on the coast of Campania. There is no doubt that the Roman royal dynasty of the Tarquins was of Etruscan origin, and a whole series of noble Roman families which flourished later in the Republic have Etruscan names. Culturally the Etruscan influence made itself felt chiefly in Roman religion; in particular, the cult of the Trinity of the Capitol (Jupiter, Juno, Minerva) was borrowed from Etruscan cities, and the Temple of Jupiter on the Capitol, dedicated in 509 B.C., together with its wooden image of the god, was, according to reliable tradition, created by Etruscan artists; the originally imageless cult of the Roman gods experienced a general change under Etruscan influence. It was from Etruria too that Rome received the custom of the augury of political and military enterprises from the entrails of sacrificial animals (while augury from the flight of birds, although devoted to the same purpose, was probably an original Roman institution). Attempts have been made to discern Etruscan elements even in Roman law and in particular in the system of the Roman state; but here we are left with more or less uncertain hypotheses, since we have no reliable information on corresponding Etruscan institutions. However, we may be certain that some of the symbols of Roman magistral power were borrowed from the Etruscans.

The content of Greek influence over Rome is easier to appraise, although no great clarity exists as to the route which it took. Up to about the year 1900 many scholars assumed a direct influence of Greek culture on Rome, and this influence was associated with the Greek colonies of lower Italy, in particular with the mighty city of Cumae in Campania. Today, on the other hand, the predominant view is that the Etruscans were mediators, at least in the earlier period. Thus the origin of the script used by the Romans, the Latin alphabet, is generally assumed to be the Etruscan alphabet, which of course in its turn was borrowed from the Greeks. The Greek gods, too—Apollo, Hermes-Mercury, Athena-Minerva, Artemis-Diana—which had already become domesticated at Rome by the sixth century B.C. were probably brought there by the Etruscans. Thus, in spite of the break caused by the half-barbaric Etruscan civilization these were in fact genuine rays of the Greek spirit that reached Rome in its early history. In the legal sphere, where Greek influence becomes noticeable around the middle of the fifth century in the Twelve Tables legislation (although it may go back even further), Etruscan mediation cannot be proved, for we have no notion of the Etruscans' own legal system. But in all these cases of foreign mediation we are dealing only with isolated elements which were absorbed by the strength of a vigorous population and transformed into their own institutions and forms of thought. Not until very much later was Rome hellenized in a deeper sense, when Greek influence penetrated the whole of spiritual and material life.

II. *Economic and social conditions*

Rome in its early period was a community of farmers. It is possible that the advantageous position of the city on the navigable Tiber (which at this point moreover was easily bridgeable) and on the ancient *via Salaria* into the Sabine country was an early encouragement to trade and industry; but during the entire early period and for a long time thereafter political and economic power was associated with the ownership of land. This lay at first almost exclusively in the hands of a comparatively small number of noble families (*patricii*) who also, as knights (*equites*), formed the core of the Roman army. They were separated from the mass of the Roman people (*plebs*) by a huge social gulf; according to the law of the Twelve Tables marriage between patricians and plebeians was not allowed (although, according to tradition, this was changed in the year 445 B.C. by a *lex Canuleia*); and the plebeians were excluded from offices of state until the struggle of the orders in the fifth and fourth centuries, and from some priesthoods at all times.

A considerable proportion of the *plebs* seems originally to have consisted of small dependent farmers who lived on patrician-owned land. The patrician landowners were themselves farmers and not mere absentee landlords; they conducted their farming with their sons and a few slaves and thus they needed for themselves only a fraction of the land they owned. The rest they allowed plebeians, who had themselves little or no land, to occupy by way of *precarium*; these plebeians thus became their *clientes* and were obliged to lend them support in war and politics. In return the patrician lord was obliged to afford his clients protection and help in every necessity. How strictly this duty of the *patronus* was regarded may be seen from a provision of the Twelve Tables (VIII. 21) which outlawed the *patronus* who abandoned his *cliens*.

This original form of *clientela* seems to have disappeared early, presumably through the economic and social rise of the *plebs* which had begun by the fifth century B.C. But very similar relationships of loyalty and protection persisted into later times and remained at every period a characteristic feature of Roman life. These social phenomena influenced the political development of Rome to such a degree that the nature and working of the Roman state cannot be understood if we disregard them. As late as the time of Cicero and Caesar political battles were conditioned by them; and Augustus founded his authority upon, among other things, ancient Roman notions of social and political dependence. And at the very end of Roman history we find again, in the relationship between landowner and half-free tenant (*colonus*), almost the same form of client-status as existed in the earliest period.

The patrician nobility was organized according to clans (*gentes*), a system which was perhaps peculiar to it. The members of the *gens* were united by a common name and a common cult for as long as they were still descendants of the original patricians in Rome, and up to the late Republic a right to inherit and to be a guardian was associated with *gens*-relationship. There is no doubt that these were only the relics of the very important position occupied by the *gens* in the early period: there are, for instance, certain indications that patrician land was once in the collective ownership of the *gentes*. At any rate the *gentes* with their following of clients were bodies of great strength and unity, and composed a very powerful (sometimes too powerful) element within and alongside the system of the state, which by comparison took a long time to assert itself.[1] On one occasion it seems that a *gens* undertook a single-handed feud against Rome's neighbours (see the account in Livy 2. 50 of the fall of the Fabii in the fight against Veii); and as late as the fourth century one can observe how certain powerful and noble *gentes* and their dependants keep recurring throughout whole generations in the magistracy-lists.

The absolute dominance of the patrician nobility was assured so long as the cavalry recruited from its ranks remained the basic fighting arm of the Roman military levy. But this situation changed

[1] According to a widely accepted theory of the Italian legal historian Pietro Bonfante, the *gentes* were a form of political organization older than the state, and the state in fact arose out of a federation of *gentes*. This theory cannot be examined here; but it can be said that it is not susceptible of any strict historical proof.

with the introduction of hoplite tactics; brought from Greece, they spread all over Italy and, as we know from archaeological finds, were adopted in Rome before the end of the sixth century. Henceforth the core of the army was provided by the heavily armed infantry recruited from the more well-to-do plebeian farmers. This class, which had formerly been nothing but a disorganized horde of baggage-carriers in the field of battle, now became the principal bearer of the burdens and spoils of war. As in many Greek commonwealths some generations earlier, so too in Rome this revolution in military methods brought political change with it, and the *plebs* joined battle with the patrician families in a struggle for political equality. This struggle, which lasted about a century, ended with a certain degree of democratization of the Roman state. But this was in appearance only: in reality the aristocratic political leadership remained unbroken. The only difference was that a certain number of plebeian families, which had in the course of time risen to wealth and political importance, now shared political power with the patrician families.[1]

The part played by slavery in the rustic society of the early Roman period was fairly small, not to be compared with its role in the later Republic and Empire. The unfree serf ate the same bread as his master, and at the same table, and was protected against personal injury by a statutory composition of half the amount prescribed for the case of a free man (Twelve Tables, VIII. 3); if he were set free he was still required to be loyal to his former lord, just like a *cliens*, and (unlike the practice of later times) did not acquire citizenship. A peregrine in Rome was in principle without rights,[2] just like a freed slave, and needed the protection of an influential citizen, unless he happened to belong to the racially kindred Latins or to some other community to which *commercium* had been granted, i.e. a position of equality with Roman citizens in private legal relations.

Although the production of the necessaries of life by domestic industry was certainly the rule, the exchange of goods for money was a very ancient aspect of Roman economic life. The description .

---

[1] Many of the distinguished plebeian families, moreover, derived from the nobility of neighbouring communities which had been closely connected with the Roman nobility and finally migrated to Rome.

[2] In the Twelve Tables a foreigner is called *hostis*; he was thus described by the same word as was afterwards used only for 'enemy'. The word *peregrinus*, meaning 'foreigner', is later, and indicates one who has come over land (*per agros*).

of money as *pecunia* (from *pecus*) betrays the fact that cattle were once used as the medium of exchange; and, at the time of the Twelve Tables, fines were still reckoned in terms of cattle and sheep. But from about 1000 B.C. onwards copper (*aes*) appears in Italy as a medium of payment. Later it was stamped with a mark as a sign of purity, and from the third century B.C. onwards in Rome was minted, or rather cast, in clumsy coins weighing a pound each (*as librale*). Of course foreign and especially Greek coins may have been in circulation a fairly long time before this.

III. *The state*

1. *Populus Romanus.* The Romans never thought of the state in the abstract way we do today. It was not for them an impersonal power standing in opposition to the individual, whose actions were dependent on its permission, but rather the individuals themselves —that is, the citizens—collectively. For this reason they knew no other name for it than the name of the community, *populus Romanus*; this phrase was used for as long as the republican tradition lasted, which was well into the Empire, as the technical description of the Roman commonwealth.[1] At the same time it was customary in official documents to mention the Senate as well as the *populus* and indeed before it (SPQR: *senatus populusque Romanus*); we see reflected here the mighty position of power enjoyed by the Senate in the middle and late Republic.

2. *The popular assemblies.* The body of citizens which gave the state its name was also, in the Republic at least, its supreme political organ. In its assembly (*comitia*, from *com-ire*, to come together) decisions were taken on war and peace, magistrates were chosen, and statutes passed. On these occasions, however, the people functioned not as an unorganized mass but divided into groups. In the fully developed republican constitution there were three separate modes of grouping the whole community, modes which clearly arose at different periods and were of different natures.

Only the oldest mode, the curiate assembly (*comitia curiata*), can

---

[1] *Res publica* (*res populi*) was not a technical description of the state as such, although the usage of the word in authors of the late Republic and Empire is often not far away from the modern notion of the state. Basically the phrase means the affairs (or the property) of the *populus*, i.e. of the state. It means 'republic' in the modern sense only where it is used by authors of the Empire in contrast to the dominance of the emperors; though here the expression usually used is *libera res publica*. See W. Suerbaum, *Vom antiken zum frühmittelalterlichen Staatsbegriff* (1961), pp. 1 ff.

be definitely dated to the period of the kings. In its historical form it can perhaps be traced to the sixth century B.C., but its origins probably lie much further back, and may well be contemporaneous with the first emergence of a Roman commonwealth.

In this assembly the citizens grouped themselves according to their *curiae* (*curia* presumably = *co-viria*, 'group of men'). These *curiae*, thirty in number, were themselves organized in three groups of ten each, and each group formed a third (*tribus*) of the whole community; like the *phratries* (brotherhoods) of the Greek cities, they were bodies of a sacral character with their own cults and religious organs. The influence of the patrician *gentes* was predominant in them, and indeed many scholars think that the plebeians did not belong to the *curiae* at all; though this is unlikely, since the curiate organization seems to have been the basis of the oldest Roman military system, from which the plebeians can scarcely have been excluded. Each of the three *tribus* provided one squadron of cavalry (later the number rose to two and more squadrons); and each *curia* may have originally provided a hundred infantrymen (*centuria*).

The only functions of the *comitia curiata* in the Republic were in the field of sacral law; and this assembly met usually under the presidency of the *pontifex maximus*, the head of the state religious system.[1] And since the curiate organization no longer had any real existence, the *comitia curiata* of the Republic operated without any real participation of the citizens. The assembly in practice consisted merely of thirty officials, each of whom had to represent one *curia*. As to the sphere of operation of the *comitia curiata* in the regal period it is difficult to be certain; it certainly played a part in the inauguration of the king and in some of his religious ritual activities, and probably even at that time its principal importance lay in the religious field. It seems at least doubtful whether it ever had the power of making specifically political decisions, e.g. as to war and peace.

On the other hand, the *comitia centuriata*, the second mode of assembly, had from the very beginning a real political character.

---

[1] Sometimes, however, under the presidency of a consul or praetor, but only if this magistrate after election by the *comitia centuriata* (see below) obtained the benefit of the *lex curiata de imperio*, which gave him the formal right to exert his power of command, particularly referable to war. Probably even this purely formal act had a meaning connected with sacral law. It may have arisen from the co-operation of the *comitia curiata* in the inauguration of the kings.

For this the citizens were divided into 'hundreds' (*centuriae*), the military origin of which is perfectly obvious. For as long as there existed a Roman citizen army, the infantry was arranged in centuries; and a whole series of warlike ceremonies which always remained peculiar to this form of the popular assembly confirms the supposition that the *comitia centuriata* was in essence none other than the heavily armed infantry force drawn up for the exercise of political functions. It must therefore have emerged shortly after the introduction of hoplite tactics, i.e. towards the end of the sixth or beginning of the fifth century. By the time of the Twelve Tables the *comitia centuriata* seems to be already known (Tab. IX. 2: *comitiatus maximus*).

In the only form of the constitution of which we have any real knowledge, the Servian constitution (so-called because according to tradition it was introduced by the last king but one, Servius Tullius), the centuriate organization had certainly lost its military character and had become simply a system of voting and imposing taxes. In it the citizens were divided according to their property into classes, each of which contained a fixed number of centuries irrespective of its actual numerical strength. The total number of 193 centuries was distributed among the classes in such a way that the more prosperous classes—the knights able to equip a horse (*equites*), together with the next highest class—had an absolute majority with ninety-eight centuries.[1] This was because the votes of the individual citizens were counted only within each century: their majority produced the vote of the century concerned; and the end result of the voting was obtained from the majority of the centuries. Since, in addition, the centuries were not called up simultaneously but in their class-order and the voting only continued until a majority vote was achieved, the less well-off citizen normally had no opportunity to make any real use of his right to vote. This organization of the citizen body cannot have served any military purpose at this stage: it is obviously a result of simple political voting arithmetic, the intention of which was to ensure the preponderance of the wealthy in this, the most important, form of popular assembly. The highest magistrates (consuls, praetors, and censors) were chosen by the *comitia centuriata*; it also passed

---

[1] Under a later reform of the centuriate organization (of which both date and details are equally uncertain) the balance seems to have been shifted to some extent in favour of the lower classes.

statutes (*leges*) on the proposal of the convening magistrates, as a rule the consuls, and gave formal decisions on peace and war. According to the provisions of the Twelve Tables mentioned above, it alone was competent in political trials in which the life of the accused citizen was at stake (i.e. when the trial was *de capite civis*).

In contrast to the *comitia centuriata*, the *comitia tributa*, the third and probably latest form of the Roman citizen assembly, had a clearly civil character from the very beginning. Here the citizens were organized according to their residence in the different districts of the Roman state; these were called *tribus*, like the three divisions of the citizen body in the *comitia curiata*, but had no recognizable connection with the latter. Around 400 B.C. there were twenty such districts. Four of these, the *tribus urbanae*, lay in the centre of the city, while the others, called after patrician families, were situated in the immediate neighbourhood of Rome (*tribus rusticae*).[1] Between the fifth century and the middle of the third century the number of districts grew to thirty-five, through the setting-up of new rustic *tribus* on conquered territory. This was the final figure, although the area of the Roman state kept on increasing until it eventually incorporated the whole of Italy. It was the custom to assign to one of the existing *tribus* communities which had been received into the Roman citizen body, as well as individual persons who had been granted Roman citizenship. In this way the *tribus* division tended more and more to lose its local relevance and became in the end a purely personal organization of the citizens.

In the *comitia tributa* the members of a single *tribus* formed a voting body with the same function as a *centuria* in the *comitia centuriata*. The decisions resulted from a majority of the *tribus* and not from a majority of the citizens entitled to vote, and since—at any rate in the early period—the rustic *tribus*, numerous though individually weaker in numbers, contained the farming class, while the urban *tribus*, few but individually stronger in numbers, contained the urban and mostly landless population, the conservative element long retained a clear preponderance in this form of the popular assembly, in which the lesser magistrates were elected,

[1] Already in the year 312 B.C. the censor Appius Claudius Caecus had allowed landless citizens (who until that time had remained outside the *tribus*) to be registered in all the *tribus* then existing (Livy 9. 46. 10 ff.). The later censors, however, restricted them to the four urban *tribus*. It was not until the social changes after the Punic wars and the reception of new citizens that the composition of the rustic *tribus* was transformed; though these still retained a higher prestige than the urban *tribus*.

laws enacted, and fines inflicted for contravention of statutes. The less well-off citizens do not seem to have won a decisive voice in the *comitia tributa* until the second century B.C.

The citizens formed themselves into *curiae*, *centuriae*, or *tribus* only for the purpose of voting on the bill proposed by the presiding magistrate or on an election proposal (*rogatio*). Mere communications from the magistrate, as well as speeches by persons introduced by the magistrates, were made in an unorganized assembly (*contio*). But the popular assemblies met only at the call of a competent magistrate and possessed no right of initiating legislation (unlike the Athenian democracy, for example); their only power was either to accept or reject the proposals laid before them.

3. *The kingship*. At the summit of the Roman commonwealth in the earliest times stood the king (*rex*), who exercised not only the military and political leadership but also the representation of the community *vis-à-vis* the gods. The political might of the kingship immediately before its fall (traditionally dated 510 B.C.) is reflected in the powers of the republican magistracy which replaced it. The outward attributes which the republican magistrates inherited from the kings point to a position of superiority and a far-reaching authority: for example, the purple garment, which the republican magistrate put on only on the occasion of a triumph after a victorious campaign, but which presumably was worn by the king on all ceremonial occasions; also the official servants (lictors), who went in procession in front of the magistrates, constantly ready for the execution of punishments with their axes and bundles of rods (*fasces*); and the magistral seat on a high stage (*tribunal*) and 'carriage-chair' of carved ivory (*sella curulis*) used in judicial proceedings. The Romans themselves traced these marks of kingly power back to the Etruscan models (see e.g. Livy 1. 8. 3), and there is much to be said for the suggestion that the political power of the kingship illustrated in these forms reached its highest point of development in the reigns of the last Etruscan kings.

Other antiquated features of the kingship come into view on a consideration not of the republican magistracy but of the priesthood which succeeded the kings on the sacral plane. The (life-long) holder of this office was called *rex sacrorum*: this was not a new office, different from the kingship, but was the old kingship itself; for as long as a Roman state cult remained it continued to exist in its sacral function because only a king possessed the necessary

magic power. The way in which this *rex sacrorum* was chosen
obviously goes back to ancient ideas about the rightful king's
closeness to the gods and about his magical powers, and may
therefore be applied to the early Roman kingship with a high degree
of probability. The king was neither elected nor nominated by his
predecessor but was revealed by the gods through a sign (especially
through the flight of birds). Thus the *rex sacrorum* of republican
and imperial times, having been taken (*captus*) by the president of
the college of pontiffs learned in the sacral law (the *pontifex maximus*), was presented to the gods, in the presence of the *comitia
curiata*, for their approval by means of a sign (*auguratio*). It is
certainly no accident that Roman tradition reports such *auguria* in
the case of Romulus and Remus (Livy 1. 6. 4 f.) and of Numa
Pompilius (Livy 1. 18. 6 ff.). A special partly religious, partly magical charisma, similar to the old Germanic *Königsheil*, was thus the
basis of the kingly power, and the sacral function of the king was
originally just as essential as his political and military functions,
with which it was indissolubly connected. During the later (Etruscan) kingship, however, a more rationalized interpretation of its
political power must have arisen; for otherwise the fall of the
kingship, i.e. the restriction of its power to its sacral function,
would hardly be comprehensible.

4. *The republican magistracies.* The yearly elected magistrates
(*magistratus*: superiors) who took over the government after the
expulsion of the last Etruscan ruler held merely the military command and political power, and this situation is not altered by the
fact that their entry into office and their conduct of their office
always remained associated with religious acts (the taking of
auspices). The area of religion remained under the priests, among
whom the college of *pontifices*, as the highest expert authority,
advanced more and more into the foreground in such a way that
its president became the king's superior.

The earliest development of the chief republican magistracy is
very much disputed in its details. By contrast to Roman tradition
—according to which the dual occupancy of the office goes back to
the first year of the Republic (510 B.C.) and the holders of the office
were from the beginning called consuls—a common modern opinion
is that originally the number of office-holders was something other
than two and that they differed from each other in rank. Support
for this idea is provided, among other things, by the fact that Roman

tradition, even from the last decades of the fifth and the beginning of the fourth centuries, reports large colleges of magistrates with memberships of varying size, with military and political leaders in the place of consuls (*tribuni militum consulari potestate*). The consular constitution undoubtedly became usual after that period. The question naturally arises whether it was really a revival of an older system, which had been obsolete for generations and could hardly have still had a place in the political consciousness. As against such doubts, however, there is the evidence of the *fasti consulares*, the list of names of all the principal magistrates, which has been for the most part epigraphically preserved. This represents a very secure basis for the unambiguous tradition of the original duality of the republican consulship. It is a source which has repeatedly shown itself reliable in other respects and its evidence can hardly be finally contradicted by the other hints available to us. Thus the most likely thing is that the highest Roman office was occupied by twin magistrates from the very beginning of the Republic. However, the oldest name for the holders of this office seems to have been not *consuls* but *praetors*. The law of the Twelve Tables speaks of the praetor, not of the consul, and the text of an old statute preserved in Livy (7. 3. 4 ff.) calls the magistrate who was at that time highest in rank *praetor maximus*.[1] Praetor (from *praeire*, to precede) denotes the military commander, thus emphasizing the most elementary and, in primitive social conditions, most important function of the magistrate. Still, the authority of the praetor almost certainly also had a civil side from the very beginning. This covered the areas which were later described as *coercitio* (executive power) and *iurisdictio* (jurisdiction) and which, together with the function of military command (*imperium* in the narrow sense), made up the concept of all-embracing authority (*imperium* in the wider sense). In addition, as instruments of their political leadership, the praetors had the power to convene the people in assembly, the power to propose elections and bills to be voted on (*ius agendi cum populo*), and the right to summon and consult the senate (*ius agendi cum senatu*).

On campaign (*militiae*) the holder of *imperium* could, up to the

---

[1] This passage of Livy is also used to disprove the originality of the consular constitution. It must be admitted that the notion of *praetor maximus* accords ill with a system of two magistrates, in principle of equal rank, who changed around only in the exercise of their official powers.

second century B.C., inflict corporal punishment at his discretion on the disobedient citizen and could even have him executed. But 'at home (*domi*), i.e. within the city boundaries marked by the first milestone out of Rome, a Roman citizen threatened with corporal or capital punishment could 'invoke the help of the people' (*provocatio ad populum*) unless of course he had previously been found guilty in a formal trial. This right of *provocatio* presumably arose in the course of the struggles between the patricians and the plebeians, and when these ended it was formally recognized in 300 B.C. by a *lex Valeria*.[1] This imposed a limit on the right of magistrates with *imperium* to exercise their *coercitio* within the city boundaries of Rome; this limitation could be enforced by other magistrates of similar or higher rank, and in particular by the tribunes of the people, whose intervention (*intercessio*) was commonly invoked in such cases (*appellare*). This restriction of the *imperium* is illustrated by the usage whereby the official servants of the magistrate, when in the centre of the city (*intra pomerium*), bore with them only the ceremonial bundles of rods, omitting the axes they carried outside the city boundary.

Other factors, too, effectively limited the apparent omnipotence of magistral *imperium*. The duration of office was in principle restricted to one year (the so-called principle of annuality); and at any one time two or more magistrates with similar powers functioned alongside one another (the so-called principle of collegiality). Collegiality prevailed in particular after the introduction of the consular constitution; and so at least from the early fourth century (*leges Liciniae Sextiae*, 367 B.C.) there was collegiality between the twin bearers of the highest *imperium*, who were now called consuls.[2]

The principle led to odd and dangerous consequences; for example, to a daily changing supreme command whenever both consuls took the field together and not in different theatres of war; and the right of each to nullify the official acts of the other through his *intercessio*. It is one of the mysteries of the Roman state that this system produced no more calamities than it did. In situations of crisis, of course, the dangers of collegiality could be excluded by

---

[1] Roman tradition knows of three *leges Valeriae de provocatione* (509, 445, and 300 B.C.), of which, however, probably only the last is historical. The Twelve Tables' clause about criminal procedure before the *comitia centuriata* has nothing to do with the right of *provocatio*.

[2] Mommsen interpreted *consules* as 'colleagues' by means of deriving the word from *consalire*, 'to leap together'; nevertheless, it is more probable that it is connected with *consulere* and describes those magistrates who were accustomed to consult the Senate.

the appointment of a dictator; and each consul could make such an appointment. The dictator in his turn could nominate a commander of cavalry (*magister equitum*) as his assistant. For the duration of his office, which was limited to six months and in any case ended with the going out of office of the consul who had nominated him, the dictator possessed the highest military and civil powers, while the *imperium* of the consuls was in abeyance (Polybius, 3. 87. 7) or was only exercised in so far as the dictator permitted it.[1]

Besides the two consuls, after the *leges Liciniae Sextiae* of 367 B.C. there functioned a third bearer of *imperium* who thenceforth bore alone the old title of praetor. He was subordinate to the consuls (*minor collega consulum*) although his *imperium* was in every way similar to theirs. In the normal course the function of *iurisdictio* belonged to him and not to the consuls; and in a case of need he could take the place of consuls who were dead, absent, or otherwise engaged, for other military or political functions. As the burden of jurisdiction as well as of military and political leadership began to increase, from the middle of the third century onwards, new praetorships were created; their holders were used partly in the administration of justice in the city of Rome, and partly for the carrying on of war and government in Roman possessions overseas (unless the importance of a particular theatre of war demanded the sending of a consul). It is indicative of the structure of the republican city state and of the political thinking of the Romans that the growing volume of business was not met by the creation of special offices, as afterwards under the Principate, but that the idea of a unitary and all-embracing *imperium* was adhered to.

Of course there were from very ancient times a number of offices which had not only limited duties but also limited powers in the fulfilment of these duties. Their holders certainly possessed official authority commensurate with their spheres of operation (*potestas*) but had no general power of command (*imperium*). The oldest of these offices is the quaestorship. It was created about the middle of the fifth century B.C.,[2] perhaps as a model derived from the Greek cities in Italy for the administration of the state treasury (the

---

[1] The dictator system is regarded by many modern authors as the original republican system of government, which was revived in later times for emergencies.

[2] In the year 447 B.C. (according to Tacitus, *Ann.* 11. 22) popular elections of quaestors took place for the first time. These treasury quaestors have probably nothing to do with the *quaestores parricidii* (= murder investigators) who were mentioned in the Twelve Tables (IX. 4) and who must have had functions of a judicial kind.

aerarium populi Romani), and was at first, like the consulship, a dual office. In the same century, however, according to tradition, two further quaestors were added, who were to serve in wartime as administrators of the military treasury and assistants of the commander. From 267 B.C. onwards eight quaestors were elected each year, from Sulla onwards twenty, and these new posts were for the administration of Italy and the provinces. Later than the quaestorship is the office of the curule aediles. Together with the plebeian aediles, who were originally special officers of the *plebs*, they policed the streets and markets; but, unlike the plebeian aediles, they exercised jurisdiction in market disputes and in certain matters of public order. Being thus administrators of justice they were entitled (unlike the plebeian aediles) to the judicial chair (*sella curulis*), and their title derives from this distinction.

The censorship was also a magistracy with a special sphere of duties. The two censors, who were elected only once every five years and remained in office for eighteen months, had to supervise the citizen roll and keep it up to date; in particular, they had to fix the distribution of the citizens into the classes of the Servian constitution and into *tribus*, and to carry out the formal reception of past magistrates into the Senate (*lectio senatus*). It was their duty also to arrange for the contracting of public works and for the letting out of state-owned lands. Their office enjoyed special prestige, in particular because, as well as being charged with the classification of citizens and the *lectio senatus*, they functioned in a certain sense as judges of morals. From the mid third century onwards it was almost the invariable rule that only ex-consuls (*viri consulares*) were chosen as censors; and the censorship was regarded as the crown of a great political career.

All these magistracies were offices of honour (*honores*), from whose holders the expenditure of considerable sums of money for the common good (and later for the amusement of the citizens) was expected: expenditure which could be met out of a military commander's booty only if he were victorious. Salaries were drawn only by constables, messengers, and scribes, who were not magistrates in the Roman sense, but merely subordinate assistants of the magistracy. Their social standing was so low that freedmen were usually employed in these offices. The practical influence of these magistrates' servants (generically called *apparitores*, from *apparere*, to be at someone's orders, to wait on someone) was also in general inconsiderable, since the magistrates exercised their office personally and by word of mouth whenever possible. Not until the Principate did the beginnings of a bureaucracy emerge.

5. *The Senate.* The third component of the Roman constitution, along with the popular assemblies and the magistracies, was the 'Council of Elders' (*senatus*). There is no doubt that it already existed in the period of the kingship. While at that time it was probably a gathering of the heads of the patrician nobility, it changed during the Republic more and more into a council of ex-magistrates. To have occupied a magistracy became a normal prerequisite to reception into the Senate, and with the gradually increasing number of magistracies there arose what was nothing less than a definite expectancy of a seat in the Senate (in principle tenable for life). Around 216 B.C., when after the battle of Cannae it was necessary to replenish the gravely thinned ranks of the Senate, this expectancy existed only for ex-consuls and ex-praetors; but a hundred years later ex-aediles were included. Shortly afterwards ex-tribunes of the *plebs* were added, and, from Sulla onwards, ex-quaestors. The ex-magistrate did not, it is true, count strictly as a member of the Senate (*qui in senatu sunt*) before the next censors had carried out a *lectio senatus*; but he was allowed, immediately on the ending of his year of office, to take part provisionally in sessions of the Senate and to cast his vote, and was reckoned one of those *quibus in senatu sententiam dicere licet.*

The Senate was organized in classes according to rank, and the classes corresponded to the offices previously held by the members. In the first class there stood, accordingly, the ex-consuls (*consulares*); there followed the ex-praetors, ex-aediles, etc. Since it was the practice of the presiding magistrate to ask the senators for their opinions according to this order of rank,[1] the senior members tended to lead the discussion. All the power and experience of the politically dominant stratum of Rome was concentrated in the Senate, which amid the yearly change of magistrates was the one point of stability in Roman political life; and this is the reason for the immense power that this body enjoyed for centuries. Without possessing any legislative or executive power of its own, the

---

[1] From the end of the third century B.C. until Sulla there was an official leader of the Senate (*princeps senatus*) who had the right of expressing his opinion first. He was one of the oldest and most respected of the *consulares*. In the last century B.C. the custom was to consult first the consuls-designate (i.e. those who had been elected for the following year but had not yet entered upon their office).

Senate, as a standing source of advice (*consilium*) for the magistrates, held the real leadership of the state firmly in its own hands.
Its resolutions, clothed in the form of advice and therefore called
'counsels' (*senatus consulta*), embodied the most important political
decisions; and through its right of administering the community's
finances together with a clever exploitation of the limitations on
magistral power arising from annuality and collegiality it was able
to bend the resistance of the magistrates to its will. The period of
the Senate's ascendancy was the proudest period of Roman history;
and its decay marked the decline and fall of the republican system.

6. *Political result of the struggle of the Orders. Special organs of the
plebs.* At the beginning of the Republic only members of the patrician nobility were capable of holding magistracies or seats in the
Senate; and the plebeians had to win admission to the magistracies
by way of the grave social struggles of the fifth and fourth centuries.
They achieved this step by step; even after the consulship had been
opened to them (367 B.C.) other magistracies still remained closed
for a long time. The patrician monopoly persisted longest in the
priesthoods: the office of *pontifex maximus* was not occupied by a
plebeian until 254 B.C., and some (politically insignificant) priesthoods remained for ritual reasons always reserved to patricians.

It is possible that plebeians were received into the Senate before
they were admitted to magistracies, since the holding of the latter
was, especially in early times, not absolutely necessary for obtain-
ing a place in the Senate. But the patricians retained in the Senate
certain privileges which were never abolished. The ancient form
of address *patres* belonged by law only to patrician senators. Only
the patrician senators possessed the right to approve decrees and
elections of the *comitia* (*auctoritas patrum*); a right of control which
was originally very important but which became very much less
so as soon as the practice was adopted of discussing in the full
Senate proposed bills and elections even before their introduction
in the popular assembly, and of having them authorized by the
patres forthwith. Lastly, a most special privilege of the patrician
senators was the ancient institution of the *interregnum*, which
certainly goes back to the regal period: if on account of deaths or
resignations there were no holders of *imperium* in office, then the
power of government (the *auspicia*) devolved back upon the
patrician part of the Senate; patrician senators took over the government (each of them for a maximum of five days) with the duty

of carrying out as soon as possible an election of new consuls. Even as late as the age of Cicero this procedure was a living institution.

The political equality won by the *plebs* was, broadly speaking, enjoyed in fact by only a comparatively small number of plebeian families which succeeded in reaching the consulship and in being recognized by the leading patrician families as their partners in political power. They united themselves with these to form a new ruling aristocracy, the so-called *nobilitas*, which for a very long time kept its ranks firmly closed against penetration by members of upstart families (*homines novi*).[1]

Decisive for the success of the *plebs* in the battle for admission to the magistracies was, without doubt, the possession by the *plebs* of an effective political organization of its own. The beginnings of this organization lay presumably in some cult of a religious kind, as is hinted by the name of what were probably the earliest special officers of the *plebs*, the aediles (from *aedes*, temple), who seem to have been originally the administrators of the sites of plebeian cults. On the other hand, they played hardly any part at all in the political struggle of the *plebs*, and were entrusted at an early date with general official duties of a police character. By contrast with them, the office of the *tribuni plebis* had probably at all times the purpose of defending plebeian interests against the ruling patrician families. A *coniuratio*, i.e. a solemn oath sworn by the entire *plebs*, to the effect that they would avenge with death any attack on the tribunes, gave the latter an immunity (*sacrosanctitas*) for the duration of their office. To lend aid to the individual citizen and to protect him against oppression and injustice (*auxilii latio*) was always their special duty. As an entity the *plebs* was organized in a *concilium plebis* arranged according to *tribus* (*concilium* from *conkalare = convocare*). The decrees of this body, convened and presided over by the tribunes, and including by far the greater part of the citizens, lent plebeian demands the necessary force.

After the end of the social struggles the special organs of the *plebs* remained in existence and managed to incorporate themselves in a peculiar way into the constitutional life of the whole community. Decrees of the *concilium plebis* (*plebis scita*) became

---

[1] The gradual climb of a family to the consulship (and thus to the *nobilitas*) was no rarity, but the winning of the consulship by a man without senatorial ancestors was most unusual. It happened only fifteen times in a period of 300 years.

binding on the entire people;[1] indeed, in the middle and late Republic this was the normal form taken by legislation. The tribunes of the people (whose number, originally probably varying, was later fixed at ten) were accorded the right of interceding against the official acts of all magistrates (except a dictator); any of them could thus cripple the activity of every ordinary holder of office. They were allowed to attend meetings of the Senate, at first only on the special tribune's bench which was set up at the door of the senate chamber, but finally won the right to summon and consult the Senate themselves (*ius agendi cum senatu*). The dangers which lay in the institution of the tribunate of the people were held in check for a long time through the united firmness of the patrician-plebeian aristocracy and through the extraordinary strictness and sobriety of Roman political thinking; indeed, it was in the tribunes and their right of *intercessio* that the Senate found a particularly reliable means of enforcing its will against over-confident magistrates. When, in the second half of the second century B.C., tribunes of the people appeared who were ready to oppose the will of the majority of the Senate and who pursued revolutionary goals with demagogic methods, it meant the beginning of the crisis within political life which ultimately led to the fall of the Republic.

[1] According to tradition this was statutorily recognized three times (449, 339, and 286 B.C.); but only the latest of these statutes seems credible (the *lex Hortensia de plebiscitis*).

2

THE *IUS CIVILE* OF THE EARLY PERIOD

I. *The code of the Twelve Tables*

THE first point in Roman legal history which is at all fixed is the famous legislation of the Twelve Tables, in which the Romans themselves perceived the basis of their entire legal life (*fons omnis publici privatique iuris*, Livy 3. 34. 6). Unjustified doubts have been raised as to the historicity of this work of legislation;[1] the traditional date assigned to it (451–450 B.C.) is probably at least approximately accurate, and the connection, insisted on by Roman historians, with the struggles of the patrician and plebeian orders which began about this time is credible. The Twelve Tables were the work of a commission of ten men (*decemviri legibus scribundis*); during the continuance of their activity all political power was entrusted to them and the ordinary magistracies were in abeyance.

Only fragments of the text of the Twelve Tables are preserved, and these only in the form of quotations in the literature of the late Republic and the Empire. It is largely uncertain how much has been lost, and in what sequence the individual fragments originally stood in the context of the whole; modern attempts at reconstruction, like that of Schöll (*Legis XII Tabularum reliquiae*, 1886), according to whose arrangement the Twelve Tables are cited today, are altogether hypothetical and sometimes quite improbable. Some of the legal texts handed down as being parts of the Twelve Tables may in fact be of later origin; and even the genuine bits are without doubt modernized in form, since the original text of the code, drawn up on twelve wooden tablets, perished at an early date (probably in the burning of Rome by the Celts in 390 B.C.) and the later Republic knew the wording of the code only in a form which had been more or less assimilated to the Latin of a later era. For

---

[1] In particular, by the Italian historian Ettore Pais and the French legal historian Édouard Lambert. The prevailing opinion is against them. But individual writers, nevertheless, continually utter opinions which are not very far away from this radically critical attitude towards the traditional view.

this reason the existing fragments are linguistically not difficult to understand; while if we had the unchanged Latin of the Twelve Tables' period we should probably have the greatest trouble in understanding it.[1] On the other hand, the legal meaning of the Twelve Tables fragments is often uncertain and disputed; in such cases the solution may be sought through evidence found elsewhere in literature or through comparison with other legal systems, in particular with Germanic and early Greek law.

Greek law, moreover, as has been already indicated in another connection, exerted a certain influence on the composition of the Twelve Tables, an influence of which antiquity itself was conscious; thus, for example, in the law of neighbouring landowners and of corporations Roman jurists saw a correspondence with Attic law (Gaius, *D.* 10. 1. 13 and *D.* 47. 22. 4).[2]

Yet the material influence of Greek law is restricted, so far as we can see, to such details as in no way detract from the peculiarly Roman character of the whole. This, again, does not exclude the possibility that the impulse to create such a legal code came from contact with Greek culture; a possibility which indeed seems supported by certain details of the (generally not very credible) tradition about the way in which the Twelve Tables came into being.

11. *The law of the Twelve Tables*

The Twelve Tables were—as the surviving fragments clearly show—a comprehensive codification of the law in force at that time. They included provisions about the course of legal proceedings, including the execution of judgement, and about those areas of law which are today sharply distinguished into civil and criminal but were still a unity in the eye of the ancient Roman legislator. On the other hand, they did not deal with the political system of the community or with the constitution of its courts. Thus, the legislators intended only to codify the *ius civile*, i.e. those rules

[1] A sample of the very oldest Latin is provided by an inscription from the Forum, much discussed and of still unsettled meaning, Dessau 4913 = Bruns, *Fontes*, p. 14 (end of sixth or early fifth century B.C.). See F. Leifer and E. Goldmann, *Zum Problem der Foruminschrift unter dem lapis niger* (*Klio*, Beiheft 27, 1932; older literature is cited there).

[2] These correspondences do not, however, prove (as the Romans supposed) that Attic law in particular was the direct model for the Twelve Tables, for the same provisions about the law of neighbours turn up also in the municipal code of Alexandria (preserved in a papyrus, Pap. Hal. 1. 79 ff.) and they may equally well have existed in the legislation —now lost—of the Greek cities of southern Italy.

which were applicable to the rights and duties of the individual citizen, but to do so as completely as possible. This limitation of subject-matter corresponds entirely with the purpose attributed by Roman tradition to the Twelve Tables, namely the safeguarding of the small man in particular against the arbitrary behaviour of the patrician nobility in legal relations and the administration of justice. It is not possible to say with certainty how far the legislators, in pursuit of this aim, carried out reforms in the law as they found it, since to a large extent only conjecture is possible about the law of the preceding period. Still, several individual provisions in which a certain social purpose can be seen may be attributable to measures of this kind.

The codification of the entire body of law (with the exceptions noted above), which until then had been very largely unwritten,[1] represented an enormously difficult task in the conditions of this early period. Even in the modernized form in which we possess the fragments of the Twelve Tables one can see how the legislators had to wrestle with the primitive and still untamed national speech in order to produce the correct expressions for the rules they laid down. The sentences are of extreme brevity, very similar in form and very simple in their structure. An 'if' clause, used to define the conditions for the application of a statutory rule, is followed by the rule itself in the imperative mood. The subjects governing the verbs are mostly unnamed; and often they change within the same set of sentences, so that the reader has to guess from sentence to sentence, from the context, who is the person in mind.[2] Much of what the legislators only hinted at, in particular the legal terms

---

[1] It may be presumed that before the Twelve Tables there were some norms and forms of sacral and civil law which were reduced into writing for the private use of the college of pontiffs. At least some of what the Romans called 'king's laws' (*leges regiae*) may go back to these priestly codes, which were later published, according to tradition, by a *pontifex* called Sex. Papirius (whence the phrase *ius Papirianum*).

[2] As an illustration we append (with a translation as far as possible literal) the provisions about summoning one's opponent to court, an act which the plaintiff had to carry out himself, without official help: 'Si in ius vocat, ni it, antestamino. Igitur em capito. Si calvitur pedemve struit, manum endo iacito. Si morbus aevitasve vitium escit, iumentum dato. Si nolet arceram ne sternito': 'If he summons to law, if he does not go, he shall call up witnesses. Then he shall seize him. If he evades arrest or resists (tries to flee?) he shall lay hands on him. If sickness or age is a weakness, he shall provide a beast to carry him. If he does not wish, he shall not provide a tilt-wagon.' The sense of *pedem struere* was disputed even among the late republican interpreters of the Twelve Tables. The 'laying hands' on the defendant (*manus iniectio*) is an act of formally assuming power over the defendant, while *capere* clearly means no more than 'seize'.

which they used, was certainly familiar to their contemporaries, but provided the occasion for controversies even to late republican jurists, and also make harder the task of the modern legal historian seeking to understand the text.

A large part of the code—according to the usual modern arrangement, the entire content of the first three Tables—concerned the law of procedure. Alongside a very ancient and strictly formal system of procedure (the *legis actio sacramento*)[1] this contained also a later and simpler system (the *legis actio per iudicis postulationem*), which, however, was only applicable to certain types of claim.

In the field of private law, as is not surprising in view of the rustic character of the early Roman commonwealth, rules concerning family rights, inheritance rights, and neighbours' rights predominate—in other words that part of the law of things which is most important in a farmer's daily life. By contrast, there is in the surviving Twelve Tables' fragments very little mention of commercial transactions or contracts; and indeed it can hardly be supposed that the code contained much about these matters, for this department of legal life was clearly very little developed. The Twelve Tables contain a harsh form of debt-contract, in which the borrower, through the receipt of the money weighed out to him before witnesses, literally gave himself into the power of the creditor (whence the transaction's name, *nexum*, 'binding'). If he could not free himself punctually by repayment he fell into a condition of debt-bondage without the necessity of the judgement of a court. Alongside this archaic legal institution (which, however, was not abolished until towards the end of the fourth century B.C.) there also stood in the Twelve Tables a simple form of debt-promise (*sponsio*) which arose through mere question and answer and which could be enforced by means of the simplified procedure of the *legis actio per iudicis postulationem*.

In the following pages some degree of detail must be given about the criminal law of the Twelve Tables, because it is in this that the position of the code in cultural history can be particularly

---

[1] The parties were obliged, as soon as they had arrived at a precise statement of their legal allegations, to enter upon a procedural wager; and in disputes concerning ownership each party had to deposit a sum of money with the *pontifices*. This was forfeited to the state (and was applied to the expenses of the state cult) if the depositor lost the case. If the claim concerned some wrongdoing deserving of death, then the place of the money deposit was probably taken by a ceremonial oath. Both the money deposit and the oath were called *sacramentum*.

clearly seen. Here, too, we find combined both archaic features and features which point towards the future. The code, so far as can be seen, was in very large measure based on the idea of the right of an injured party to private vengeance. Punishment was inflicted by the state only in the case of high treason (*perduellio*) and perhaps also in the case of certain grave delicts of a sacral kind, in other words only in the case of such crimes as were committed directly against the commonwealth. Even the punishment of a murderer (*parricidas*) was left to the victim's kin (his agnates). It seems that the Twelve Tables contained no express provision about the punishment of a murderer; though an old rule, which probably dates from the era before the Twelve Tables, lays it down that in a case of unintentional killing ('if the spear has rather flown from the hand than been thrown') the killer has to surrender a ram to the agnates of the deceased.[1] This ram was a sort of representative object of vengeance—a 'scapegoat'—as Labeo, one of the leading jurists of the time of Augustus, confirms; the intention was that it should be led away and put to death; and from this it may be inferred that the agnates were entitled to wreak blood-vengeance on the man who had 'killed consciously and with malice'.[2] But they were entitled to do so only after his guilt had been judicially established. The surviving fragments of the Twelve Tables say nothing about what happened if the murderer evaded vengeance by flight; but we may suppose that the later practice in the case of a fugitive charged with a capital crime, that of prohibiting him from fire and water (*aqua et igni interdictio*) by magistral decree, goes back to the law of the Twelve Tables. The purpose of this interdiction was to withdraw from the fugitive all assistance, even that of his relatives and friends, and so to make it impossible for him to remain on Roman soil. Thus his only course was flight abroad—which, in the early Republic when the Roman state did not yet extend very far, was not at all difficult. As late as the second century B.C., according to the Greek historian Polybius, some communities in the immediate vicinity of Rome, such as the Latin cities of Praeneste and Tibur and the Greek city of Naples, had in

---

[1] The sentence 'si telum fugit magis quam iecit, aries subicitur' is ascribed by tradition sometimes to the *leges regiae*, sometimes to the Twelve Tables.

[2] The much-discussed sentence traditionally belonging to the *leges regiae*: 'si qui hominem liberum dolo sciens morti duit, parricidas esto', probably means, that *only* a person who knowingly and deliberately kills a free man is a murderer (and is consequently exposed to blood-vengeance).

consequence of old treaties of alliance the right to receive fugitives. They were thus protected from pursual, but were no longer allowed to set foot on Roman soil and so were obliged to live thenceforth in exile.

Unlike the case of murder, in which the avenger's right of putting the wrongdoer to death did not seem to need any special mention, the Twelve Tables expressly provided the death penalty for a series of other crimes; and here the mode of executing the penalty in each case reflects more or less exactly the nature of the crime. The intentional fire-raiser was to be burnt alive; the man who stole crops by night was to be hanged at the site of his crime as a sacrifice to Ceres the goddess of the harvest; the false witness was to be thrust into an abyss. Here again we are not dealing with a public punishment of the wrongdoer, but with the injured party's right of vengeance against the man whose guilt had been established by a judgement. In the case of theft this aspect of capital punishment is beyond doubt; indeed, the victim of the theft was entitled to kill the thief without any formality if he caught him at night—or even by day, if the thief put up armed resistance: the only requirement was that in such a case the victim of the theft had to summon the neighbours by means of a loud cry for help (*endoplorare* = *implorare*) so that no doubt could exist as to the propriety of the killing. But in all cases he could bring the thief caught red-handed (*fur manifestus*) before the judicial magistrate, who would then immediately hand the thief into his power, the wrongful deed being manifest. The victim of the theft might then kill the thief, might sell him as a slave to foreigners (*trans Tiberim*, where the territory of the Etruscan city of Veii began), or might accept a ransom for him. But if the thief had not been caught in the act, then the Twelve Tables did not allow the victim to wreak physical vengeance; he could merely demand a money penalty from the thief, as a rule twice the value of the stolen object. The code also laid down money penalties for lesser physical injuries; but here these penalties were fixed by the code itself once and for all. For the breaking of a bone (*os fractum*, Tab. VIII. 3) the wrongdoer had to pay 300 *as* if the injured man were free, 150 *as* if he were a slave; for less serious injuries (simple *iniuria*, Tab. VIII. 4), 25 *as*. On the other hand, in the case of more serious physical injuries which rendered a main limb useless (*membrum ruptum*), the code laid down in principle only physical retaliation by infliction of the same injury (*talio*), though this applied only if the parties had failed to agree on a money composition and thus to settle their dispute by means of a peaceful settlement (*pactum*).

The claims for money penalties based on the lesser delicts which the Twelve Tables thus recognized formed the point of departure for the development of the 'private criminal law' of the late republican period and the Empire; this was ultimately regarded as part of the law of obligations, and from it there emerged the law of delicts of the German civil code and of the other civil codes influenced by Roman law. In place of claims directed to private vengeance and based on murder and other serious delicts, criminal prosecutions became possible from the second century B.C.; they could be initiated not only by the victim or his relations but by anybody else as well, and they had as their object the public or state punishment of the criminal. There thus arose a law of crime and criminal procedure which was no longer part of the *ius civile*, but was reckoned as belonging to the *ius publicum*. To the legislators of the Twelve Tables, however, an interpretation of criminal law in which the state played a part was still entirely foreign. For them the natural and only result of a crime was the victim's right of vengeance, and they were merely concerned to restrict the right of physical vengeance to the more serious crimes, to keep this right under judicial control, to isolate the wrongdoer who had been found guilty, and thus to protect the commonwealth from the effects of devastating family vendettas. To this extent the criminal law of the Twelve Tables, seen as a whole, bears a very archaic character.

Certain other delicts regulated by the Twelve Tables also seem archaic and strange to the modern way of thinking, namely those which show the firm belief of the early Romans in the destructive power of magical spells: the enchantment of grain standing on the stalk so that the ears became empty (*fruges excantare*, Tab. VIII. 8a); the enticement (*pellicere*) from someone else's land to one's own of the mysterious powers which cause seeds to fructify (Tab. VIII. 8b); the whispering of evil incantations against the person of another (*malum carmen incantare*, Tab. VIII. 1). The code seems to have treated all these offences as deserving of death. It is also thought that magical ideas lay behind a curious provision about searching the house of another for one's stolen goods (Tab. VIII. 15a): the searcher had to go through the house naked carrying a basin and a halter (*lance licioque*). Other Indo-European legal systems and also ancient Jewish law contained provisions for the formal searching of a house; but these odd requirements, for which no really satisfactory explanation has yet been advanced, are found only in the Twelve Tables.

III. *Legal development after the Twelve Tables*

For a period of about two centuries, this consisted very largely of interpretation of the text of the Twelve Tables, and in legislation by the popular assembly, which—so far as private or criminal law is concerned—was at first extremely scanty, but became somewhat commoner after the end of the fourth century B.C.

The interpretation of the Twelve Tables and of the traditional stock of forms for legal proceedings and transactions remained until the beginning of the third century a jealously guarded monopoly of the college of pontiffs already mentioned. Their activity, which represents the beginning of Roman jurisprudence and which will later be more closely examined from this point of view, went on, consistent with the formalistic spirit of the early period, mostly by way of literal interpretation, but it was none the less able to develop the law in some significant points. Through a clever use of the wording of the code and through the contriving of complicated forms, the *pontifices* created means to satisfy the new requirements of legal life. Probably the best-known example of this creative activity is the form of emancipation of a son from what in principle was the lifelong power of his father; this was a transaction cleverly compounded of *seven* formal acts based on the Twelve Tables' rule that the father was to lose his power over the son if he alienated him three successive times as a bondsman to someone else. The statutory rule, whose real purpose no doubt was to limit a father's exploitation of his son's labour, was used for a completely different purpose, unknown to the legislators of the Twelve Tables, namely to make lawful a voluntary abdication of *patria potestas*. Like many other products of priestly legal technique, this complicated system remained in use for over 500 years.

Statutes (*leges*) were passed by the citizens on the proposal (*rogatio*) of a magistrate empowered to convene and preside over an assembly of the people (i.e. one who had the *ius agendi cum populo* or *cum plebe*). As a rule, of the various modes of popular assembly, only the *comitia centuriata* was used for legislation. It, too, lost importance in this respect after the *lex Hortensia* (286 B.C.) had made decrees of the *concilium plebis* binding on all citizens. Thenceforth the great majority of statutes were passed by the *concilium plebis* on the proposal of a *tribunus plebis*; and the statutes which are important in the development of Roman private and procedural law are mostly *plebiscita*. The number of such statutes in proportion to the total of republican statutes is, however, very small: in the four centuries between the Twelve Tables and the end of the Republic we know of only about thirty statutes which had any lasting significance in the history of private law and procedure. Some of these, it is true, contained important innovations. Among them are the *lex Poetelia de nexis*,[1] a statute of the *comitia*, introduced by the consuls of the year 326 B.C., which abolished voluntary debt-bondage; and the *lex Aquilia de damno iniuria dato*, a *plebiscitum* said to be of the year 286 B.C., in which the casuistic provisions of the Twelve Tables about injury to property were replaced by a new system which was both comprehensive and of the greatest significance for the further development of the law of delict. Other important statutes in the law of procedure, of succession, of gift, of guardianship, and of surety, belong to a later period, after the Punic wars.

None of these statutes is known to us directly and our knowledge of the approximate wording of the *lex Aquilia* is exceptional. For this reason the content and historical field of application of individual statutes are often disputed. The actual political backgrounds of the laws are also as a rule hidden from us; wherever the sources do give reasons for the passing of a statute (as in the case of the *lex Poetelia*) these sometimes seem suspiciously like a good story and nothing more. Still, it is clear that the majority of private-law statutes were influenced by socio-political trends; and here a part was played by the desire not only to protect debtors and the victims of usury, minors and children, but also to guard the well-being of the family against prodigality and the testamentary dispersal of its goods. The language and technique of legislation, in order to ward off the effects of subtle juristic interpretation, changed more and more from the lapidary simplicity and brevity of the Twelve

---

[1] Roman statutes are entitled after the family names of their proposers. A double title (e.g. *Poetelia Papiria*) usually points to a comitial statute proposed (as was usual) by both consuls together, while a simple title (e.g. *lex Aquilia*) points to a *plebiscitum* proposed by a tribune.

Tables to pedantic and circumstantial long-windedness. We know the end result of this development, the legislative style of the late Republic, from a number of voluminous *leges* which have been preserved in inscriptions. Among them are, for example, the *lex Acilia repetundarum* (122 B.C.), one of the numerous statutes intended to protect Rome's subjects, in particular the provincial populations, from oppression by Roman magistrates; and the *lex agraria* of 111 B.C. whose purpose was to put an end to the Gracchan system of land-settlement.

Part Two

THE LAW OF ROME AS A GREAT POWER
AND OF THE ROMAN WORLD EMPIRE
FROM THE MID THIRD CENTURY B.C.
TO THE MID THIRD CENTURY A.D.

3

THE STATE, ECONOMY, AND SOCIAL DEVELOPMENT

1. *City state and Empire*

BY 265 B.C., with the more or less completed subjection of Italy, Rome had become one of the most powerful states of the time; and the victorious struggle with Carthage which reached its climax in the Hannibalic war (219-201 B.C.) made her the mistress of the western Mediterranean. It was only hesitatingly and under the pressure of circumstances that in the second century B.C. the Roman government extended its area of power to the east: there, since the time of Alexander the Great, Greek culture had been flourishing in immense states formed on foreign soil, while the Greek mother-land was politically powerless and in a progressive economic and cultural decline. Without any extreme exertions, and despite the serious inner crises of the Roman state, the frontiers of Roman domination were pushed forward, in a period of barely 150 years, to the Euphrates and the Black Sea. Rome was now no longer just a great power among other great powers, but the supreme ruler of the entire civilization around the Mediterranean—and this, according to the ideas of antiquity, meant the world. The Roman Empire (*imperium Romanum*) and the earth (*orbis terrarum*, οἰκουμένη) were thus from the end of the Republic onwards regarded as equivalent.

Looked at from a legal point of view, this gigantic Empire was a highly complicated structure, a system of relationships of alliance and dependence in the centre of which stood the city of Rome. This system was the result of a marvellous political method developed through the experience of centuries, which, although it could be very considerably adapted to fit the conditions of particular cases, still exhibited some firmly fixed principles. The highest of these principles was *divide et impera*; the Romans, it is true, did not formulate the notion in these words, but applied it none the less with great consistency in the most diverse contexts.[1] Political units whose existence might have been dangerous to Roman domination were broken up. Alliances between allies and subjects of Rome herself were almost never tolerated, so that each dependent community had legal relations only with Rome, and no oblique relationships in the Roman network of alliances existed. In addition, Rome was able to set off against one another the various peoples and communities of the Empire, indeed even the different classes of the population within the subjected communities, by carefully preserving or creating political and social gradations. In this way Augustus, for example, after he had incorporated Egypt into the Empire in 30 B.C., immediately restored the Greco-Macedonian ruling class, which had begun to intermarry with the natives, to the position of a closed society enjoying economic and cultural privileges. The diversity of alliances and forms of subjection by which Rome differentiated the political position of the dependent communities and races rested on the same principle, as will be seen shortly. A further principle of Roman imperial policy was as far as possible to avoid interfering with the internal affairs of her subjects; they retained their own system of self-government and their native law, and in religious matters Rome practised the most extreme toleration. The former policy may of course be explained partly by the relative incapacity to develop inherent in the governmental system of the Roman city state, and the latter by the tolerance inherent in ancient polytheism; but both together went far towards making Roman domination weigh less heavily on Rome's subjects. The constant aim of ensuring the absolute military security of the subjected area may be regarded as the third principle of Roman imperialism. This involved the rounding-off of the imperial frontiers, often carried out with iron consistency, and the building of a network of strategic roads and fortified strongpoints with which Italy (in the earlier Republic) and the frontier provinces (in the Empire) were covered.

For a perspective of the organization of the Roman Empire a distinction must be drawn between Italy and the parts of the Empire outside Italy (*provinciae*).

[1] Historians dispute this and, conversely, emphasize the uniformity which Roman domination brought to Italy and to many provincial areas which had previously been politically divided. One view does not of course exclude the other; and the author continues to regard as accurate the account given above.

1. *Italy.* Italy consisted, until the beginning of the first century B.C., of two main areas, the immediate area of the Roman state (*ager Romanus*) and the territories of the allies (*socii*).

(*a*) The *ager Romanus* had long since, in the course of the struggles for dominance over Italy, grown beyond the territory of a city state; around the middle of the third century B.C. (and thus at the beginning of the period to be dealt with in this part of the book) it already included an area which was a little smaller than modern Belgium and extended, as a basically uniform mass, from Campania to southern Etruria and then north-eastwards through central Italy to the Adriatic. After the Hannibalic war, which had seriously shaken the Roman system of alliances, there were added numerous districts which had once been mere allied territories, particularly in lower Italy; these were incorporated in the *ager Romanus* as a punishment and in order to strengthen the Roman position of dominance; and finally, at the beginning of the second century B.C., a part of the southern Po basin was added, so that now a good half of Italy (reckoned northwards to the Po and not counting the islands) belonged directly to Rome.

Part of the *ager Romanus* consisted of the territories of originally independent communities which had completely forfeited their separate existences as states, but whose population had been at the same time adopted into the Roman citizen body (*municipia*). These new citizens were at first merely given equal status with the older citizen body so far as private law and civil burdens were concerned, and lacked all political rights, in particular the right of voting (*civitas sine suffragio*). Not until they had been long tried and gradually latinized were the rights of full citizenship granted to nearly all these communities. Besides the *municipia* there existed also on the *ager Romanus* a number of urban settlements which had been founded at the outset of the Roman career of conquest, and then, since the beginning of the second century B.C., maintained as strongpoints of Roman domination (finally as agricultural centres) and peopled with citizens (*coloniae civium Romanorum*, see also (*b*)). Apart from these there were only markets and places of assembly for the Roman farmers living in scattered settlements (*fora et conciliabula civium Romanorum*). In the *ager Romanus* only Rome itself was a city in the legal sense, since the *municipia* and colonies of citizens had apparently until the end of the Republic no full self-government, but merely certain organs for the carrying out of sacral functions and for the administration of the communities' property.

(*b*) By contrast, the *allied* communities were political structures with full autonomy: they had their own territory, their own law, and their own government, in which Rome only exceptionally interfered. Their relationship with Rome rested on treaties of alliance, according to which they were, in general, obliged to give military support (at their own cost and with their own system of military organization) but were not obliged to make direct financial contributions. Moreover, the terms granted to individual communities were diverse. The Romans drew a basic distinction between 'equal' and 'unequal' treaties of alliance (*foedera aequa* and *iniqua*). Those communities with which Rome had concluded a *foedus aequum* were sovereign in the legal sense, and this was demonstrated, for example, in the fact that a Roman magistrate setting foot on the territory of such a city was obliged by protocol to do without his lictors, since here his power of command was in abeyance. In practice, of course, an allied city, sovereign in this way, might still be so subject to Roman influence that its political role could hardly be distinguished from that of a community under a *foedus iniquum*. These latter, non-sovereign allies, recognized Roman supremacy (*maiestas populi Romani*) expressly in their treaties of alliance and were accordingly legally obliged to obey the directions of the Roman government.

The Latin communities occupied a special position among the Italian allies. Originally this category included only the racially related neighbour-cities of Rome, which were also Rome's oldest allies. Their citizens were not only on the same footing as Romans from the point of view of private law, but were entitled also to vote in the Roman popular assemblies, and up to the second century B.C. used to receive full Roman citizenship on migration to Rome. But after the last insurrection of these Latin cities properly so called (*prisci Latini*, old Latins) in 340 B.C. only a few of them remained in existence as independent commonwealths; most were changed into the status of *municipia*.

On the other hand, in the course of the Roman subjection of Italy, a second group of communities enjoying 'Latin rights' became of considerable importance; these consisted of fortified settlements (*coloniae*) which Rome had founded with the double purpose of providing for her excess population and of gaining military and political strongpoints on the conquered territory of former enemies. Some of the oldest Roman colonies, mostly in the immediate neighbourhood of Rome, were not indeed organized as independent and allied city communities, but remained within the ordinary Roman citizenship; accordingly they belonged to the *ager Romanus* and were, in law, nothing more than parts of the city of Rome (*coloniae civium Romanorum*). Other colonies, on the other hand, which were founded not by Rome alone but in co-operation with her Latin allies, received for this very reason the character of independent commonwealths: and this form of polity afterwards became the rule, because it lent those strongpoints which were far from Rome and surrounded by only recently subjected enemies a greater internal strength and greater readiness to fight. A person who had been settled in such a colony, whether he had been a Roman or an 'old Latin', lost his previous citizenship and became a citizen of the new community. This community now entered into a relationship of alliance with Rome which was exactly the same as that of the other allies, except that it derived not from a special treaty of alliance but directly from the act of founding. The members of these colonies enjoyed by comparison with Roman citizens approximately the same rights as the 'old Latins'; they were called for this reason *Latini coloniarii*, and the colonies themselves *coloniae Latinae*. It was not until the huge increase in Roman power had reduced every other form of citizenship to insignificance that Roman settlement policy returned to the foundation of *coloniae civium Romanorum*; the great agricultural settlements which arose in northern Italy, south of the Po, at the end of the third century and at the beginning of the second century B.C., and also the few colonies founded in the late Republic, all remained within the Roman citizenship.

2. *The provinces.* Outside Italy Roman policy followed the same methods which had been tried and proved in the subjection of Italy. But the geographical position of the Roman dominions outside Italy, and the conditions which the Romans met with there, made necessary different and special kinds of administration. While Italy was governed and indeed (so far as the *ager Romanus* was concerned) administered directly from Rome, yet in the oldest of Rome's overseas possessions (Sicily, Sardinia and Corsica, and Spain) the constant presence of governors was thought necessary. Accordingly, these and all other acquisitions outside Italy

(including Celtic Upper Italy, which was not thought of as part of Italy) were organized in special governmental areas (*provinciae*), for whose administration at first ordinary magistrates were dispatched. In general, one of the consuls went only if in a particular province there were important military tasks to be accomplished, otherwise praetors were sent; and for this reason the number of the praetors had to be increased. The number of provinces kept growing, and at the same time the load of business which had to be discharged by the magistrates remaining in Rome also increased, so a hand-to-mouth remedy was found whereby at first the period of office of some governors was prolonged (*prorogatio imperii*). Finally, however, as part of the Sullan reform of the constitution in 81 B.C., a further year was added to the single year of office of consuls and praetors in which they were given a province to administer 'in place of a consul or a praetor' (*pro consule, pro praetore*).

This development of the office of governor shows the technical difficulties which a commonwealth, originally organized as a city state, had to cope with in the government of a huge Empire.[1] There was of course no question of an intensive administration of the provinces by Roman officials. Governors had at their disposal only a small staff of assistants and therefore had to restrict themselves basically to the preservation of Roman supremacy and military security, and to the protection of and administration of justice for the Roman citizens and Italian allies who were in the province. Even the levying of the tribute imposed on the province was not the job of the organs of state: the right of collecting it was auctioned out to Roman financiers who combined into syndicates (*societates publicanorum*) for these gigantic and very lucrative deals. Local administration, the administration of justice as between the natives of the provinces, and many other tasks were in general simply left to the political organs of the subject people.

These peoples had a contractually based relationship of alliance with Rome only in rare cases; and such cases mostly arose in the era before Rome had laid claim to formal sovereignty over the area and organized it as a province. By far the greater number of

---

[1] Consciousness of these difficulties led the Roman government repeatedly to hesitate to extend the area of its immediate jurisdiction, and (particularly in the eastern Mediterranean) to try to control the native chiefs and communities through a sort of client-relationship instead. A few client-principalities of this kind—e.g. Herod's kingdom in Palestine—still existed in the early Empire.

the urban communities in the provinces, although reckoned as 'friends and allies of the Roman people', enjoyed this description only by virtue of a unilateral (and thus revocable) resolution of the Senate followed by registration in the list of *amici* and *socii* of the Roman state. These municipalities, unless granted special exemption from burdens (*immunitas*), had to pay a yearly levy (*tributa, stipendia*) to Rome as well as supplying quarters and provisions for the governor, his retinue, and his armed forces, though provisions in kind were usually recompensed by a sum fixed by the governor. In principle, they were also liable for military service, but governors did not usually bother, except in acute emergency, to call up these provincial levies of doubtful military worth.

Recognition as a 'free city' (*civitas libera*), which some provincial communities enjoyed, had already by the late Republic come to mean little more than exemption from the burden of billeting a Roman army of occupation. Certain sections of the provincial population, above all in the areas not politically organized as cities, presumably did not even enjoy the precarious status of 'allies' just described, but were in a condition of permanent subjection which had resulted from an act of mercy after surrender (*dediticii*), and if they were mostly left to their own devices, it was purely as a matter of convenience for so long as they gave no trouble. The inhabitants of many rural districts, especially in Asia Minor, were subordinate to the urban communities to which they had been allotted (*adtributi*), without possessing the citizenship of these communities.

The Roman citizens who settled in the provinces, mostly as traders, in increasing numbers during the Republic conducted their litigation in principle in the court of the governor. But they presented themselves at the court sittings which the governor held in different cities of his province even when they had no lawsuits pending; the more respectable among them, particularly those with the property-qualification of an *eques*, took part in the administration of justice in the governor's court as assessors and as jurors in civil cases. The presence of the Roman citizens residing in the area gave these sittings their name: *conventus* (sc. *civium Romanorum*). In this can be clearly seen the fact that the judicial activity of the governor mainly concerned his fellow citizens, though, if the interests of Roman sovereignty were involved, no doubt he would also at all times have summoned provincials to his court. Looking at the matter as a whole, on the basis of the scanty—and, geographically speaking, very unevenly distributed—evidence, one would say that already by the end of the Republic the judicial activity of the Roman governors was encroaching on the autonomy of the provincial communities. At the same time, the practical working of the law may have differed a good deal from one province to another, since each province was usually given its own basic statute (*lex provinciae*) by the general who had conquered it and by a senatorial commission usually constituted for this purpose alongside him, and in drawing up this *lex provinciae* the practice was to keep as near as possible to existing conditions in that territory.[1]

3. *Weakness of the republican administration of the Empire*. The organization of an immense Empire resting on the narrow basis of a city state, here described only in the broadest outline, was just as extraordinary a political achievement as its conquest had been a military one. Still, in the course of the last two centuries B.C. it became increasingly clear that the city-state constitution of Rome had outlived its usefulness. Even the capital city itself, which by the second century B.C. had grown to the dimensions of a large modern city through being the political and economic centre of a world Empire, presented administrative problems which the primitive directness of the republican magistracy was no longer able to solve.

The most important cultural result of the republican era, namely the Romanization of Italy which had been achieved through Roman settlement policy and the centuries-old military bond between Rome and her Italian allies, gradually created a national unity of Roman character out of the diverse populations of the peninsula, and made meaningless the distinction between the ruling Romans and the ruled half-citizens and allies. The reception of all Italians into the full Roman citizenship became inevitable: a measure on

---

[1] In Sicily, for example, as we know from Cicero's speeches against Verres, a system of taxation was still in force at the end of the Republic which had been created by King Hieron II of Syracuse in the second half of the third century B.C. (*lex Hieronica*). Sicily also had a judicial system, set up by the proconsul P. Rupilius and a senatorial commission in the year 131 B.C., according to which lawsuits between citizens of the same provincial community were left to the community's own local jurisdiction, but those between citizens of different provincial communities, or between provincials and Roman citizens, fell under the jurisdiction of the governor (Cic. *in Verr*. 2. 2. 32).

which the Roman government failed to decide at the right moment and to which it was eventually compelled by the extraordinarily bloody and dangerous rebellion of the Italian allies in 91-89 B.C. But once it had been completed, it only made the break-up of the Roman city-state framework stand out in clearer relief. The 'city area' of Rome now included all of Italy; the radical centralization of political life in the capital city, dictated by the idea of the city state, had to be relaxed, and a certain measure of home rule allowed to the *municipia* and colonies in general. The urban popular assemblies had lost their significance as the political organization of the whole people as soon as the most solid elements of the citizen body, namely the farmers and inhabitants of country towns, who lived far from Rome, were no longer able to participate and their dominant place in the assembly field was taken by the urban mob.

In the administration of the provinces, too, serious weaknesses appeared, caused to a considerable degree by the inadequacy of the methods of government of a city state. Above all, the annual change of magistrates proved fatal to administration and, even more so, to the solution of military problems in the provinces; it accounts for the repeated catastrophes in wars whose ultimately favourable result for Rome could never have been in doubt. More and more frequently such failures led to the creation of extra-ordinary commands with full powers; these essentially contra-dicted the republican system and naturally had the result of tempting ambitious generals to take the law into their own hands and ulti-mately even to overturn the constitution. The lack of any proper control over the conduct of governors, together with the system of tax-farming, favoured the ruthless bleeding of the provinces for the personal benefit of the Roman upper class, and thus contri-buted decisively to the collapse of political and commercial morals. Even the 'recovery'-procedure against extortionate magistrates, introduced in the early second century for the benefit of the provincials, and which through constant statutory adaptation (*leges repetundarum*) had developed more and more into an apparatus for political trials,[1] was not really able to prevent the plunder of the provinces. On the contrary, it became a dangerous weapon in internal struggles for power at Rome between the senatorial

---

[1] Cf. the *repetundae* trial of C. Verres (*propraetor* of the province of Sicily in 73 B.C.) of which we have an exact knowledge through the prosecution speeches of Cicero.

aristocracy and the money-aristocracy (the *equites*) and within the senatorial nobility itself.

No improvement of these conditions could come about without a removal of the barriers which Rome's city-state constitution imposed on the development of imperial administration. But since, according to the political notions of antiquity, a free constitution was possible only within the narrow framework of a community whose citizens could assemble at all times for the personal exercise of their rights, such a reorganization of the Empire could hardly take place except on the basis of a monarchy. Monarchy as the constitutional form of the Hellenistic empires had proved its effectiveness in the field of administrative technique; and Greek philosophy since Aristotle had given it a theoretical basis and taken from it the odium of a barbarian form of government. The ruler-cult associated with Hellenistic monarchy, which grew out of both oriental and Greek ideas, offered a means of making Roman domination seem more reasonable and thus of initiating an inner strengthening of the Empire. However, one grave problem had to be solved at the foundation of the Roman monarchy: how to overcome the forces of republican tradition, still very much alive despite all its symptoms of decay, and the consciousness of freedom and pride of domination which inspired the senatorial aristocracy.

11. *Economic and social development of Rome at the end of the Republic*

The expansion of Roman dominion over Italy was followed until the third century B.C. by an ever greater strengthening of the Roman farmer class. Time and again broad stretches of land were yielded to Rome by the defeated Italians and used for the foundation of fortified agricultural settlements (*coloniae*) or distributed by lot to land-hungry citizens. When, afterwards, the tempo of Roman conquests increased, a good deal of land remained undistributed in the hands of the state. Part of this *ager publicus* was leased out for the benefit of the state treasury; another large part was, in the course of time, auctioned off cheap to citizens with capital, particularly those from the ruling aristocracy, or was occupied by them without any title but under the state's tacit toleration. It was probably mainly on such lands that there arose for the first time large properties worked by slaves, where farming concentrated on the grazing of cattle, but also, if the ground were favourable, on the growing of olives and vines; while the raising of grain, in the absence of agricultural machinery, could be more advantageously carried on on a small scale and was thus left to small farmers and leaseholders.

The loss of life and the devastations of the Hannibalic war, which hit the farming class hardest; the competition from the Roman possessions in Sicily and Africa which had been won in the Punic wars and which produced cheap grain in huge quantities and could transport it more easily by sea to the Roman market than could the remote districts of Italy which depended on land transport; the attraction exerted by the rapidly growing metropolis of Rome itself—all these things brought about the ruin of the Roman farming class in the second century B.C. It is true that the pursuit of agriculture was not abandoned, but to a large extent the independent peasant proprietor was replaced by tenants depending on great landowners, and the ranches and plantations of the urban Roman capitalists increased in number. The capital city, which already in the third century B.C. had been more and more drawn into the trade of the Hellenistic world, soon became a commercial centre of the first rank and, above all, the dominant money-market of the whole ancient world.

The immense fortunes which flowed to Rome through wars and the plundering of the provinces were concentrated in the hands of two relatively small sections of the population: the senatorial aristocracy and the *equites*. The members of the senatorial class took part in the activities of trade and finance—but in secret, as these occupations were beneath them, according to the notions of society; their wealth, mostly invested in land, was generally inherited or won through political activity; above all, it came from the booty assigned to successful generals or from—more or less —voluntary gifts of the provincial populations to their governors. Alongside these senatorial families, some of which had been famous and powerful for centuries, a second aristocracy of *nouveaux riches* businessmen and financiers arose from the ranks of urban Romans and prominent citizens of the *municipia*. These drew gigantic profits (often invested forthwith in land) from army contracts, tax-farming and other state concessions, from usurious deals with politicians short of money and with provincial communities stripped bare by plunder, and from trade both inside and outside Italy. This capitalist stratum was called the 'knight class' (*equites*) because those citizens whose property was sufficient to allow them to serve in the cavalry with their own horses had, since early times, formed what was in some respects a privileged class within the Roman citizenship. The senatorial aristocracy, divided as never before into mutually warring groups: the *equites*, who had indeed no direct part in political business, but could enforce their economic interests both through relationships with senators and through their influence on the politically conditioned criminal courts: and the ever-growing and restless mass of the penniless metropolitan proletariat, the profitable object of demagogic machinations: these were the main elements in the increasingly tumultuous struggles within Roman politics in the last century of the Republic.[1]

111. *The crisis of the Republic*

These struggles, which were to lead to the collapse of the Senate's domination and to the establishment of a monarchy, began with the far-reaching legislation of social reform of the *tribuni plebis* Tiberius and Caius Gracchus (both of whom came from the senatorial aristocracy). In the years 133–121 B.C. they tried to restore the agrarian basis of the Roman state; their idea was to take all that part of the *ager publicus* which was in the hands of great landowners without legal title, divide it up into inalienable parcels, and assign them to landless citizens. Put into effect by revolutionary means and with the help of the Roman mob, the Gracchan reforms provoked a reaction of the ruling class which soon stopped the settlement work which had begun (*lex agraria* of 111 B.C.) and thus deprived the whole undertaking of lasting effect. The confrontation which the Gracchan revolution had called into being between the leaders of the Roman aristocracy who wished to support the senatorial regime (the *optimates*) and certain political lone wolves who tried to reach their political goals with the help of the broad mass of the people (the *populares*) remained the dominant element in further developments.

But now the main question was no longer chiefly that of social

[1] No influence was exerted on the political development of the late republican period by the repeated revolts of the slave population whose size had grown enormously through the Roman wars of conquest and through the flourishing slave-trade in the eastern half of the Empire. These slaves often led an existence unworthy of human beings, especially when they were used in gangs on ranches or in industry. Their insurrections in Sicily and southern Italy were put down with great cruelty.

or political reform; it was rather the question of who was to exercise power in the state. The political struggles of that time have probably certain demagogic methods in common with the struggles of modern monster political parties, but very little else. For these were not class struggles, but basically struggles for power among the Roman aristocracy; and it is certainly no accident that none of the great 'popular' leaders came from the common people, while the most important of them, the Gracchi and Caesar, came from the foremost families of the senatorial nobility.[1] In addition, there were no doubt more or less demagogic programmes, but no parties in the modern sense. In their place the real basis of political influence was supplied by the various relationships of trust and political friendships which from the beginning had conditioned Roman society. As the outcome of these struggles, which were waged with the most ruthless and brutal methods and eliminated the best part of the Roman aristocracy, monarchy loomed ever clearer. As we have noted earlier, it became inescapable. Extraordinary military commands and extraordinary law-making powers, political alliances, and bloody civil wars among rivals struggling for power: these were the steps on the road to monarchy, which emerged at first merely as the factual supremacy of the strongest.

This penultimate stage was repeatedly reached before anyone succeeded in establishing monarchy as a lasting system based on law. Sulla was already the unlimited ruler of the state in 82 B.C.; but, true to his political origins in the optimate camp, he preferred to restore once more the régime of the senatorial aristocracy and then to retire voluntarily from political life. His all-embracing reforming legislation was intended to secure the senatorial régime, e.g. by cutting down the powers of the *tribuni plebis*, limiting consuls and praetors to the urban occupations of political leadership and the administration of justice,[2] and permitting a second tenure of office (*iteratio*) only after ten years; but they could not prevent the crisis of the Republic.[3] Caesar was the second man upon whom, after victory over Pompey and the Senate, political supremacy had

---

[1] Even C. Marius, who is commonly thought of as having worked his way up from the ranks of the common soldiers, came, in reality, from the knight-class.

[2] Not until their second year in office did these magistrates now take over the administration of provinces as proconsuls and propraetors. However, consuls and praetors kept their military imperium *de iure* up to the end of the Republic; and consular power took precedence over that of the pro-magistrate whenever a consul appeared in a province.

[3] His innovations in the field of criminal law and procedure were more lasting.

devolved: he died under the daggers of fanatical republicans as he was on the point of bringing that supremacy to its logical conclusion. It was his great-nephew and adopted son C. Octavius, son of a senator of only praetorian rank and of municipal origin, who became the founder of the Roman monarchy: he is known to us by a name of honour which the Senate bestowed on him in the year in which the new order was founded, *Augustus*;[1] and we call the constitution which he created—monarchical in essence if not in outward form—the Principate.

IV. *The Principate*

1. *Its nature*. The creator of the Roman monarchy was faced with the grave task of reconciling his situation in some more or less satisfactory way with the traditions of the republican period and with the republican outlook of, at any rate, the leading sections of the Roman citizen body. It was in dealing with these impalpable things that Caesar had failed when, with his usual consistency, he entered upon a course of action which, if we can judge it properly, must have led forthwith to an unambiguously monarchical order. Warned by the failure of his adoptive father, Augustus now sought and found the solution of the problem in a peculiar compromise, a compromise which gave his creation a rather vague nature and one not capable of being defined in clear terms.

Seen from the standpoint of formal constitutional law, the new order (28–27 B.C.)[2] seemed expressly and ceremoniously to restore the Republic which had been shaken to its foundations in the turbulence of the last century B.C. But there were a number of reservations which, however carefully and unobtrusively conceived, gave Augustus and his successors absolute control over the destinies of state and Empire. Thus this restoration of the Republic meant the creation of a new monarchical power, albeit a power not so much built into the constitution as erected beside it. The newly organized republican constitution bestowed indeed upon the bearer of the monarchical power a whole series of functions of the greatest

---

[1] The word is untranslatable, because its meaning oscillates between religious and purely human ideas. It can actually mean 'holy'; but just as easily 'distinguished', 'imposing'. A reading of the pages which follow may show why the choice fell upon just such an ambiguous *cognomen*.

[2] Cf. *Mon. Anc.* 34: 'In consulatu sexto et septimo, bella ubi civilia extinxeram, per consensum universorum potitus rerum omnium rem publicam ex mea potestate in senatus populique Romani arbitrium transtuli.'

political significance; but these functions, looked at from a formal point of view, were a collection of details; in the form in which they appeared they were conditioned as far as possible by the inherited notions of the constitutional law of the Republic, and for this very reason were not adapted to expressing the essence of the new monarchy in terms of constitutional law.

Augustus' creation can be understood, therefore, only as a force standing outside the republican order, whose vocation of trust was to support and supplement it. Augustus did not wish to be regarded as a constitutional ruler; he wished only to be the first citizen (*princeps*, whence Principate) of a free city, who would be enabled by his supreme political prestige (*auctoritas*)[1] to assist the republican government in the maintenance of public order and in the administration of Rome's world Empire. A single man now took upon his shoulders the burden which had proved too heavy for the constitutional organs of the city state; but this man had the gifts of political genius, material means out of the ordinary and, not least, the special favour of the gods. This is the idea of the Augustan Principate. Consistently with this idea, the officials whom the princeps employed for the carrying out of the tasks which he had taken over were, legally, not civil servants at all but his own private officials; and the treasury from which he financed his administrative activities (the *fiscus Caesaris*) was his own private exchequer (though of course the preponderant part of the state's revenue was fed into it). A more delicate formula for the abolition of republican freedom and a more effective disguise for the new order than this conscious refusal to be incorporated into the constitution could not have been found.

At the same time Augustus could seek support in ideas already widespread at the time of the Republic's crisis, which rested partly on a romantic view of the old Roman state, partly no doubt also on the political theories of Hellenistic philosophy. We can see them at work in the writings of Cicero on political philosophy, and it is very instructive to observe how the ideals championed by this passionate republican were made to serve as a basis for overturning the republican order. An extraordinarily clever and vigorous

---

[1] Cf. *Mon Anc.* 34: 'Post id tempus [i.e. after the restoration of the Republic in the years 28–27 B.C.] auctoritate omnibus praestiti, potestatis autem nihilo amplius habui quam ceteri qui mihi quoque in magistratu conlegae fuerunt.' (*Quoque* must be understood as the ablative of *quisque*.)

political propaganda hammered home the notion of the Principate into the contemporary consciousness: great literary figures like Livy, Horace, and Virgil entered into the service of the idea; splendid edifices and festivals illustrated the essence and the achievements of the new régime, and the images and mottoes on the Roman coins brought them daily before the people's eyes. Even Augustus' great account of his services (*res gestae divi Augusti*), which was published in the Senate after his death and perpetuated by inscriptions in Rome and the provinces, is primarily a piece of official propaganda: it is to a large extent preserved (the so-called *monumentum Ancyranum*)[1] and represents the most direct source for Augustus' political thought.

So far only one side of the Principate has been indicated, viz. its relation to the Roman state and the Roman citizen body. But the Principate showed another face to the subject provincial populations. To them the artful juxtaposition of Republic and Principate, carefully calculated to meet the ideals and sensibilities of the Roman citizen body, was naturally quite unimportant. To interest them in the new order—and an effort to do so was made both under Augustus and to an even greater extent later—it was necessary to produce a simpler image. They were to learn to worship the princeps as the humane and just lord of the civilized races, as their saviour from the oppressions and trials of the preceding period, the bringer of peace and father of mankind; as the wise ruler in the sense of Hellenistic political philosophy or as the ancient oriental type of the god-being. For this reason the religious cult of the living Caesar was in the eastern provinces (unlike Rome) not only tolerated but from the beginning openly promoted.

Since the propaganda of the Principate did not consist of mere conventional phrases but rather rested on the living ideals of the Empire's population and gave expression to the central notions of the new order, a certain contradiction at once began to appear in its dual nature, which came increasingly to dominate the political development of the early centuries A.D. This was the contradiction between the notion, inherited from republican times, of the universal dominion of Rome, and the idea of a cosmopolitan world

---

[1] It bears this name because the version of the statement first discovered—and the most complete—was an inscription on the temple of Augustus at Ancyra (the modern Ankara). Fragments of another inscription of the same content were later found in the ruins of the city of Antioch in Pisidia.

empire in which all nations would be equally subjected to the régime of an absolute ruler.

The formal character of the monarchy founded by Augustus rested for a long time on the conception of a 'first citizen' in a republican state, a conception which in turn rested entirely on the personal *auctoritas*—prestige plus charisma—of Augustus himself. Traces of this idea are still recognizable in the vocabulary of the 'Dominate' and even of the Byzantine kingdom. But in the conscious eye of the empire's population, including the Roman citizens themselves and their most influential elements, the Principate had already in the course of the first century A.D. become an ordinary part of the constitution and indeed the central feature of the whole political system. One sign of this, among others, is the fact that the jurists of the second and early third centuries A.D. attributed the power of the princeps to the will of the people, and accorded the force of law to all his dispositions (Gaius *Inst*. I. 5; Pomponius *D*. 1. 2. 2. 11; Ulpian *D*. 1. 4. 1). The old republican accolade of a victorious general—*imperator*—established itself as the form of address and official designation for the princeps; Augustus himself had adopted it instead of his *praenomen* Gaius, and it then became a permanent component of the princeps's name, just like the names Caesar and Augustus.

2. *Its relation to the republican constitution*. It is now time to outline in more detail the relation of the Principate to the republican constitution. The republican constitutional organs continued to exist: the magistracies, the popular assemblies, and the Senate. Augustus and his successors themselves took on the consulship from time to time, and they belonged to the Senate as its senior members (*princeps senatus*). In this way the republican organs of government were made still to appear the real incumbents of the state power. In practice, however, the overwhelming might of the princeps came increasingly to deprive the republican constitution of breathing-space. Thus, in particular, it could no longer truthfully be said that the consuls continued to direct the political life of the state or even that they held the military command; the princeps alone now concerned himself with these tasks. The granting to the consuls of certain functions of a juridical kind did not go far to restoring their effectiveness as a political force, and the consulate quickly sank to the status of a mere decoration, bestowed on the members of prominent noble families and on the deserving

assistants of the princeps. This showed itself externally in the fact that it became customary to have several pairs of consuls in office successively within the same official year, each pair for a few months or even a few days.

The lesser magistracies held their ground at first better than did the consulship; in their case the princeps had no reason to take upon himself their special functions, so that the praetors, for instance, kept in principle the same criminal and civil jurisdiction that they had enjoyed in the later Republic. But their decrees were now subject to appeal to the princeps; and from the mid first century A.D. onwards the princeps could, if he liked, hear all important cases before his own tribunal. Most important of all, there now developed—at first in the field of criminal justice though later in the field of civil justice as well—an extraordinary jurisdiction of imperial officials, who tended increasingly to supplant the 'ordinary' courts controlled by the praetors. The aediles lost their police functions to new organs created by the princeps, the urban quaestors were replaced in the administration of the treasury by a similarly appointed *praefectus aerarii*, and, about the middle of the first century A.D., the right of intercession enjoyed by the *tribuni plebis* was decisively curtailed.

While the magistracies continued to exist into the late Empire, even if only as weak and pale reflections of their erstwhile greatness, the second element of the republican constitution, the popular assembly, quietly disappeared from the realm of political realities soon after the reign of Augustus. As early as the time of Tiberius the election of magistrates was transferred from the people to the Senate, at any rate so far as any real choice between several contenders was concerned;[1] it seems that even in later times a formal act of the people took place by which the Senate's 'suggestions' of single candidates were approved, but this could be nothing more than an honorific ceremony. A little later popular legislation disappeared and its place was taken in practice by senatorial

[1] From an inscription found in 1947—the so-called Tabula Hebana, reproduced e.g. in *Historia*, i (1950), 105 ff.—we know that through a *plebiscitum* of A.D. 5 an electoral body of senators and *equites* was formed whose purpose was to carry out a pre-election (*destinatio*) from among the candidates for the magistracies; this electoral body, originally organized in ten *centuriae*, was increased by a further five *centuriae* in A.D. 19. Since, however, the Roman historians do not mention this institution, and since Tacitus (*Ann.* 1. 15) expressly reports that in A.D. 14 (!) the elections were transferred from people to Senate ('tum primum e campo comitia ad patres translata sunt'), this pre-election system cannot have been long in practical use.

resolutions. After this the role of the people was limited to that of theatrical 'extras' in the ceremonial acts of state whose dignity was thus intended to be augmented by the lustre of old republican tradition. Since the popular assemblies, as has already been seen, had long ago lost their significance as political organs of the entire citizen body and had indeed become an uncomfortable and dangerous constitutional element by reason of the preponderance of the urban proletariat, this development cannot be thought of as surprising.[1]

By contrast with the magistracies and the popular assemblies, the Senate experienced a very significant extension of its competence, through the transference to it of electoral and legislative powers and through its criminal jurisdiction, recognized from the time of Tiberius, over members of the senatorial order. None the less, in spite of the consideration with which it was treated by Augustus and his successors and the genuine and repeated attempts by the emperors to hold it to a real co-operation in the discharge of public business, the Senate too very soon lost all power of independent expression of opinion and became a mere speaking-tube for the imperial will. The elections always corresponded with the uttered or even merely presumed will of the princeps, and the legislative proposals of the princeps or of his representatives were usually accepted without any serious discussion. In the second century A.D., therefore, the custom arose of citing, not the actual resolution of the Senate, which even by that time was hardly more than a formality, but the proposal of the princeps (*oratio*) instead. Later still, from the fourth century onwards, the Senate was thought of as merely the place for promulgating imperial edicts. The emperor himself hardly ever appeared any more in the Senate, but had the statute read out by one of his officers, and the only reminiscence of what once had been the real vote of the Senate was the shouts of applause and good wishes (*acclamationes*) with which the senators greeted the imperial message.[2]

While the republican constitution thus kept only the semblance of power and decayed even further, there became assembled around

---

[1] That Augustus was at least originally willing to preserve popular elections is shown by his interesting attempt, among the citizens living outside Rome, to let at any rate the municipal councillors (*decuriones*) of the citizen colonies participate in the elections by means of a written ballot.

[2] A drastic example is provided by the publication-regulations for the *Codex Theodosianus*, which specifically lists the endless series of *acclamationes*.

the person of the princeps a new organization for the state, which in the course of time was more and more extensively developed.[1]

As has been seen, the position of the princeps had its centre of gravity outside the inherited republican order and in a political ideology which could not be comprised in technical legal terms. To this sphere belong the *cognomen* bestowed upon Octavian by the Senate: 'Augustus', the honorific title 'father of his country' (*pater patriae*), the elevation of the deceased princeps to divine honours (*consecratio*) and finally the designation *princeps* as well (which, by the way, never appears among the titles and offices of the emperors). The principate was anchored in the sphere of republican constitutional law essentially by only two offices, which were formed on the model of republican magistracies without themselves being magistracies: the princeps's tribunician power (*tribunicia potestas*) and his *imperium proconsulare*. The tribunician power which was bestowed on him for life gave him all the powers of a tribune, i.e. personal immunity, the right to convene the popular assembly (though only in the form of the *concilium plebis*) and the Senate, and the right of veto against the official acts of magistrates. These powers enabled the princeps to undertake any necessary interference in the politics of the capital city; though according to the notions of the republican constitution they did not represent *imperium* but were rather results of the protective function of the tribunes for the benefit of the citizens or, to be more precise, of the *plebs*; so that the lifelong bestowal of these rights on the princeps did not need to be interpreted as a derogation from the republican scheme of state authority. In addition, it gave him an instrument whereby he could play the role of the small man's champion by the use of the tribunician right of assistance (*ius auxilii*); and, in particular, whereby he could exercise purely judicial functions by means of receiving appeals against the decisions of the magistrates charged with jurisdiction.

The proconsular *imperium* gave the princeps a supremacy over the provinces (differently conditioned in each case, as we shall see in a moment) and over the army, which had from the end of the second century and the beginning of the first century B.C. become a force of long-service mercenaries. On this there rested (in so far as it rested on anything within the republican constitution) the

[1] The most important stages in this development were the reigns of the emperors Claudius, Domitian, and Hadrian.

princeps's position of actual power. As provincial commands lasting for a long period and exceeding the normal competence of governors had repeatedly shown themselves in the last two centuries of the Republic to be a necessity, the proconsular *imperium* of the princeps was nothing out of the ordinary. It could be looked on as an indispensable requirement for the preservation of the Empire and of peace; and since it was operative only in the provinces, the urban Roman citizen hardly felt it. Indeed efforts were made to keep it as far as possible from his view: Augustus' account of himself says nothing about it, and the official titles of the earlier principes refer only obscurely to it by means of the title *imperator* which was borne like a *praenomen*.[1] This veiling of the proconsular *imperium* may explain the fact that the nature and extent of this authority are not fully clear even to modern research.

Augustus took into his own hands the administration of some of the provinces—the more important ones, in the military sense, where armies were stationed. He left the rest to the republican organs, and they were ruled by proconsuls under senatorial supervision just as in republican times; though the princeps could always interfere in their government, and could do so without consulting the Senate in advance.[2]

3. *The administrative apparatus of the princeps.* Apart from his share in provincial administration the princeps also took over certain duties in the metropolis, the carrying out of which by republican organs was either impossible or undesirable in the interests of the Principate: for example, the maintenance of an adequate police force and fire-brigade, and the control of the urban corn and water supplies. The exchequer of the princeps (*fiscus Caesaris*), from which the expenses of all these branches of administration were met, attracted a large proportion of the entire revenues of the Empire, particularly from the provinces directly ruled by the princeps, and left the old treasury of the Republic (*aerarium populi Romani*) far behind it in importance.[3] Financial administration,

---

[1] Trajan was the first to include the title *proconsul* in the recital of his offices.

[2] This is evidenced by the edicts of Augustus found in the senatorial province of Cyrene (cf. e.g. Stroux-Wenger, *Die Augustusinschrift von Kyrene*, 1928).

[3] It does not seem that the *fiscus Caesaris* arose at the beginning of the Principate as a unitary and comprehensive organization. We know in the time of Augustus only of some individual provincial *fisci*, which were administered by freedmen of the princeps; probably it was under Claudius that decisive progress was made in building up and co-ordinating the fiscal administration. The jurists of the late second and third centuries represent the *fiscus* as an authority with its own legal personality, capable of litigating in its own name,

correspondence between the princeps and his subordinates, and the attending to numerous petitions which reached the princeps in particular from the population of the provinces demanded extensive central offices in the neighbourhood of the princeps and, in addition, certain auxiliary organizations, for example, an expeditious and reliable state post-office (*cursus publicus*). There thus arose a far-reaching administrative apparatus which in the course of time developed more and more branches and increasingly pushed the republican organs aside. By contrast with the unitary but many-sided republican *imperium* there now prevailed a rigid compartmentalization; and the offices created by the princeps were not unpaid offices of honour like the republican magistracies, but had large salaries attached to them (*salarium*: 'salt-money'); their tenure was not limited to a year but lasted for so long as the princeps pleased.

The princeps allowed the two leading classes of Roman citizens —the senatorial aristocracy and the *equites*—to share in the duties of his administrative sphere; and a fixed group of offices was reserved for each of these classes. A senator from the highest rank of consulars administered the post of *praefectus urbi* created by Augustus, whose job it was to maintain peace and order in the capital city and, connected with this, increasingly to exercise powers of a judicial kind. The chief superintendents of public buildings, aqueducts, and main roads (*curatores operum publicorum*, *aquarum*, *viarum*) were also senators. Most important of all, the chief posts of command in the army, from that of the general of a legion (*legatus legionis*) upwards, together with most of the governorships in the princeps's provinces, were in principle filled exclusively by men from the senatorial class. The governors of this class were called *legati Augusti pro praetore* and had by reason of delegation from the princeps the same power in the area of their province as a republican magistrate had, including the command of the troops stationed there. A lesser number of provinces were governed by governors from among the *equites*; these were usually small provinces, whose governors were called *praefecti* at the beginning of the Principate, but from the time of Claudius onwards bore, like other officials of the same rank, the formal designation *procurator*.[1]

though represented for this purpose from the time of Hadrian by special officials called *advocati fisci*.

[1] Such a *procurator* from the *equites*-class was Pontius Pilate; he administered the small province of Judaea.

Yet the large and especially important province of Egypt was an equestrian province: Augustus did not wish, on account of its economic importance as the granary of the Empire and chief source of food supplies for the city of Rome, to entrust it to a member of the senatorial nobility, and he sought also to secure the province by other exceptional measures. For example, members of the senatorial class could not set foot there without the special permission of the princeps. The position of the governor of Egypt (*praefectus Alexandriae et Aegypti*) was one of the highest offices which an *eques* could achieve. Certain metropolitan equestrian offices, called prefectships, had approximately the same standing: thus, in Rome, the office of commander of the imperial body-guard (*praefectus praetorio*), usually held by two *equites* at once on account of its dangerously powerful character, and the office of chief of police (*praefectus vigilum*), the post of head of the corn supply (*praefectus annonae*), and that of postmaster-general (*praefectus vehiculorum*). A large number of further equestrian offices arose with the gradual development of the individual branches of government, in particular of the financial administration; their incumbents usually received the rank of *procurator*.

Up to the second century A.D. the central departments operating directly under the princeps were not filled with senators or *equites* but were administered by imperial freedmen. They were originally purely internal auxiliary organs of the princeps in his personal administrative activity, but developed from the time of Claudius a firmer organization and a more independent position. The 'chief of accounts' (*a rationibus*) of the princeps, who originally occupied no greater position than the corresponding private employees of other well-to-do Romans, now became a sort of imperial minister of finance; the princeps's correspondence was now kept up, according to its formal character, by two separate offices *ab epistulis* and *a libellis*, to which a further special office for keeping the imperial archives (*a memoria*) was added. It is peculiarly relevant and is a result of the highly personal character borne, and necessarily borne, by the régime of the princeps, that these leading offices were in the hands of freedmen, men highly educated and experienced in affairs, mostly of Greek origin and responsible for much of great significance in the administration of the Empire. Not until Hadrian (A.D. 117–38) were these posts, too, always filled by *equites*. The building up of the imperial financial administration increasingly

suppressed the pernicious system of tax-farming. This development benefited not only the state revenues, but also those who
owed taxes, particularly since the *fiscus* was subject to the law courts
just like a private citizen. The permanent supervision maintained
by the princeps over the entire administration of the Empire, and
particularly over the administration of justice, promoted the
certainty of the laws and reduced corruption, though without
suppressing it completely.[1] On the whole, the Empire was not only
more intensively but also far better administered in the first two
and a half centuries of the Principate than it had been under the
Republic.

4. *The succession.* The weakest point in Augustus' ingenious
scheme was the problem of the succession to the Principate. Since
the monarchical power of the 'first citizen' was rooted not in the
constitution but in a political ideology, there could be no question
of statutory regulation of a system of succession. Above all, any
such thing as recognition of a succession in the family of the
princeps was simply irreconcilable with the official theory of the
continuation of the Republic. Election by the most important of
the republican organs of state, the Senate, could by reason of the
powerlessness of this body usually be no more than a formality;
and if it were otherwise, it would have been undesirable, for the
princeps made understandably strong efforts—at least in the first
century of the new order, and again in later times—to secure in
practice the succession to his position within his own family, even
if there were no legal means of ensuring this. Finally, there was
always the possibility that the army, the strongest support of the
monarchy, would express its wishes with regard to the succession
and if necessary would enforce them with armed might.

Thus with the death of every princeps there arose a more or less
critical moment for the inner peace of the Empire. The problem of
the succession was solved, however, according to the circumstances of the individual case: sometimes by way of inheritance,
sometimes through election by the Senate, but after the end of the
second century almost always through the decision of the army, or,
more properly speaking, of the armies, which stood, widely separated from one another, on the boundaries of the Empire and

---

[1] We possess numerous reports from the period of the Principate of *repetundae* prosecutions of corrupt and extortionate governors. They usually took place in this era before the
Senate or, if imperial officials of *eques*-rank were involved, before the princeps himself.

which frequently raised up rival contenders among whom a decision had to be reached by means of civil war. The only means, and
certainly not an infallible one, against the dangers inherent in the
succession, was the idea of the co-regency. Augustus had admitted
his chosen successor to share in the affairs of government even
during his own lifetime, and also in external ways indicated that
he was the future princeps. Later even clearer cases of co-regency
are met with, and even isolated cases of joint reign, in which two
principes ruled simultaneously with the same powers. Experience
taught that to hand on the Principate to a blood-descendant could
easily bring the wrong man to the leading place in the world
Empire; while on the other hand, in view of all the difficulties
inherent in the succession, the sense of legitimacy which a relation
of the preceding princeps would enjoy proved an almost indispensable advantage. At the end of the first century A.D. (from Nerva
onwards) a practice therefore arose whereby the princeps adopted
the best of his assistants and then designated him as his successor:
a procedure which gave the Empire a series of great and noble
rulers (Trajan, Hadrian, Antoninus Pius, and Marcus Aurelius)
and in certain respects represented the most consistent implementa-
tion of the idea of the Principate.

Even if, as we have just seen, the determination of the succession
was a purely political proceeding to which no fixed legal rule
applied, yet the new princeps always needed to be legitimated by
the transference to him of those powers which belonged to him
within the framework of the republican constitution—above all
the tribunician power and the proconsular *imperium*. The decision
about this was probably taken in the first place by the Senate; but
apparently it was regarded as important to reinforce this significant act by means of a popular law (a form which for other purposes
was no longer used). This is at any rate what happened on the
accession of Vespasian, who reached power through a military
revolution, and whose statute of appointment is partly preserved
in an inscription (the so-called *lex de imperio Vespasiani*: Bruns,
Fontes, no. 56).

5. *Achievements of the Principate; economic and social conditions;
outgrowing of the city state.* The Principate made possible for more
than 200 years the peaceful development of the Empire and of the
whole ancient civilized world; the succession-struggles after the
deaths of Nero and Commodus represent in perspective only short

and insignificant episodes in this long period of peace; and the foreign wars were waged on the distant frontiers of the Empire, even if, as in the campaigns of Trajan and Marcus Aurelius, they sometimes subjected its economic strength to a dangerous strain.

The generous personal régime of the principes benefited the provinces above all: these had suffered very greatly in the conditions of the late Republic and now, especially in the first century A.D., experienced a period of great material prosperity. Italy herself shared only for a while in this economic boom, for in spite of all measures of reform the severe social damage sustained in the late Republic could not be enduringly repaired. Augustus tried by means of a series of basic statutes to revive decayed marital and class morals, to avert the dangers of childlessness, and to check the increase of foreign elements in the citizen population caused by immense manumissions of slaves of the most heterogeneous origins.[1] He also founded settlements in Italy which were intended primarily to provide for veterans of the last civil wars (and were carried out only by means of a brutal clearance of the previous owners); in the long run these settlements probably led to a not inconsiderable increase of the small peasant-proprietor class in the sense of the programme once pursued by the Gracchi.[2] Later, Nerva, Trajan, and their immediate successors set up comprehensive foundations for the education of children of poor citizen families; the capital of these foundations was placed at the disposal of Italian farmers in the form of perpetual loans at a low rate of interest, and thus served simultaneously to combat childlessness and to support agriculture. But in spite of all these measures large-scale ranching and with it the depopulation of Italy made further strides, and the economic lead over the provinces in wine, oil, and industrial production which Italy had held at the beginning of the Principate was gradually lost. A consciously directed economic policy such as is known today and such as was known even in Hellenistic Egypt was never applied by the emperors of

---

[1] The *leges Iuliae de adulteriis coercendis* and *de maritandis ordinibus* of 18 B.C. and the *lex Papia Poppaea* (A.D. 9) were directed to the raising of the standards of marital morals and the combating of celibacy and of childlessness. The *lex Fufia Caninia* (2 B.C.) and the *lex Aelia Sentia* (A.D. 4) represented a (certainly rather faint-hearted) attempt to limit manumissions of slaves. Details about the contents of these statutes will be found in treatises on Roman civil law.

[2] It probably often happened that these veterans, inexperienced or out of practice in agricultural work, leased out their land and then led modest *rentier* existences in the cities.

the Principate period. They concerned themselves with immediate problems like the corn supply for Rome, for which Augustus had created a government monopoly and which then increasingly developed; but they gave no special attention to the individual branches of the economy according to a unified plan, and the overwhelming impression given by the economic life of that time is of liberalistic *laissez-faire*. Thus a trend began which in the long run was bound to lead a transference of the economic and finally of the spiritual and political centres of gravity from Italy to other parts of the Empire, especially to the eastern part.

For the moment, however, Rome and its people were still the centre of the world Empire, a Roman citizen counted as a sharer in world domination and Roman culture was displaying an immense power of expansion. The whole western part of the Empire was more or less thoroughly Romanized in an astonishingly short space of time. In some parts of Spain, North Africa, and southern France this Romanization had already begun in the last century of the Republic, promoted by the advance of the Roman merchant, the setting up of Roman citizen colonies, and the bestowal of Latin rights on individual communities. Under the Principate it made progress, among other things through the settlement of veteran soldiers in the frontier areas of the Empire (which probably contributed to the gradual desolation of Italy). Following upon the Romanizing of the provinces, numerous individuals and also whole communities or even provinces were accorded Roman citizenship or 'Latin' rights. There is no need to point out that in this way the city-state structure of the Empire, still maintained in form, now finally lost its meaning, and that Roman citizenship increasingly developed the significance of the citizenship of an Empire.

It was only in the eastern provinces that Roman culture made no appreciable conquests, since here Greek culture prevailed, a match for that of Rome and indeed in many respects still superior to it; in addition, it had for long been respected and spared by the Romans, and by many emperors, above all Hadrian, actually fostered. However, Roman and Greek civilization were increasingly thought of as a unity, and thus east and west grew to a certain extent together into a compact cultural whole.

The economic and cultural basis of the Romano-Hellenistic world Empire was the innumerable urban commonwealths, big and small. Although these did not possess the freedom of political self-determination, as they had done in the era of the old Greek and Italian city states, they had at least a large measure of self-government (though one admittedly unprotected against encroachments by organs of the Roman state); and, in spite of the differences in legal standing which had arisen when the Roman Empire was being founded but were now fading away, all still had a share in the same liberal economic life and in the same civilization and culture. Men from the upper stratum of provincial citizen communities began as early as the first century A.D. to climb as high as the Roman Senate. Towards the end of the second century a good half of the senators came from the provinces, and a considerable number of them were of Greek or oriental origin. With Trajan (A.D. 98–117), who was born in the old citizen colony of Italica near Seville, and Hadrian (117–38), also from Italica, the Principate itself came into the hands of Spanish Romans; and only a few of their successors had their homes in Italy.

In this way the organization of the Empire, laid down in republican times and resting on the right of conquest of the city state of Rome, was increasingly overtaken by developments; and, looked at in the large historical context, it was nothing but a necessary result of this development when Antoninus Caracalla, by a famous edict of A.D. 212 (the *constitutio Antoniniana*), extended the Roman citizenship at one stroke to the whole Empire. This edict came into being for unimportant reasons of contemporary policy, probably above all through lack of money,[1] but it is none the less a milestone in the history of the Roman Empire. It has been preserved for us on a papyrus in the Giessen collections (Pap. Giss. 40) though in such a mutilated form that important questions must remain unanswered. One special class of the population of the Empire, the *dediticii*, was perhaps excluded from the grant of citizenship, but it is not yet established beyond doubt which elements of the population belonged to this class.

With the *constitutio Antoniniana* the idea of the supra-national world Empire had finally triumphed over the idea of the supremacy of the city state of Rome. The republican constitution which Augustus had artificially preserved and which in the course

---

[1] It is presumed that Caracalla wished by the extension of the citizenship to increase the yield of the 5 per cent inheritance tax (only levied on Roman citizens) which Augustus had originally introduced for the support of the army.

of time had become more and more a thin and hollow pretence was ripe for final collapse. It was now possible for the first citizen of the city of Rome to become absolute ruler of all the nations of the world; his seat was no longer necessarily in Rome, but was determined exclusively by economic and cultural factors and by the military and political needs of the Empire. Economic distress, which began as early as the second century A.D., together with external and internal political catastrophes in the third century, completed this structural change comparatively rapidly and thoroughly, and allowed the old order to survive only in the shape of a few venerable relics and a number of petrified formalities. The nature and structure of the late Roman state in the form which it took more and more clearly from the end of the third century onwards will be briefly considered at the beginning of the last section of this work.

4

CRIMINAL PROSECUTIONS

1. *The emergence of the* iudicia publica

THE 'private criminal law' of the Twelve Tables reflected the conditions of a primitive commonwealth of modest dimensions and rustic character. It was bound to prove increasingly inadequate as Rome developed into a metropolis dominated by powerful social tensions; and the growth of the urban proletariat and of the slave population was certainly accompanied by a rise in criminality which demanded vigorous measures for the maintenance of public security. There thus arose, probably in the course of the third century B.C., but no later than the beginning of the second century, a drastic police-jurisdiction directed against those guilty of crimes of violence, arson, poisoning, and theft. All of these were liable to the death penalty (though in the case of the thief, only if he had been discovered in the act of stealing or bringing the object home). Even the mere carrying of weapons with criminal intent, and the buying or selling or even possession of deadly poison, were equally capital offences. A criminal arrested by these police authorities was punished officially, though the procedure could be initiated by a private citizen by means of laying an information (*nominis delatio*), in which case it was usually the informant's business to produce the evidence of the alleged crime. The *praetor urbanus*, as the possessor of the general function of jurisdiction, was the person competent to exercise this police justice; but he left the punishment of slaves and of criminals from the lower stratum of the free population to the *tresviri capitales*, magistrates of lower rank,[1] who also had the task of policing the city, of superintending the state prison, and of carrying out executions. Criminals who confessed or who had been caught in the act were apparently put to death by the *tresviri* without any court trial; and, in the case of

[1] The office was created at the beginning of the third century B.C.; it was later counted as part of the so-called Vigintivirate, which included also some of the *praefecti iure dicundo*, the *decemviri stlitibus iudicandis*, and the officials whose job it was to keep the streets of Rome clean.

slaves, confession was induced by means of torture. But if the accused denied the crime alleged against him, then the advisory committee (*consilium*) of the *triumvir* who was dealing with the matter decided as to his guilt or innocence. Only such cases as concerned citizens of some standing, and who had not confessed, were dealt with by the praetor himself or by an investigator (*quaesitor*) appointed by him. In this case the verdict of a *consilium* was always necessary. The punishment of those found guilty was then the praetor's affair; he could not substitute another punishment for the death penalty fixed by law, but no doubt could allow the person condemned to escape into exile and would then pronounce the *aqua et igni interdictio* against him.

Trials for political crimes in the early Republic were conducted, as has been seen, by *tribuni plebis*, aediles, or quaestors. But in the period after the second Punic war this procedure soon proved to be outdated, since the popular assembly no longer consisted mostly of careful and thoughtful farmers, as it had previously, but was dominated by an urban mob exposed in large measure to demagogic influences. In addition, politics and government had become so complicated that the ordinary citizen was often no longer in a position to judge the matters alleged as part of the crime. It consequently became more and more common for the Senate to entrust the investigation and trial of political offences, particularly derelictions of duty by provincial governors and other magistrates, to the consuls or to one of the praetors and their *consilium*, which consisted of senators and was therefore expert in the field. These extraordinary courts (*quaestiones extraordinariae*) were also set up for dealing with offences committed by large numbers of criminals which could not be handled in the normal course of public criminal justice, and for the repression of movements dangerous to the state.

All these criminal tribunals (*iudicia publica*) probably bore the signs of improvisation up to the end of the second century B.C. They were formed as the occasion arose, and the choice of the *consilium* which had to decide the question of guilt lay presumably either with the presiding magistrate or with the Senate. In the sole case of proceedings for extortion committed by Roman officials in Italy or the provinces (the *repetundae* procedure) there had been, since the *lex Calpurnia repetundarum* (149 B.C.), a special list of judges, valid for the whole official year, out of which the *consilium* was formed by co-operation between accuser and accused. This proceeding was under the presidency of the *praetor peregrinus*. Other 'standing' courts of this kind (*quaestiones perpetuae*) could apparently not be created until the *consilia* of the criminal courts were freed from the necessity of including only senators (of whom there were at that time normally only 300); and this limitation was removed by the *lex Sempronia iudiciaria* of C. Gracchus (122 B.C.) under which *equites* were admitted to seats on the tribunals. This statute represents the beginning of the development of the system of jury-courts which administered ordinary criminal justice in the late Republic and early Empire.

11. *The jury-courts of the late Republic and early Empire*

The standing courts already in existence at the end of the second century and probably created by the *lex Sempronia* were renovated and increased in number by Sulla in the course of his constitutional reforms. There were now courts for high treason and disobedience to the superior organs of state (*quaestio maiestatis*),[1] the embezzlement of state property (*quaestio peculatus*), bribery at elections (*quaestio ambitus*), extortion in the provinces (*quaestio repetundarum*), murder by violence or by poisoning and the endangering of public security (*quaestio de sicariis et veneficis*), forgery of wills or of coins (*quaestio de falsis*), and serious wrongs including the infringement of domestic peace (*quaestio de iniuriis*). Others were added later, such as the *quaestio de vi* for violent offences of every kind, and the *quaestio de adulteriis* for adultery and the seduction of respectable unmarried women. These depended partly on the criminal legislation of Augustus which completed the development of the *iudicia publica*. Praetors presided as a rule over the individual *quaestiones*.[2]

---

[1] *Maiestas* means authority (properly speaking 'being greater'), and *crimen* (*laesae*) *maiestatis* thus means an offending of authority. The statute of Augustus seems to have placed the protection of the state and of the republican authority in the forefront, though it is not entirely clear whether it mentioned the princeps as such. In the course of the first century of the Empire, however, an attack on the person of the princeps came increasingly to be the chief instance of the crime of *maiestas*, and the application of the statute was very far-reaching.

[2] Before Sulla entrusted the presidency of the *quaestiones* to the magistrates who had formerly been provincial praetors, these courts were usually presided over by *iudices quaestionis*. This office was filled between the aedileship and the quaestorship. It continued in existence until the reforms of Augustus, since even after Sulla's time the number of praetors was not sufficient to provide presidents for all the *quaestiones*.

We have a fairly exact knowledge of the procedure of these jury-courts from the speeches of Cicero, although of course here it is seen only from the perspective of the advocate. The trial was officially initiated not by the presiding magistrate or by a public prosecutor, but always required the laying of informations (*nominis delatio*) by a private person. This laying of informations now became a real prosecution; though if the competent judicial magistrate received them (and this question was decided at any rate in certain cases not by the magistrate himself but by a *consilium* formed from the judges of his *quaestio*) the person laying the informations obtained the rights and duties of a litigant; it was now his business to convict the accused of the crime before the court. Every citizen of good reputation was, in principle, permitted to initiate a prosecution (except in the case of the procedure before the *quaestio de iniuriis*); and it is here that we see the special character of the 'public' criminal process as contrasted with the private suit of the Twelve Tables which was open only to the party injured or (in the case of killing) to his kin. The motives of the prosecutors were naturally very varied. Besides an injured party's thirst for vengeance, which might be satisfied in a *iudicium publicum* as well as in a private action, enmities which had nothing to do with the crime in question played a great part; so also did political ambition, and, above all, greed for money, for the criminal statutes promised rewards of considerable size for the victorious prosecutor: indeed, in the case of capital condemnation the prosecutor actually received a proportion of the confiscated property. Without doubt there were many people who made a business of instituting prosecutions, and very few who in instituting them thought only of the public interest. An attempt was made to combat the grave abuses to which this system of prosecution gave rise, by providing that, if the prosecutor's charge were shown to be unfounded, he himself was immediately subjected to a proceeding for 'calumny' (*calumnia*), condemnation in which involved public infamy and, in particular, a prohibition from ever again instituting a prosecution.

If the judicial magistrate had accepted an 'information', he next ordered the *consilium*, i.e. the sworn jury which had to decide the question of the guilt or innocence of the accused, to be formed by lot from the judge-list of the *quaestio* concerned; and in the course of this process both the accuser and the accused had the right to reject a certain number of judges. The members of the *consilium*

chosen in this way—their number was different at different times
and in different *quaestiones* but might be as high as seventy-five—
were sworn in before the beginning of the trial. The trial itself was
dominated by the accuser's initiative, even more so than is today
the case in English prosecutions. The accuser called and examined
the prosecution witnesses, the accused did the same with the witnesses from whom he expected favourable testimony. Sharp cross-
examination took place. The judges listened in silence, and were
forbidden to speak to each other. The presiding magistrate restricted himself to ensuring an orderly conduct of the trial, in
which duty he was usually very easy-going. The fairness with
which the rules of Roman criminal procedure afforded the accused
scope for making his defence is most impressive and might even
seem to us exaggerated. He could sometimes have as many as six
advocates appearing for him. To them and their client express
statutory provisions accorded extremely generous speaking time
measured by the clepsydra and amounting to half as much time
again as was at the disposal of the prosecution. The *consilium*
reached its verdict, as a rule, by means of voting tablets which
were secretly placed in an urn. An equality of votes meant acquittal;
and if a large number of judges abstained from voting, a fresh trial
was held. In a *repetundae* case, in which the political and usually
also the financial existence of former magistrates was at stake and
numerous individual occurrences usually had to be investigated,
a second trial was actually prescribed by law in all cases.

On foot of the vote of the *consilium* the judicial magistrates
announced either that the accused had, according to the belief of
the court, committed the act alleged against him (*fecisse videtur*)
or had not committed it. In principle, no punishment was pronounced at this stage, for this was already clear from the statute
on which the prosecution was based. It was only in those cases
where the punishment consisted of a money fine the amount of
which depended on the damage which the accused had done that
an assessment of the penalty was needed. This was the job of the
consilium, and it therefore had to meet again, after the verdict of
guilty, for a further proceeding about the amount in issue (*litis
aestimatio*). The carrying-out of the punishment was a matter for
the presiding magistrate. In the last century of the Republic the
death penalty was, so far as can be seen, no longer carried out on
persons condemned in the *quaestio*-procedure, persons who as a

rule were *honestiores*, i.e. belonged to the upper classes; instead, the magistrate gave them an opportunity to escape into exile. On the other hand, slaves and criminals belonging to the lower orders of the free population (*humiliores*), who had been condemned for a capital offence by the police-court of the *tresviri capitales* (which evidently existed up to the end of the Republic), were doubtless as a rule put to death. Only in this way was it possible to restrain professional criminality, particularly since punishment by way of deprivation of liberty was still unknown in republican criminal law.

III. *The development of 'extraordinary' criminal jurisdiction and the decline of the jury-courts under the Principate*

As has already been indicated, Augustus did not abolish the late republican jury-courts but on the contrary renovated them and increased their number. Thus they remained under the Principate the organs of 'ordinary' criminal justice (*ordo iudiciorum publicorum*). But Augustus simultaneously subjected the police system and police justice to a thoroughgoing reform by appointing a senator of consular rank to the permanent post of urban chief of police (*praefectus urbi*) and by creating a strong force of police quartered in barracks, the *cohortes vigilum*. The *praefectus urbi* and also, though with a limited jurisdiction, the commander of the *vigiles* (*praefectus vigilum*) replaced the *tresviri capitales* as the organs of police justice. Outside the city of Rome and its environs, too, Augustus took energetic steps to put down crime, particularly gangsterism which had grown greatly in the lax conditions of the late Republic and during the civil wars in Italy. He covered the country with military posts, probably mostly garrisoned with men drawn from the praetorian guard, the only military unit stationed in Italy and thus under the command of the *praefecti praetorio*. Probably the commanders of the individual military posts always had a jurisdiction over criminals from the lower orders (especially slaves) while other criminal cases were sent on to the *praefecti praetorio*.

It may be assumed that this organization of the police-system by Augustus represented not only a decisive advance in the combating of crime, but also an important improvement in criminal justice. Police jurisdiction no longer lay in the hands of young magistrates of inferior rank who changed each year and thus had little time to gather experience. It was now exercised by tried men, some of whom were even prominent jurists,[1] and whose duration of office in any case made possible a certain stability in the administration of justice. Compared with the jury-courts the procedure before the *praefectus urbi*, at least, was in many respects superior. It was more concise and quicker, and while in the jury-courts, on account of the complicated statutory requirements about procedure and of the parties' respective positions of power, there were endless delays,[2] the parties before the *praefectus urbi*, in particular the accuser, could count on a rapid decision. And just as the *praefectus urbi* was usually superior in knowledge and experience even to the praetors who presided over the jury-courts, so too the *consilium* of consulars and other senators was in general more useful than the judges of the ordinary criminal courts. Finally, the prefect's court was not, like the jury-courts, a special court before which only certain statutorily defined offences could be tried; on the contrary, judgement could be passed on every offence against public order and security. Unlike the ordinary courts, there was no need, before the court of the prefect, for several different trials if the same delinquent had offended different criminal statutes. The prefect could even punish offences for which no ordinary criminal prosecution was provided by statute, and in respect of the punishment to be inflicted he had a freer hand than the magistrates presiding over the *quaestiones*. All this may explain how the 'extraordinary' criminal jurisdiction (*cognitio extra ordinem*) of the *praefectus urbi* began even in the first century A.D. to supplant the 'ordinary' jurisdiction of the jury-courts; though some of the latter were still in existence in the second century. The last report which we have concerning them comes from the period of the Severan emperors and refers to the *quaestio de adulteriis*; probably this court lasted longer than the others because it was concerned with offences which were especially far removed from the sphere of the *praefectus urbi* who

[1] The post of *praefectus urbi* was occupied by the jurist Pegasus in the reign of Domitian; and in that of Marcus Aurelius by the celebrated Salvius Julianus; one *praefectus vigilum* was Q. Cervidius Scaevola.

[2] We possess in a papyrus a speech of the Emperor Claudius about abuses in the ordinary courts and, in particular, about litigation delayed by the parties (see J. Stroux, *Eine Gerichtsreform des Kaisers Claudius*, 1929). At the time of the Emperor Septimius Severus more than 3,000 adultery cases were pending before the *quaestio de adulteriis*, of which only a minority were dealt with.

concerned himself originally only with offences threatening public order and peace.

Alongside the jury-courts of the *ordo iudiciorum publicorum* and the extraordinary courts of the *praefectus urbi*, the *praefectus vigilum*, and (in the parts of Italy outside Rome) the *praefectus praetorio*, the Senate and the princeps also functioned as organs of criminal justice. The criminal jurisdiction of the Senate going back to Tiberius[1] was basically limited to members of the senatorial order. This was doubtless meant as a privilege; persons of senatorial rank were not to be judged in the publicity of the jury-court procedure and by jurors who were mostly of lower rank. However, since the Senate was becoming increasingly obedient to the real or even presumed will of the princeps, this privilege proved in many cases to be fatal for the accused, particularly when a political accusation was in question (trials for *maiestas*), and it was thus often more advantageous for the accused if the princeps took the case before his own court. This explains the fact that from the middle of the first century the Senate as a court loses importance by comparison with the court of the princeps.

According to the system created by Augustus, the princeps had the power of exercising jurisdiction at least within the framework of his *imperium proconsulare*, which, however, extended only to the provinces and the army, and indeed in theory perhaps only to those provinces which he himself administered (the so-called imperial provinces). Normally, his jurisdictional powers were exercised there by his legates. However, whenever the princeps himself was present in one of these provinces he was without doubt entitled to take over himself the role of judicial magistrate. It was also natural for the inhabitants of the province, particularly the resident citizens, to appeal to him as the real possessor of the jurisdiction applicable to them against decisions of his representatives. It seems doubtful whether the princeps could lay claim to the right of jurisdiction in Rome also on the strength of the official (republican) powers which had been bestowed on him.[2]

---

[1] As early as Augustus a procedure before the Senate instead of before the *quaestio* was in certain conditions permitted in the case of a trial for *repetundae* by a decree of the Senate (the *senatus consultum Calvisianum*) preserved in an inscription along with the Cyrenaean edicts.

[2] An affirmative answer to this question depends on whether the consular power was in fact bestowed on Augustus (as the historian Cassius Dio asserts) or merely the honorary privileges of a consul.

It is, however, certain that as possessor of the *tribunicia potestas* he was entitled to exercise a sort of supervision over the administration of justice. Even the tribunes of the republican era used to investigate the decrees of judicial magistrates on the appeal (*appellatio*) of a litigant and if necessary quash them by their right of *intercessio*, without of course being in a position (as the emperor later was) to set another decision in place of the one quashed.

The question of how and when the court of the princeps, starting from these constitutional conditions, developed into a settled institution is difficult to answer, because the Roman historians on whom we have to rely for information up to the late second century have handed down only a very incomplete, vague, and often prejudiced account of imperial justice. Augustus seems to have acted the judge in various contingencies, though he hardly claimed a general judicial competence, and in particular he seems to have refrained from interfering in the administration of ordinary civil and criminal justice (which he himself had reformed). The same is evidently true of Tiberius. Only under subsequent emperors, above all Claudius, does the real development of the imperial court of justice seem to have taken place. It reached its high point in the period from Hadrian to the emperors of the Severan dynasty. The emperor could now bring before his own tribunal every legal dispute, whether on foot of an appeal against the decision by another court, or as first and last instance at the request of the parties or probably even by his own decision. Although many emperors devoted a great deal of time to jurisdiction, still at no stage can more than a small fraction of all cases have come before their court. However, since their decisions departed in many ways from established patterns, these judgements (*decreta*) came to be regarded as authoritative, particularly in the field of civil law, and tended to be both cited and followed as though they were statutes.

We are very poorly informed about the details of the procedure before the 'extraordinary' criminal courts of the imperial era (including the emperor's own court).[1] Prosecutions could certainly be instituted officially; but even here the system of privately instituted prosecution was the norm. The proceedings were conducted

---

[1] The reports about the proceedings against Christian martyrs are not helpful about the ordinary procedure, because the martyrs had avowed themselves openly as being of Christian faith, i.e. were self-confessed, and their cases did not, accordingly, need to be decided before the *consilium*.

with greater speed and elasticity than in the jury-courts. We have, however, no reason to doubt that the accused was given enough time to make his defence. The principle that it was not the presiding official but his *consilium* who reached the verdict seems to have applied to extraordinary criminal justice just as to trials before jury-courts. Admittedly, we have definite indications of this only in some reports about the imperial court; but it is scarcely to be imagined that other court-presidents could in this respect have behaved more independently than the princeps.

In regard to the punishments which the presiding official could impose on the confessed criminal or on one found guilty by the *consilium* there existed in the extraordinary criminal justice of the imperial era a greater discretion than in proceedings before the jury-courts. While the latter remained tied to the republican and Augustan criminal statutes, which provided either money fines or capital punishment (i.e. in this context, exile), the official judges entrusted with extraordinary criminal jurisdiction could order a defendant to be sent to a school of gladiators or to forced labour in mines or other public works (*condemnatio in metallum, in opus publicum*), though this punishment was inflicted only on (free) persons of low social standing. The same thing held, as a rule, for the death penalty, which in the case of prominent citizens (municipal councillors and upwards) was seldom executed even by the extraordinary courts except for serious political crimes. For such persons the normal capital sentence was deportation to an island (with or without imprisonment while there); in less serious cases mere relegation was thought enough, i.e. banishment from Rome and Italy or from the province in which the condemned person had lived. Relegation and deportation took the place of the permitted exile, as the latter had lost its significance through the extension of and structural changes in the Empire.

The jury-courts of the Republic had shown signs of developing something like the rule of law and the principle of impartial criminal justice, and with their disappearance this tendency was also partly submerged. But the extraordinary procedure was more effective, more flexible and, looked at as a whole, probably more just, above all *vis-à-vis* the small man who had had very little benefit from the achievements of the jury-court procedure. It is true that he was still liable to very much harsher punishments than the members of the upper classes; but he was no longer as liable to the death sentence as in republican times, and, in addition, he probably had in general a better opportunity for making his defence before the court of the *praefectus urbi* or the *praefectus vigilum* than before the *tresviri capitales* of the Republic. In the second and early third centuries A.D. imperial legal decisions and opinions directed the practice of criminal law and procedure along the path of careful establishment and assessment of guilt[1] and of punishment differentiated accordingly. The late classical jurists dealt with public criminal law in fairly exhaustive treatises, although apparently not with the same thoroughness as civil law, which had a very much older scientific tradition behind it. Associated with the modest remains of this criminal law literature of the imperial age which were included in the Justinianic legislation there arose, after the revival of Roman law in the late Middle Ages, the first beginnings of European criminal jurisprudence.

[1] It is from Trajan that the observation comes that it is better that a guilty person should go unpunished than that an innocent person should be punished (Ulp. *D.* 48. 19. 5 pr.).

5

THE DEVELOPMENT OF CIVIL LAW IN THE
ROMAN WORLD STATE AND EMPIRE

1. *International legal relations and the* ius gentium

As we have seen, from about the third century B.C. Rome stood as
a great political and economic power in the centre of the stream of
Hellenistic world traffic. Roman merchants soon reached the east
of the Mediterranean world and foreign traders came in much
greater numbers than before to Rome and Roman Italy. For legal
relations between persons belonging to different states there prevailed in Rome and generally in the ancient world the dominating
principle of the *personal* application of laws. The law of each state
basically applied only to citizens, not to foreigners. A foreigner who
had not been accorded, on foot of treaties between states, a more or
less comprehensive equal status with a citizen (*commercium*)—and
in some circumstances even *conubium*, an equivalence of rights of
marriage—had in the case of a legal conflict to make use of the help
of a citizen, his 'protector' (*hospes*, πρόξενος).[1] In the east, dominated as it was by Greek culture and speech, this legal isolation of
individual states had been at least to some extent overcome in
practice by the formation of a commercial code common to all the
Greeks and based on the mutual relationship of all Greek legal
systems. But the old Roman civil law with its peculiar forms stood
at first like a foreign body in international legal relations, a foreign
body moreover which seemed to resist adaptation: for if Hellenistic
commercial law had been pragmatically shaped and was in a high
degree elastic, old Roman civil law was dominated by the formalistic
interpretative art of the *pontifices*, and was rigid, narrow, and
capable of being made to fit changed circumstances only with the
help of very complicated forms and acts. Again, writing was very
widely used for important legal transactions in the Hellenistic
world, but Roman law recognized the validity only of spoken words

---

[1] Within the Greek world the institution of προξενία developed gradually into a settled
institution which has certain similarities with the modern system of consulates.

arranged in quite definite formulas; and while Hellenistic commercial law arrived at its own freedom by means of contacts between members of different states, the Roman *ius civile* remained in principle closed to foreigners.

The entry of Romans into the full stream of world commerce was thus bound to lead to innovations of great consequence in Roman legal life. Rome, too, found herself compelled to afford legal protection to the foreigner as such—as had for long been usual in the Greek world. We do not know when this first happened, but we do know at least one definite step towards the proper protection of foreigners in Rome: around the middle of the third century B.C. commercial traffic with Rome had grown to such a degree that a special magistrate was appointed to handle cases between foreigners, or between a foreigner and a Roman. He was called 'the foreign praetor', *praetor inter peregrinos* or *peregrinus*, in order to distinguish him from the city praetor (*praetor urbanus*), the original magistrate for cases between Roman citizens. We know hardly any details of his jurisdiction, but it may be presumed that it played a considerable part both in liberating legal procedure from the formalism of the Twelve Tables and also in the recognition of certain formless contracts (sale, hire, contracts for work and services, mandate, partnership). At any rate, these contracts, unlike the old Roman transactions creating liability, could be concluded even by non-citizens without *commercium*. Their obligatory force rested, as later jurists used to say, not on the *ius civile*, the law peculiar to Roman citizens, but on the *ius gentium*; this was a way of expressing the idea that such contracts were recognized by all nations and could thus be validly concluded not only between Romans but also between Romans and foreigners and between foreigners themselves.

The notion of the *ius gentium* has thus a wider significance than the modern notion of 'international law' which is derived from it. The latter is restricted to describing the complex of norms which by virtue of international treaties or common agreement as to the law jointly operate to control the relations of states with each other. Norms of this kind did indeed count as part of the *ius gentium* and therefore this expression is used where historians (especially Livy) speak of the sacredness of international treaties or of the immunity of ambassadors. But the idea of *ius gentium* extended also to other areas of the legal system, particularly private law. Because it was

known that contracts of sale, service, loan, and so on were customarily concluded and observed among other nations too, it was
assumed that the obligation arising from such transactions rested
on legal principles which were everywhere in force in the same
way. It is true that this theory, which probably arose in late republican times, was not built upon any thorough knowledge of
foreign legal systems, about which the Romans probably never
bothered themselves very much. For example, they apparently
never realized that the legal structure of sale in the Greek world
was quite different from its structure in their own legal system.
What they thought of as *ius gentium* and applied to Romans as well
as foreigners was in reality Roman law both by nature and by
origin. For great though the changes may have been which economic life and legal practice experienced through the influence of
world commerce and of Hellenistic common law, a simple adoption of foreign legal norms into Roman law was not in fact the consequence of these influences, or if so it was only to a very limited
extent. Seen as a whole, commerce with foreigners and contact
with foreign legal systems provided merely the impetus for the
creation of new rules of law in which the typically Roman nature
of the old *ius civile* perpetuated itself. This independence of legal
thought does not seem surprising in the case of a people which
was just then in the act of conquering the whole of Italy from the
narrow base of the countryside of Latium, and which later, in the
Principate, set its stamp on the whole of Spain and France and
other districts of the Empire. We shall see that even when the
Romans no longer played the leading role in the political and cultural life of the Empire, Roman law still basically preserved its
own national character.

11. *The Law of the Empire and native law*

With the expansion of the Roman Empire the sphere of application of Roman law grew correspondingly. It is true that in the
Roman world Empire of the late Republic and Principate the
principle of the personal application of laws still held. The only
people who lived according to the Roman *ius civile* were Roman
citizens, wherever resident. The subject peoples used in principle
their own native law, and when they litigated before their own
courts it was this law which was applied. If, voluntarily or involun-
tarily, they sought their rights before Roman courts, the case was

conducted according to Roman forms, and in general it is probable that Roman principles of *ius gentium* were applied, at any rate in the field of commercial law: for the reason that Roman courts neither knew the provisions of the subjects' own legal systems nor were able or willing to open their minds to the different sets of notions of such legal systems.

In the form of the *ius gentium*, therefore, Roman legal culture stretched in all directions far beyond its own narrow field which was properly the community of Roman citizens. At the same time, however, this narrow sphere of Roman law kept being itself extended through the extension of the citizenship. After the social war in the eighties of the first century B.C., which led to the reception of all the Italian allies into the Roman citizenship, Roman law alone operated in Italy. The foundation of citizen colonies overseas had begun at the end of the Republic, together with the bestowal of citizenship on individuals, whole communities, and even provinces. Under the Principate this extension went on with ever greater generosity, so that the legal community of Roman citizens went deep into the provinces.[1] Finally, when the *constitutio Antoniniana* of A.D. 212 adopted into the citizen body the mass of the population of the Empire which had up to then been excluded, it seemed that the whole *imperium Romanum* must have become a unified area in which from then onwards only Roman law, whether *ius civile* or *ius gentium*, must have been applied.

The latter view, once more or less universally held, was disproved at the end of the nineteenth century by the discoveries of Egyptian papyri. These showed that in this province both before and after the *Constitutio Antoniniana* an uninterrupted legal tradition prevailed which, looked at as a whole, rested throughout on the pre-Roman legal system and consisted of both Greek and native Egyptian elements. That things cannot have been very different in the other parts of the Greek half of the Empire was then shown by a careful examination of the imperial laws of the third century A.D., in particular of the numerous surviving constitutions

---

[1] However, we know a case of individual bestowal of citizenship in the time of Augustus in which the new citizens were expressly given the choice of whether they would bring their legal proceedings before Roman magistrates, or before the court of their own community, or before the courts of *civitates liberae* (see inscription from Rhosos on the borders of Cilicia and Syria, Riccobono, *F.I.R.A.*, i. 55. 53 ff.). Without doubt this choice of court also meant a choice of the law to be applied. We do not know whether it was usual or exceptional to combine a privilege like this with the bestowal of citizenship on individual provinces.

of Diocletian. These imperial laws are predominantly so-called 'rescripts', i.e. legal opinions which the emperors gave in concrete cases in answer to the inquiries of private persons or of officials or judges. We can see how the emperors, in very many of the rescripts in reply to questions which can only be understood by reference to the notions of the Greco-Hellenistic legal world of the East, urged the principles of Roman law and the decisions which Roman law provided. This means that the legal life of the Greek half of the Empire, even after the *constitutio Antoniniana*, was in fact very largely dominated by native schemes of legal thought. The 'national law' of the Greek East thus asserted itself in the face of the Roman imperial law. And indeed it could scarcely be otherwise. By the *constitutio Antoniniana* only the political status of the former subjects was changed. But the right of self-government of the erstwhile foreign communities continued unchanged and, along with it, probably their own administrations of justice as well, though to an extent which cannot be defined. Roman law must have been more or less strange to these local tribunals, if only for the reason that they mostly understood no Latin; and for this reason they quite naturally applied their own traditional rules of law. The scribes, too, who because of the widespread use of writing in the legal transactions of the Greek East were very important in legal life, continued to use their old formulas and attempted to reconcile them with the requirements of the law only outwardly.[1] Roman law was probably effectively applied only where the judges actually knew it; and this probably happened in the east at first only in the Roman governor's court.

Of course, we notice how in the provinces (even of the Greek half of the Empire), as early as the middle of the second century A.D. and specially· after the end of it, 'Roman jurists' (νομικοὶ Ῥωμαῖοι) appeared; they advised parties and judges and drew up documents which were supposed to be watertight according to Roman law. But apart from the fact that their abilities were

---

[1] A well-known example of this is as follows: the Roman law of contract had no such thing as the modern principle of 'freedom of contract' and allowed only certain definite types of contract, including the *stipulatio*, an oral question-and-answer agreement which had a purely formal character and could have every conceivable content (sale, gift, loan, etc.). The Hellenistic scribes understood of the nature and effect of the stipulation only this much, that every transaction was valid in which the parties had exchanged question and answer. Accordingly they used to add to their own native contractual forms the phrase καὶ ἐπερωτηθεὶς ὡμολόγησα ('and having been asked I acknowledged it').

probably very modest and not to be compared with those of the great metropolitan jurists, their number may have been comparatively small and their effectiveness may therefore not have been very widely felt. Their activity was probably limited to those places where the application of Roman law was observed in any case, i.e. basically the court of the Roman governor. Roman law may have extended its sphere somewhat, but it never entirely supplanted the native law until its own law-schools sprang up in the east of the Empire, especially the school of Berytos (Beirut) in Syria. But this development belongs to the last period of Roman legal history, the age of the Dominate; and in the study of the Dominate it will be seen that the survival of the native legal life of the east was not without influence on the development of Roman law.

The shape of relations between Empire law and national law in the eastern half of the Empire is much clearer than are the corresponding developments in the west. Here we not only lack the massive sources for the practical legal life of the Empire which we possess for the east in the papyri; we are also without the least idea of the legal systems which were once in force in pre-Roman times in these areas. It may at any rate be assumed that Roman law succeeded in establishing itself more fully in the west than in the east. Roman culture did not meet here, as in the Hellenistic area, with an equally developed or even superior civilization, and it therefore encountered no lasting resistance. Southern France, parts of Spain and Northern Africa, were to a considerable extent occupied by Roman or Italian settlers; and the extension of Roman citizenship among the natives began here much earlier and was more rapidly completed than in the east. Latin became the language of the whole western half of the Empire, and with it Roman civilization gained such a firm foothold that Spanish, Gaulish, or African authors increasingly set the tone of Roman literature in the period of the Principate. In such conditions it was natural for Roman law to be much more thoroughly applied than in the never-latinized east. It is possible of course that in the late Roman 'vulgar law' which in the fifth and sixth centuries A.D. was in force in Spain and southern France (the only areas in which we can see anything of the development of western provincial law) traces of pre-Roman national legal practices are embedded: but it seems unlikely that we shall ever be in a position to prove this.

III. *Sources and strata of law*

The old Roman *ius civile* was based on the Twelve Tables, interpretation of the Twelve Tables, and subsequently enacted popular
statutes. Since popular legislation encroached on the sphere of
civil law only with hesitation, usually for some special political
reason and always only in narrowly defined and isolated areas, it
was unable to do justice to the great economic and social changes
in Roman life after the third century B.C. The most significant
innovations in the private law of the late Republic were achieved,
accordingly, in the field of the application of law. The leading role
here lay in the hands of the jurisdictional magistrates, which in
Rome mainly meant the two praetors charged with the administration of civil justice. The rules newly applied in the jurisdiction of
these magistrates were placed in opposition to the *ius civile* under
the title 'magistrate's law' (*ius honorarium*). The greater part of the
ius honorarium applied also to legal relations with foreigners and
was thus simultaneously *ius gentium*; though in the course of time
there arose also principles of magistrate's law which helped to
develop the statutory law applying only to citizens and which were
therefore themselves applied only to citizens. On the other hand,
there were certain statutory provisions (which were thus *ius civile*
as opposed to *ius honorarium*) which were also binding on foreigners.
Both pairs of ideas, *ius civile–ius gentium* and *ius civile–ius honorarium*, thus overlap. They rest on quite different perspectives: the
former concerns the personal sphere of application of legal norms,
the latter concerns their source.

Magistral jurisdiction nominally kept its power to create law into
the second century A.D., though in practice it was probably not
exercised beyond the time of the early Principate. At times, especially no doubt in the last two centuries of the Republic, it was the
dominant element in Roman legal development. But then other
factors joined it and finally replaced it. One of these was jurisprudence, which by the end of the Republic had risen to great
heights of achievement and which under the Principate remained
for all of two centuries the most productive element in Roman legal
life. The other was imperial legislation, which even in the first two
centuries A.D. grew in importance. Consistent with the nature of
the Principate, it was at first disguised as quasi-magistral creation
of law or as senatorial legislation; in the late period it came out into

the open and, as other forces died out, took over the entire further development of Roman law.

The work of all these law-creating factors is reflected in the structure of the Roman legal system. From the moment when magistral jurisdiction took it in hand, Roman law developed from a unitary mass of material to a system of different juxtaposed and superimposed legal strata of a more or less peculiar nature. When classical jurisprudence began its work it found, alongside the *ius civile*, the *ius honorarium* already in a state of strong development: the *ius civile* strict and rigid in its basis though certainly modernized in some details by later legislation and by borrowings from magistral law; the *ius honorarium* progressive and free, subject to constant further development. Both stood in contrast to one another, as in English law common law stood beside equity, the latter derived from the practice of the Chancellor's court. Classical jurisprudence took the contrast between *ius civile* and *ius honorarium* for granted, but in seeking out the many points of contact between both masses of law and in developing both of them in common it gradually obliterated their boundaries. Thus the late classical jurists of the late second and early third centuries A.D. were the last who still had clearly before their eyes the structural difference between *ius civile* and *ius honorarium*. Then, when the cultural collapse of the third century had broken the threads of tradition and destroyed the lofty level of jurisprudence, both masses of law coalesced in the eyes of later antiquity into the unity of a single 'jurist's law'. *Ius civile* and *ius honorarium* as concepts had almost disappeared: all that was seen now was what the hands of the classical jurists had transformed them into. But even in the era of classical jurisprudence imperial law had begun to take shape as the third and newest stratum of Roman law. Although at the time it was not yet clearly conceived of as a firm body of law of a new kind, yet it developed during the late period into a unitary and peculiar group of rules which now provided the contrast with the 'jurist's law' of classical jurisprudence. Even the law of the later Roman period, therefore, was not a unity consisting of legal norms of equal value, but a stratified law.

The existence side by side of different, interacting, but in their structure always separate legal strata is a phenomenon to which our eyes must first become accustomed before understanding it. It is the outcome of a growth which was natural and rarely disturbed by rational planning—something which we can observe in many other details elsewhere in Roman law. If the legal systems of the present day—except for English law—resemble a garden laid out and cultivated according to a definite plan, in Roman law, on the contrary, to a certain extent the conditions of nature prevail; organisms which are dying away stand immediately beside new shoots forcing their way upward. Every legal institution still shows, even after a long time, the traces of its origin in this or that stratum of the general development, and can for that reason be fully and properly understood only by reference to its history. In a word, Roman law, in the same way as English law, is a legal system particularly rooted in history; and, viewed in its proper context, it shows the indelible marks left by the processes which formed it. The abstract system of Roman law principles which modern science, in particular the theoretical German jurisprudence of the nineteenth century, has distilled from the Roman sources shows, it is true, hardly anything of this peculiar structure of ancient Roman law. In it the historical strata of Roman law are forced into a timeless and rationalizing system and thus their significance is not infrequently distorted. Modern research is concerned to free itself from this unhistorical way of looking at the matter, which means not only that our historical knowledge is being made more accurate, but also that an essential contribution is being made to the study of the system of civil law and of the body of concepts in the modern codifications which rests upon it.

In the following chapters (6-8) we shall subject the origin and development of the three legal strata of *ius honorarium*, jurisprudence, and imperial law to a somewhat closer examination.

6

CIVIL JURISDICTION AND THE
IUS HONORARIUM

1. *The jurisdictional magistrates*

AS we saw in considering the structure of the republican constitution, the administration of justice (*iurisdictio*) was one of the functions of the unitary and comprehensive magistral office. This is
how matters always remained in principle so long as the republican
magistracies were something more than mere titles. Actually the
highest magistrates, the consuls, did not themselves exercise jurisdiction after the *leges Liciniae Sextiae* of 367 B.C., but left it to the
third and lesser bearer of *imperium*, the praetor. Accordingly, in
that period of the Republic which is better known to us, and in the
Principate, the praetorship was the magistracy properly charged
with jurisdiction. Apart from the special competence of the curule
aediles in market disputes, the praetorship's function was the entire
administration of civil and criminal justice in Rome and in Roman
Italy.[1] After 242 B.C. two praetors divided these duties between
them: the holder of the older praetorship, who was now called
praetor urbanus, retained the jurisdiction among citizens, while
the newly added *praetor peregrinus* was competent in cases between
foreigners or between a foreigner and a Roman. Thus the *praetor
urbanus* had a huge sphere of business. Still, there was only a
limited increase in the number of the urban Roman jurisdictional
magistrates. In the context of the Sullan reforms the praetors who
had previously been used as provincial governors were given presidencies in the jury-courts (*quaestiones*), the numbers of which
were being augmented at that time. From that period onwards the

---

[1] There were, none the less, auxiliary judicial organs to take some of the praetor's burden.
The police-court of the *tresviri capitales* looked after a large, indeed very probably the
greater, part of criminal trials in Rome; in other criminal matters the praetor could have
himself represented by *quaesitores*. *Praefecti iure dicundo* were dispatched to Italian country
towns on the *ager Romanus* in republican times; these were partly chosen by the people,
partly appointed by the praetor. In the last century B.C. and under the Principate there
was a local jurisdiction of municipal magistrates.

competences of the *praetor urbanus* and *praetor peregrinus* were restricted mostly[1]—and, after the judiciary laws of Augustus, entirely
—to the administration of private law.

In the provinces the governor (of whatever rank) or, in his stead,
the quaestor, exercised both civil and criminal jurisdiction among
Roman citizens, and also among foreigners, so far as such cases
came before him by virtue of the province's statute (*leges provinciae*)
or by the operation of his discretion.

11. *The nature of magistral jurisdiction and its importance for the
development of private law*

Ius dicere has the same etymological sense as *iudicare*. But while
the latter word was applied to the settlement of a legal dispute by
means of judgement, the Romans used *ius dicere* and its derivatives
to describe the activity of the jurisdictional magistrate, who did
not himself pronounce the final judgement but merely had presi-
dential or introductory functions in the case. The judgement was
in the procedure of the Republic and in the 'ordinary' procedure
of the Principate always pronounced by sworn judges.

The oldest form of Roman court was probably a bench of several
jurors presided over either by the magistrate himself or by a representative appointed by him. This type of court lasted in the criminal
sphere into the Empire. But even in the case of private law disputes
about matters of high value (particularly inheritances) there still
existed at the beginning of the second century A.D. a jury-court of
this kind, the court of the 'hundred men' (*centumviri*). Its great
antiquity is attested by the facts that it was only in this court that
the old emblem of state authority, a wooden lance (*hasta*), was set
up and that the proceedings before it remained always tied to the
formalities of the *legis actio* procedure. In the Empire this court too
met and passed judgement under the presidency of a magistrate.[2]

---

[1] Certain criminal matters for which there was no permanent *quaestio* fell within the
competence of the *praetor urbanus* even in the last century B.C. Under the Principate there
seems to have been a special praetorship for such cases.

[2] It is true that the individual benches of jurors into which the whole 'college' of the
105 *centumviri* was divided were presided over not by praetors but by magistrates of lesser
rank, the '10 men for the decision of legal disputes' (*decemviri stlitibus iudicandis*). A special
praetor hastarius ('lance praetor') seems to have presided over the entire court; and probably the preliminary procedure took place before him, so that the distinction between the
proceeding *in iure* and the proceeding *apud iudices* was applied here also. It is doubtful
whether this regulation is any older than the Augustan judiciary reforms. But at any rate it
must be presumed that magistrates presided over the centumviral court in republican times.

The overwhelming majority of civil actions in the later Republic took place, however, not before the *centumviri* but as a rule before single judges (*sub uno iudice*); though in certain special cases they were also held before small colleges of arbitrators (*arbitri*) or so-called 'recoverers' (*recuperatores*),[1] who all functioned without being presided over by a magistrate. Here the only function of the magistrate was to carry out a preliminary proceeding in which he had to decide on the admissibility of the plaintiff's claim and to appoint the judge or judges by whom the case would be heard. In its beginnings this peculiar form of civil procedure goes back at least as far as the Twelve Tables, which contained a special *legis actio* for a certain class of private law claims. It was called *legis actio per iudicis arbitrivi postulationem* because the proceeding before the praetor, which was tied to certain spoken forms, concluded in an application by the plaintiff for the appointment of a 'judge or arbiter'. Presumably the heavy pressure of business on the magistrates led them comparatively early to assign more and more private actions to single judges or small groups of judges, until this finally became the rule and the old jury-court procedure under the presidency of a magistrate became the exception. The strict division of the course taken by the trial into the introductory stage before the magistrate (the proceeding *in iure*) and the actual hearing of the case before the judge or judges (*apud iudicem*) developed in this way into a special characteristic of Roman civil procedure, which did not disappear until the rise of the 'extraordinary' procedure of the imperial period.

The judges and arbitrators appointed for the decision of the case by the magistrate *in iure*, usually according to the suggestions of the parties, were private persons who at any one time were obliged only to pass judgement in the particular case for which they were appointed. But they were not mere referees, since, although in most cases they would have been suggested by the parties, they were in fact charged with their task not by the parties but by the magistrate. To this extent the jurisdictional power of the magistrate formed the basis for the procedure *apud iudicem*; it lent the authority of the state to the verdict of the judge. Apart from this more formal working of magistral power, the influence of the magistrate on the course and outcome of the case certainly seems,

---

[1] The remarkable name of these judges is explained by the fact that such colleges were originally set up as special courts to decide on reparations for damage caused in war.

at first sight, very slight. Probably it was in fact slight, so long as the proceeding *in iure* was dominated by the strict formalism of the *legis actiones*. The parties had to proclaim cause of action and defence before the magistrate according to 'formulae' whose wording was closely associated with the underlying provisions of the Twelve Tables and some later statutes (hence the expression *legis actiones*). If the claim had been raised in this way with formal correctness, the magistrate hardly had any option but to assign a judge.

But this all changed as soon as another form of procedure *in iure* arose alongside the *legis actiones* in which an informal proceeding before the magistrate replaced the parties' exchange of formal words. Not only could the parties now bring forward claims and defences which were not included in any of the few *legis actio* formulae, but the magistrate was also freed from the formalism of the *legis actiones* and was able to base his decision as to the appointment of a judge on an objective assessment of the parties' allegations. He could now also prescribe for the judge the direction he should take in investigating and deciding the case. With this the magistrate obtained what was in fact the key position in the whole course of the proceedings, although his formal function remained that of merely introducing the action.

The magistrate at the end of the proceedings *in iure* orally pronounced his decree on the assigning of a judge (*dare iudicem* or *iudicium*) and on the latter's duty to condemn the defendant (*condemnare*) in certain conditions, but in the absence of these conditions to acquit him (*absolvere*). It was the parties' business to fix the wording of this decree in written form; and for this purpose, before the proclamation of the decree began, they summoned witnesses who had then to guarantee by means of their seals what the parties had written down. From this calling-up of witnesses the whole proceeding which concluded the stage *in iure* (the central point of which was the magistral decree) was called *litis contestatio*[1] ('the attestation of the dispute'). With regard to the decree itself the phrase used was simply *iudicium dare*. Its wording corresponded as a rule to certain model formulae which were published in the edict of the magistrate

---

[1] Cf. Festus, p. 38: 'Contestari est, cum uterque reus (= party) dicit: testes estote.' See also ibid., p. 57: 'Contestari litem dicuntur duo aut plures adversarii, quod ordinato iudicio utraque pars dicere solet: testes estote.'

concerned.[1] The parties were therefore in a position to refer to these model formulae in making their applications to the magistrate; and the principal objects of the proceeding *in iure* were to decide which formula was to serve as the basis of the decree initiating the case and how it ought to be adapted to suit the allegations of the parties, in particular of the defendant. It is therefore easy to understand that Gaius, the jurist of the second century A.D. to whom we owe the greater part of our knowledge of the history of Roman civil procedure, perceived the special character of this type of procedure in the element of 'litigating by means of procedural formulae' (*litigare per concepta verba, id est per formulas*, Gaius, *Inst.* 4. 30). Following him, modern legal science speaks of 'the formulary procedure'. At the same time, the oldest of these procedural formulae were probably in use in the later *legis actio* procedures (i.e. in the *legis actiones per iudicis postulationem* and *per condictionem*). It was not the rise of the procedural formulae, but rather the freeing of the stage *in iure* from being tied to the statutory oral formulae of the *legis actiones*, that was the essential and extremely fruitful innovation brought by the so-called formulary procedure.

It may be presumed that the informal proceeding *in iure* was first allowed in cases where a claim was raised and legal protection expected but where a suitable *legis actio* did not yet exist. In other words, the rise of the formulary procedure was closely connected with the extension of the protection of legal action beyond the limits of the legal relations recognized by the old *ius civile*. To the oldest stage of this extension probably belong the claims based on informally concluded contracts of sale, hire and service, partnership and mandate. In the *legis actio* procedure these claims could evidently not be pursued unless the performance agreed upon had been assured additionally by means of a special and formal creation of liability. But in the third or early second century B.C. it was felt necessary to concede that these contracts were binding in

---

[1] In a case, for example, where the plaintiff asserted *in iure* that the defendant owed him a certain sum of money whether on foot of a formal promise of performance (*stipulatio*), or on foot of a loan, or in consequence of a payment mistakenly made, and where the defendant disputed the duty of payment imputed to him, the edict of the *praetor urbanus* contained the following model formula: *Octavius iudex esto* (Appointment of the judge). 'Si paret Numerium Negidium Aulo Agerio HS (= sestertiorum) decem milia dare oportere, iudex Numerium Negidium Aulo Agerio HS decem milia condemnato, si non paret absolvito.' The personal names are stock 'blanks' which turn up in all the model *formulae*. Agerius (= *is qui agit*) means the plaintiff, Numerius Negidius (= *is a quo numeratio postulatur et qui negat*) means the defendant.

themselves, and the praetor, on foot of an informal proceeding *in iure*, accorded a *iudicium* with a formula which directed the judge to adjudicate on the plaintiff's demand not according to strict statutory law but according to the principle of contractual good faith (*ex fide bona*). There thus arose a group of 'good faith' actions which were of great importance to economic life and gave an entirely new appearance to the Roman law of obligations.

The reference to the principle of *bona fides* was, however, only one of several means of shaping the formula which the praetor used in order to extend the protection of law beyond the limits of the claims recognized by the *ius civile*. Sometimes in doing so he based himself on the civil law and applied its remedies to situations to which in origin they were not appropriate. He then directed the judge to *assume* that the missing conditions, normally necessary for the civil claim concerned, were actually present (*formulae ficticiae*). In this way, for example, the penal actions for theft and damage to property—which according to the law of the Twelve Tables and the *lex Aquilia*, respectively, could only take place between Roman citizens—were extended to foreigners who had committed theft or had been the victims of theft.[1] The *praetor peregrinus* to whose jurisdiction such cases belonged accorded a *iudicium* by virtue of his jurisdictional power, even without any statutory basis, and directed the judge to decide in the same way as he would have decided had both parties possessed Roman citizenship. The praetor very often did not direct the judge's attention to any already existing legal norms, but described in the formula merely a hypothetical set of facts which, if established, would lead to the condemnation of the defendant. When the formula was shaped like this, the judge did not need to investigate the propriety of the plaintiff's claim either according to the principles of the *ius civile* or according to the criterion of *bona fides*; he merely had to inquire whether the factual conditions of condemnation set forth in the formula were established (hence *formulae in factum conceptae*).[2] In such cases the

---

[1] Thus before the creation of this *formula* (the date of which we do not know) the foreign thief was probably exposed to uncontrolled arrest by the citizen from whom he had stolen, while the foreigner who had been robbed was without any legal protection.

[2] An example of a *formula in factum concepta* is provided by the formula for the well-known action for deceitfully causing an injury (*actio de dolo*): 'Si paret dolo malo Numerii Negidii factum esse, ut Aulus Agerius Numerio Negidio fundum de quo agitur mancipio daret . . .' ('If it appears that it has been effected through the deceit of the defendant that the plaintiff has alienated to the defendant the land in question in this case . . .'); next

legal question, i.e. the question whether and in which circumstances the plaintiff's claim might deserve the protection of law,
was decided by the magistrate himself through the granting of the
iudicium and the drawing up of the formula. In this way he really
took the place of a legislator even if only for the individual case of
the dispute to be decided on foot of the formula.

The formulary procedure finally established itself also in the
sphere of the old civil-law claims. A *lex Aebutia*, which in all probability belongs to the second century B.C. but cannot be more
accurately dated, admitted it instead of the *legis actio* procedure
only for certain claims. But the judiciary reforms of Augustus
brought its final victory: after the *lex Iulia iudiciorum privatorum*
(17 B.C.) the oral formulae of the *legis actiones* were used in the
introductory stage of only a few special cases, chiefly in the procedure before the court of the *centumviri*.

The extension of the formulary procedure to the area of old
civil-law claims meant that the innovations of the jurisdictional
magistrates were also felt here. Objections on the part of the defendant which in the *legis actio* procedure could not have been heeded
were now given consideration by means of the inclusion in the
formula of an exemption-clause (*exceptio*) in the direction to condemn. If, for example, the defendant, as against the plaintiff's
claim based on a loan or a formal debt-promise, alleged an informal
agreement to refrain from pressing the claim for a time, or to forgo
it altogether, then the magistrate directed the judge to condemn
only if the conclusion of such an agreement was not proved.[1] In
this way the rigidity and strictness of the old *ius civile* was considerably mitigated. In many cases the magistrate even exercised
the right of rejecting from the outset claims which were firmly
based on statute but which seemed to him unfair, by refusing to
grant the plaintiff a formula and thus a hearing before a judge
(*denegare actionem*).

The only possibility of appeal against the decisions of a jurisdictional magistrate lay in the intercession of another magistrate of
equal or higher rank, and in particular of *tribuni plebis*, whose
primary duty it was to defend the citizen against injustice. The

follows the direction to the judge to condemn in these circumstances, but otherwise to
dismiss the claim (i.e. if it does *not* so appear).

[1] 'Nisi inter Aulum Agerium et Numerium Negidium convenit, ne ea pecunia (intra
biennium) peteretur' (so-called *exceptio pacti conventi*).

intercession had to be immediately proclaimed in the presence of the magistrate against whose decree it was directed. For this reason a party who felt himself to be unfairly treated used to appeal at once (*appellare*) to a tribune of the people (or to the whole college of tribunes); and intercession was granted after an investigation of the facts in the course of which the jurisdictional magistrate also had an opportunity of setting forth the grounds for his decision. It had only the effect of quashing the decree: the decree became void, but no one could compel the magistrate to set a new one in its place. This could only be accomplished by trying one's luck with another competent magistrate; in particular, on the expiry of the official year, with the successor of the magistrate who had been unsuccessfully approached.

The extraordinary importance of magistral jurisdiction for the development of Roman private law from about the end of the third century B.C. onwards will be appreciated through the examples just used in order to illustrate the technique of creation of law by the magistrates. It has been seen that numerous claims were given recognition which were entirely foreign to the old *ius civile*, and that the *ius civile* itself was corrected by the non-application of antiquated rules and its strictness relaxed by the admission of new kinds of defences. In this way the law was adapted, purely through the practice of the magistrates' courts, and without the necessity of any great help from legislation, to meet the requirements of a developing economy and of a refined legal instinct orientated according to the principles of contractual good faith (*fides*) and equity (*aequitas*). In form this huge advance was the work of a long series of annual magistrates; it was a mere accident if some of them had a better knowledge of law than the average contemporary Roman. We shall, however, see that behind the decisions of these men there stood opinions and advice which the leading jurists of the day used to give partly to the litigants and partly to the jurisdictional magistrates themselves.

III. *The edicts of the jurisdictional magistrates*

The development of law in the sphere of jurisdiction took form in the edicts of the jurisdictional magistrates. Edicts were magistral proclamations whose content and scope might be very diverse. They consisted in part of ephemeral communications and regulations which applied only to the occasion which had given rise to them, but in part also of pronouncements which retained their force for the entire period of office of the magistrate issuing them. The jurisdictional edicts belonged to this second group (*edicta perpetua*); praetors, aediles, provincial governors, and also, probably, quaestors assigned to provincial governors used to set forth publicly (*proponere*) on a whitewashed wooden tablet (*album*) the principles which they intended to follow in the exercise of their jurisdictions and the formulae which they intended to use as the basis for the granting of actions. They thus made available to litigants a basis for their applications (*postulationes*) in the procedure *in iure*. At least from the late Republic onwards litigants could, *vis-à-vis* a magistrate, rely on the contents of the edicts as confidently as on a statute, for magistrates were by a *lex Cornelia* of 67 B.C. strictly bound by their edicts. However, even after this statute it still remained in a magistrate's power to grant from case to case new remedies which had not yet been provided for in the edict.

At the expiry of the official year a new edict appeared together with a new magistrate. But, understandably, the new magistrate usually used his predecessor's edict as a model and added only those changes and supplements which in his opinion were needed. In this way, probably very early, a fixed basic stock of edictal norms was formed which was included in every year's edict and increased in size only gradually (*edictum tralaticium*). In time the various edicts became a fairly complete reflection of jurisdictional practice, a codification of magistral law, which did not indeed possess the rank of a statutory code but had the advantage over a statutory code of being capable of development: a capacity resulting from its yearly republication, since every new magistrate entering on office had the opportunity of cutting out what was antiquated and of including new remedies which then, if they proved themselves, could become standing elements of the *edictum tralaticium*. Under the Principate the productive strength of the praetorian practice probably soon began to slacken; but it was not until the year A.D. 130 that the jurisdictional edicts were fixed in their final form, when on Hadrian's orders they were subjected to a final edition by Salvius Julianus, one of the greatest Roman jurists. This edition was approved by a resolution of the Senate and for the future could be changed only by the princeps himself (*constitutio Tanta*,

18).[1] The jurisdiction of the magistrates thus finally lost its creative importance; in its place, jurisprudence and, increasingly, imperial legislation now took over the further development of Roman law.

The edicts contained model formulae both for the claims based on old civil law and for those newly created within the framework of magistral jurisdiction; the formulae of the latter type were regularly preceded by a special promise of legal protection[2] (a so-called 'edict' in the narrower sense). Other announcements in the edicts concerned the refusal of legal protection in certain circumstances (*denegatio actionis*) and *restitutio in integrum*, whereby claims which, according to strict civil law, no longer existed, could be revived. There were in addition in the edicts a number of magistral commands and prohibitions (*interdicta*) which served mostly for the preservation of peace and public order and above all formed the basis for the protection of possession; and finally forms of defence (*exceptiones*) and formulae for contracts which had to be or could be concluded between the parties in the course of litigation (*stipulationes praetoriae* or *aediliciae*).

Apart from this, our knowledge of the jurisdictional edicts is full of gaps. We possess only very scanty accounts of the edicts of the *praetor peregrinus* and the provincial governors; it seems that, under the Principate, what was basically the same edict was published in all the provinces, and that its text hardly differed from that of the urban praetor's edict. Hardly anything survives of the aediles' edicts beyond the provisions about liability for defects in the sale of slaves and animals, though no doubt it was just these parts of this edict which were important from the point of view of private law. Only the edict of the *praetor urbanus* is known fairly accurately—though only in its final form after the revision by Julian—through the large fragments of the commentaries on the edict composed by the jurists of the Empire and preserved in Justinian's Digest; so that we have no detailed knowledge of its development. General historical considerations, together with the few pieces of

---

[1] Our account of the Julian edition of the edict has been (probably wrongly) doubted by A. Guarino (in several writings, the most recent being *Storia del diritto romano*, 4th edn., 460 ff.) on the grounds that there is nothing about it in contemporary tradition. But Justinian's precise statement cannot have been merely invented, and the Julian edition is already mentioned by an historian of the fourth century, who in his turn seems to have based his account on a source belonging to the period of Diocletian and Constantine.

[2] An example is provided by the edict about *negotiorum gestio*: 'Ait praetor: Si quis negotia absentis, sive quis, quae cuiusque cum is moritur fuerint, gesserit, iudicium eo nomine dabo' (cf. *D.* 3. 5. 3. pr.).

evidence which we have about the nature of earlier editions of the edict, lead to the presumption that the main bulk of the edict had been formed in the period between the third century and 80 B.C.

IV. *Magistral law and civil law*

The 'magistral law' (*ius honorarium*) which grew from the jurisdiction of the Roman magistrates is distinguished from the *ius civile* of the Twelve Tables and even more sharply from the private law system of a modern code by its *procedural* character: rights and duties appear in it always in the form of potential actions (*actiones*), defences (*exceptiones*), and other procedural remedies. Even the old *ius civile* was to a large extent adapted by the jurisdictional magistrates into this form, so that the whole body of law in the edicts, taken over and further developed by classical jurisprudence, was more or less dominated by a procedural way of thinking.

In general, magistral law did not form a closed and separate body of law in opposition to the *ius civile*. On the contrary, it was to a large extent closely connected with civil law norms in as much as it supplemented, limited, expanded, or transformed these. Certain institutions which originated in magistral law (as, for example, the *bonae fidei iudicia*) were, moreover, afterwards thought of as being part of the *ius civile*. It was only exceptionally that civil law and magistral law became sharply opposed, as in the sphere of ownership and inheritance. This led to a duality of concepts by which civil ownership (*dominium ex iure Quiritium*) was opposed to a magistral notion of 'having things among one's property' (*in bonis habere*), and the civil right of inheritance (*hereditas*) to a magistral 'possession of the estate' (*bonorum possessio*). Only the relation of common law and equity in English law offers a parallel for this mutual interaction of two systems simultaneously in force. In English law there is an ownership 'in law' as well as an ownership 'in equity', and, as in Rome, there can be two different persons who possess ownership in the same thing, of whom one owns according to the former system and one according to the latter.

7

JURISPRUDENCE AND THE LAW OF
THE JURISTS

1. *Early history of Roman jurisprudence*

THE history of Roman jurisprudence begins with the *pontifices*, the college of priests which, as we have already seen, was an important factor in the further development of the law of the Twelve Tables. As community magicians and the makers of the Roman calendar—this was certainly their original function—the *pontifices* had probably always controlled not only the regulations governing the relations of the community with the gods (i.e. the *ius sacrum*) but also the actual formulas for the relations of the members of the community among themselves: the forms of action of ancient Roman procedure and the formulas for the conclusion of legal transactions. Just as in the case of prayer to the gods, so too in legal relations among humans everything depended, according to the opinion of early Roman times, on the use of the correct words; only if one knew the right formula could one effectively invoke a deity, or bind or loose a human being. Like all magic art, the knowledge of the *pontifices* was essentially secret: the collection of formulas listed in the archives of the college (the *libri pontificales*) was for a long time available only to members of the college, and only amongst them were the methods for applying the law handed down, methods developed and tried in the course of generations. The monopoly held by the pontifical college through this secret knowledge of legal technique continued even when the magical element in the forms governing the citizens' legal relations was hardly any longer felt. The legislation of the Twelve Tables was unable to destroy it, for apart from the fact that the code evidently did not contain the formulas used by the *pontifices*, the text of the Twelve Tables itself required interpretation by the college of legal experts if it was to meet the requirements of legal life over a long period. Not until the formula-collections of the pontifical archives were made public—according to tradition, at the beginning of the third century B.C.—and members of the college began to impart legal opinions publicly, that is in the hearing of all and by means of an open exposition of authoritative points of view, was the sole supremacy of the *pontifices* broken, at least in principle, and the way laid open for the development of a free legal science, i.e. one no longer tied to the priestly office. The fact that, none the less, the members of the pontifical college and of related priesthoods played a predominant role among the jurists of the following 150 years is merely an eloquent demonstration of the strength of tradition in Roman life.

The representatives of the free legal science now developing concerned themselves, as the *pontifices* had done, mainly with the giving of opinions on legal questions (*respondere de iure*); and, like the *pontifex* who had been charged each year with the duty of advising the citizens, they gave their advice without payment. Thus, even after the connection between legal science and the college of *pontifices* had been broken, the legal art did not become a profession through which one earned one's living; like politics, it remained a field for the activity of men of wealth and prestige, mostly of senatorial rank, who regarded working for reward as beneath the dignity of their class. Legal practice brought the jurist no money; its advantage for him lay in increased prestige, a widening circle of friends and dependants, and, on this basis, a successful political career.[1] Those who approached him for advice included not only private persons with lawsuits or some other legal business on their minds, but also—and most significantly—the organs of justice themselves: the magistrates who controlled the courts, and the *iudices* appointed to decide particular cases. These were so much the more dependent on the jurists' help, since they themselves very often possessed only scanty knowledge of the law; they were appointed not on account of any practical or technical qualifications they might have, but because of their distinguished

---

[1] These goals could also be reached by court oratory, i.e. by appearing as advocate for plaintiff (or prosecutor) or defendant, principally in criminal trials; a man so engaged was called a *patronus* or *advocatus*. This pursuit, however, was quite different from that of a jurist whose work was to give legal advice, though this does not exclude the possibility that jurists occasionally appeared in the role of advocates. F. Wieacker rightly draws attention (in 'Sein und Werden im Recht', *Festgabe für Ulrich von Lübtow* (1970), pp. 183 ff.) to the fact that the most powerful of the Roman families are scarcely represented among the jurists of the Republic; but this may be a reflection of the fact that those who enjoyed inherited power and prestige were simply not dependent on putting up a performance in order to win their way to public office.

descent, their prestige, or their connections, and indeed partly through the arbitrary drawing of lots.[1] In any council of advisers (*consilium*), too—with which magistrates and *iudices* and indeed any Roman citizen with an important decision to make used to surround themselves—the advice of a jurist was probably seldom absent and may frequently have been decisive. Much the greater part of the brilliant creations of the *ius honorarium* is probably in reality the work of the jurists, who either as individual advisers, or as members of the *consilium*, guided the innovating hand of the magistrate.

The giving of legal opinions remained the central feature of the jurists' work right up to the latest period of classical jurisprudence, in other words for more than four centuries; and all other forms of juristic activity are more or less closely connected with it. This is particularly true of one branch of activity, peculiar to the early period of Roman legal science, and which has led the historians of Roman law to call this period that of 'cautelary' jurisprudence,[2] namely the drawing up of formulas for litigation and other legal business. One of the very oldest works of Roman legal literature known to us, the *venalium vendendorum leges* ('conditions of sale for things capable of being sold') of Manius Manilius (consul in 149 B.C.) consisted—if one may judge from the title—entirely, or at any rate substantially, of a collection of model formulas for contracts of sale. In addition, we possess similar 'forms and precedents' for contracts of sale, hire, and service in a work on agriculture (*De agricultura*), the author of which, the elder Cato (consul in 195, censor in 184 B.C.), was celebrated in later ages not only as a great statesman, but as an outstanding expert in the law. Even in the last century of the Republic the jurists seem to have been engaged in framing forms for contracts. It is true that we do not know of any works from the late Republic which are exclusively devoted to this subject;[3] but some specialized forms for legal transactions which were still commonly used in the classical period,

---

[1] The praetors of each year received their several spheres of duty (jurisdiction *inter cives* or *inter peregrinos*, governorships, and—after Sulla—the presidencies of the criminal courts) through the drawing of lots. Lots were drawn also for assigning *iudices* in civil actions, unless the parties were able to agree on a particular person.

[2] *Cautio* (from *cavere*, 'to be on one's guard, to take (prudent) measures') means the contract document. The formation *cautela* occurs originally only in the special sense of 'giving security', but later developed the meaning 'clause of a contract'.

[3] Yet a book on agriculture written by a contemporary of Cicero and Caesar—M. Terentius Varro—does contain some contractual forms.

bear the names of leading jurists of the last century before Christ, e.g. the *cautio Muciana* (which concerns the law of legacies) after Q. Mucius Scaevola, and the *stipulatio Aquiliana* (a form of general set-off and receipt, with the purpose of transforming all existing liabilities between the parties into a new, unitary obligation) after C. Aquilius Gallus. Apart from a very few exceptions, we know neither the date of origin nor the authors of the individual procedural formulas used in the so-called formulary procedure; but we may take it as likely that they, or by far the greater number of them, were designed by the jurists of the second and first centuries B.C.

The eager cultivation of forms, which certainly had its roots in the faith in literal formalism characteristic of early Roman legal interpretation, naturally took a rather less prominent place as soon as jurisprudence found the way to a freer and more liberal mode of thought towards the end of the Republic. But it was none the less a most significant contribution to the development of Roman legal thought, for only through the work of formulation over centuries could the clear and brief precision of Roman legal speech be brought to its classical perfection. In the procedural formulas, cautelary jurisprudence left a precious heritage from which later jurisprudence up to the end of the classical period could be nourished.

Closely connected with the advisory activity of the Roman jurists there was also legal education, which throughout the early period of which we are now speaking certainly still consisted of practical instruction. The advising jurist was surrounded by his pupils; they listened to his opinions and were allowed to discuss with him the points for and against them. Even later, in the Empire, this *disputatio fori* formed the real centre of legal education; it was preceded, however, though perhaps not invariably, by a beginner's course with a connected series of lectures, conducted, naturally, by a private teacher of law, since until the time of east Roman legal culture in the later Empire there were no state or state-recognized schools of law with comprehensive curricula.

11. *The jurisprudence of the late Republic*

Those individual features of Roman jurisprudence which derived from the tradition of the *pontifices* survived in large measure the arrival of the Greek spirit in the Roman world. Greek philosophy and rhetorical technique became, in the last century of the Republic, standing elements in Roman education. The theory of rhetoric itself, which as early as the beginning of the last century B.C. had been expounded by Roman authors in the Latin language, immediately found a practical application in court advocacy. But the sphere of law was not the same as those other spheres, in which the Romans had not formed their own approaches to intellectual life. Here there already existed a legal art, and one moreover oriented to the practical problems of ordinary life; while the Greek philosophers, if they ventured at all upon the discussion of specific legal problems, generally stuck to a purely speculative treatment, and the Greek orators dealt with law in a way which was completely contrary to the tradition of Roman jurisprudence. It was the concern of the latter to secure an objectively correct interpretation and application of rules of law, while the Greek orators taught the art of successfully presenting whatever case the client for whom the advocate was acting at any given time might wish to make. They recommended in one case a free, in another case a literal interpretation of statute law; and they provided arguments both for the strict application of the rules, on the one hand, and for a decision in accordance with equity—and therefore against the words of the law—on the other. This kind of ambivalence in the treatment of legal problems might perhaps be a source of some stimulation to the Roman jurist; but it was absolutely incapable of taking over Roman jurisprudence.

Thus the development of Roman jurisprudence continued on its own path. Looked at as a single phenomenon, it remained something specifically Roman, and can probably be regarded as the most significant achievement of the Roman spirit and as the most important of Roman contributions to the development of European culture. At the same time, there is no doubt that Greek learning and Greek methods of thought affected the growth of jurisprudence in various ways. It has been rightly pointed out that the very emergence of a legal literature in Rome, like the emergence of all Roman literature, is associated with the stimulus which acquaintance with the literary culture of the Greeks first provided. Certainly, there is lively disagreement as to the nature, origin, and significance of Greek influences on the legal science of the late Republic and the Empire, and it may seem doubtful whether we shall ever be able to give precise answers to all the questions which arise in this context, or to give a securely founded decision on how much of what we can see of Roman jurisprudence rests on native Roman tradition, and how much is to be accounted for by the fertilizing influence of Greek scientific method. The remarks which follow are intended to give a (necessarily incomplete) picture of the complexities of the problem and of the present state of the discussion.

The strength of the old Roman tradition is seen with especial clarity in the *arrangement of legal material* in the writings of the jurists. The great works which can be reconstructed from the fragments which have survived maintain, in this regard, a certain pattern right up to the end of the classical period—a pattern which certainly cannot be described as rational either by reference to modern techniques of legal exposition or by reference to the conventional plan of a learned Greek work, and may quite possibly be explained by a tradition of reflecting the sequence of the material in the Twelve Tables. It is only in the short elementary manual of Gaius, which belongs to the middle second century A.D. (but may perhaps be based on a work of about a century earlier) that we find anything like a systematic arrangement which undoubtedly shows the inspiration, direct or indirect, of a Greek model; and this work seems to have had no successors in the later classical age.

It has been possible—with varying degrees of certainty—to establish, here and there, actual material borrowings from the doctrines of Greek philosophy. The theory of natural law, of an order far transcending the laws of individual commonwealths, goes back to Aristotle, but was introduced to Roman literature by Cicero, and was undoubtedly a familiar idea to the jurists. It may have had some influence on the development of the *ius gentium*, and may also have provided a basis for the occasional allusions to a purely 'natural' possession or a purely 'natural' obligation. But natural law doctrine does not make a direct appearance in our sources until the jurists of the late second and early third centuries A.D.; and even they use it simply as a perfunctory introductory flourish, as a sort of flimsy superstructure capping a discussion—itself conducted on lines laid down by tradition—of the positive Roman Law.

Greek notions of the physical world probably exerted a somewhat deeper influence on the Roman jurists' teachings on identity and change in things; though this influence is also controversial.

Here use was made of Greek concepts in order to solve concrete legal problems, in particular in deciding the question of who was to be the owner of the end-product in a case where things belonging to different owners had been combined or mixed, or where one man had worked another's raw material into a finished article; though it must be said that the solutions arrived at in this way are not always among the best achievements of Roman jurisprudence.

There may possibly be further instances of this kind of borrowing from Greek theory; but, if so, they are matters of detail. They are sufficient to prove that the Roman jurists both knew the results of Greek intellectual inquiry and were ready to press them into service, but insufficient to demonstrate anything like a fundamental transformation of Roman legal science under Greek influence.

Such a transformation could not have been limited to the taking over of isolated theories and conceptions; it would have had to affect the entire range of legal thought and method. It is usually supposed, indeed, that the jurists of the late Republic had learned from the Greeks the art of dialectic, and that it was this which allowed their practice in the law to pass from its primitive condition to the rank of a proper legal science; and certainly, having regard to the fundamental significance of Greek models in most other spheres of Roman intellectual life, this point of view does not seem unlikely. But it is hardly possible to prove it beyond doubt, if only for the reason that we know far too little of the older jurists to be able to measure the difference between their methods of work and those of the jurists of the late Republic and Empire. In any case, the procedural formulas evolved by the older jurists should warn us not to underestimate their art; a considerable part of these had probably been already settled before any intensive Greek influence had begun to be effectively felt in Roman thought. They already contain much of the conceptual structures and modes of operation that we find still being used by the jurists of the late republican and imperial eras. Moreover, it is significant that there is no agreement as to the quarter of the world of Greek science from which the main influence on Roman legal method is supposed to have come; some modern scholars point to the theory of rhetoric, which they think would have corresponded more closely to the practical Roman temperament than philosophy, with its more or less speculative orientation; others to the dialectical method of the philosophers, and this in turn opens up the question of the various schools and trends of Greek philosophy. All this clearly shows the difficulty of finding any exact proof that these influences were brought to bear on a discipline, such as that of the Roman jurists, which had its own objectives and which was itself unknown to Greek thought. This difficulty has, so far, been overcome only in a few isolated areas which scarcely offer an adequate basis for answering the question whether the Roman jurists owe their masterly technique to Greek models rather than to their own native tradition; for example, the (mostly infelicitous) attempts of jurists in the late Republic and early Empire to define legal concepts with the help of often fantastic etymologies can be attributed with certainty to the theories on grammar propounded by the Stoic philosophers. Another example—and a very impressive one—of the adoption of Greek method has been recently provided by the demonstration that some of the leading jurists of the first two centuries A.D. were not only familiar with Stoic principles of expository logic, but also went to some pains to display them in connection with the interpretation of legal transactions.

But treatments of this theorizing kind are a great rarity in the surviving fragments of classical works. It is impossible to say whether they may have been commoner in the unabridged form of these works; and moreover it is still far from clear to what extent these excursions into logical theory may have had a practical importance in the interpretative work of the jurists.

A generation ago, the distinguished philologist Johannes Stroux believed he was able to demonstrate a decisive influence exerted by Greek rhetorical method in the direction of freeing Roman legal science from antiquated formalism; but his thesis has encountered justifiable objections. Stroux regarded the decision in the *causa Curiana* (an inheritance lawsuit brought before the *centumviri* in 93 B.C. by one Manius Curius) as a breakthrough towards a freer mode of legal interpretation; but it is hard to see that it had any such historic importance, even though among contemporaries it became famous as a victory of the celebrated orator L. Licinius Crassus over the great jurist Q. Mucius Scaevola.[1]

---

[1] The *causa Curiana* is nowhere mentioned in legal literature (which very seldom took any notice of judicial decisions, unless they were those of the Emperor himself). Probably the jurists stuck to the strict interpretation of the disputed testamentary clause (for which Scaevola pleaded) until, more than two centuries later, the Emperor Pius decided a similar case in the same way as the *centumviri* had done.

Modern research has shown that the Roman jurists never followed any uniform doctrine in their interpretation of laws and legal transactions; their methods constantly varied, and sometimes obviously reflected an antique tradition of their own profession. This can be seen for example in the technique (practised into the time of the Empire) of extending or limiting the application of statutory rules by attributing to the legislator a use of words which differed from the normal. Side by side with this, admittedly, we meet something undoubtedly facilitated by rhetorical theory: the bold contrasting of the words (*verba*) with the sense (*sententia*) of a statute, though this first becomes demonstrable only in the jurists of the high classical period of the second century A.D. In interpreting legal transactions, particularly in the sphere of formal transactions, no departure was tolerated from the old and strict principles; though in legal relations which were freed from formal requirements and were dominated by the principle of *bona fides*, it may be that a freer interpretation had always been usual, one which looked less to the words used than to the real wishes of the parties.

Unfortunately, few of the Roman jurists of the republican period are figures who can be individually appreciated. We know a considerable number of names from as early as the third and second centuries B.C.; we know that with few exceptions the bearers of these names belonged to senatorial families and that many of them occupied the highest magistracies; we know, here and there, the titles of literary works, though only very few scattered and fragmentary traces of these works have been preserved. Only in the last century of the Republic do the historical accounts become a little better. In this period the social stamp of jurisprudence changes. The senatorial aristocracy becomes less prominent, and most jurists now come from the equestrian order, in which many of them spent all their lives: a sign that, in the midst of demagogy and political violence, the giving of legal opinions no longer offered great advantages to a political career. Many jurists of this period, too, were not native Romans, but came from Italian country towns, some of which had been received into the Roman citizenship only at the end of the Social War.

The two greatest jurists of the age and those whose scientific activity is best known to us did in fact come from old and noble Roman families, and both rose to the consulship. Both belong to the period in which the influence of the Greek spirit began to make itself felt in Rome. The senior of them, Q. Mucius Scaevola (consul 95 B.C., died 82 B.C.) from a noble plebeian family which had previously produced several important jurists, is said to have been the first to arrange the law 'according to kinds' (*ius civile primus constituit generatim*, Pomponius *D.* 1. 2. 2. 41). This does not mean that he produced a comprehensive systematization of law, but probably merely records the fact that he liked to distinguish different sorts (*genera*) of legal relationships carrying the same name: thus, for example, five kinds of guardianship (Gaius, *Inst.* 1. 188) and at least three kinds of possession (Paulus *D.* 41. 2. 3. 23). In this, and generally in his attempts at definition, we can probably see the results of Greek intellectual modes. In the celebrated inheritance case of M. Curius, however, we find him standing for the old Roman literal strictness against the rhetorical arguments based on equity. The writings of Q. Mucius remained influential until well into the Empire; his treatise on the *ius civile* (in eighteen books) remained for a long time the standard textbook on this part of the legal system, and commentaries were still being written on it as late as the second century A.D.

Servius Sulpicius Rufus (consul in 51 B.C., died 43 B.C.) a friend and contemporary of Cicero's, came from a patrician family, though one which had long been politically unimportant: his grandfather may have been a senator, but of small prestige; his father belonged to the equestrian order; and he himself reached the consulship only at his second attempt. He received (probably along with Cicero, at the feet of Apollonius Molon in Rhodes), a thorough grounding in Greek rhetoric, and practised first as a forensic orator. It was not until later that he devoted himself to a closer study of jurisprudence. His teachers were pupils of Q. Mucius; one of them, C. Aquilius Gallus (praetor in 66 B.C.) was the creator of the defence (*exceptio*) based on deceit (*dolus malus*) which lives on in the modern civil law. Servius' Greek training can be seen in his own career. If Cicero (*Brut.* 152 ff.) is to be believed, he was the very first to bring scientific method (*dialecticam* [*artem*]) to bear on jurisprudence, which led Cicero to accord him an even higher place than Q. Mucius. Servius seems to have often engaged in controversy with the latter; one of his works is actually cited by Gellius (*N.A.* 4. 1. 20) under the title *reprehensa Scaevolae capita*. However, the very modest fragments which survive from

the writings of both jurists do not disclose any fundamental differences of method, and it must not be forgotten that on another
occasion Cicero made fun of Servius' art as mere quibbling with
words. (Cicero himself attempted, evidently in vain, to transform
jurisprudence into the mould of Greek science; this work (*De iure
civili in artem redigendo*) is, however, lost.) Servius' effect on those
who came after him was hardly less lasting than that of Q. Mucius.
What is remarkable is that he was the first to write a commentary
—though a very brief one—on the praetorian edict and thus was
presumably the first to initiate the literary cultivation of the *ius
honorarium*. A pupil of his, A. Ofilius, one of those jurists who
always remained in the equestrian order, then dealt with the edict
in a much more exhaustive work. From that time onwards the *ius
honorarium* was and remained a field of juristic endeavour in no
way inferior to the *ius civile*. Ofilius and the other pupils of Servius
belong to a generation of jurists whose activity extends beyond the
end of the Republic and into the Principate of Augustus; they thus
represent the transition from republican jurisprudence (the results
of which some of them compiled into lengthy books) to the classical
age of Roman legal science.

III. *Classical jurisprudence*

1. *The Principate and jurisprudence; the* ius respondendi *and the
participation of jurists in imperial administration.* Roman jurisprudence, which emerged in the peculiar social and political conditions of the mid Republic and grew in the free and spiritually
active atmosphere of late Republican individualism, did not fade
away in the changed climate of the Principate, but on the contrary
flourished even more strongly. Indeed, the era of its greatest brilliance (unless we are deceived by the uneven character of much of
the tradition) was as late as the second century A.D.: this was a
period of Roman history in which the Empire, indeed, enjoyed a
large measure of material prosperity under the excellent administration of Trajan, Hadrian, and the Antonine emperors, but in
which intellectual life in most areas already bore signs of senile
slackening. There are various reasons for this late flowering of
jurisprudence: its timely immunization against the poison of
rhetoric, which infected all the other branches of literature and
science and allowed commitment to one's subject to be replaced
by the ideal of an artificial and formal presentation of material,

without interest in its real value; the peace and economic prosperity of the Empire; the huge expansion of Roman civilization and of Roman citizenship, factors which increased the intensity and geographical scope of Roman legal life to formerly unknown dimensions; the careful cultivation by the emperors of the administration of government and justice, and, closely connected with this, the interest taken by the emperors in jurisprudence as such.

The attitude of the emperors towards the jurists naturally changed in the course of time. Seneca's (certainly malicious) satire shows us the jurists, reduced to shadows and scarcely alive, creeping from their places of hiding after the death of Claudius; and other passages in literature show traces of a powerful repression exerted by several emperors on jurisprudence. As a whole, however, legal science was greatly advanced by the Principate. We can see how Augustus sought the co-operation of the leading jurists of his time; though it is understandable that he found no welcome with many of those who were republican at heart and to whom the new order was an abomination. The clever A. Cascellius, for example, who had already made himself unpopular through legal obstructionism[1] and his sharp tongue, is said to have spurned the consulship which Augustus nevertheless offered him; and the greatest of contemporary jurists, M. Antistius Labeo, maintained throughout his life an obdurate and scarcely concealed opposition to the régime.[2] But the distaste for the new order felt by these jurists, who had grown up in the republican spirit, was a transitional phase, and there were always others more co-operative. We find C. Trebatius Testa, who was already closely associated with Caesar, advising Augustus on an important decision of legal policy (cf. Justinian, *Inst.* 2. 25 pr.). Among the younger jurists the one who with particular willingness placed himself at the disposal of the new regime was C. Ateius Capito, Labeo's ambitious rival.

Moreover, Augustus was responsible for a measure which—however it may be interpreted—at any rate created an enduring bond between the princeps and the jurists and decisively influenced the character and mode of operation of classical jurisprudence.

[1] He declared invalid the gifts made by the triumvirs Octavian (Augustus), Antonius, and Lepidus to their followers from the properties of proscribed citizens (Valerius Maximus 6. 2. 13).

[2] According to Pomponius *D.* 1. 2. 2. 47, he, too, refused the consulship; but according to Tacitus, *Ann.* 3. 75, his political attitude prevented his being admitted to this office at all.

'Primus divus Augustus, ut maior iuris auctoritas haberetur, constituit, ut ex auctoritate eius responderent' are the words used in a scanty résumé of the history of Roman legal science which has been preserved in a work of the second century A.D. (Pomponius *D*. 1. 2. 2. 49). These words have usually been understood to mean that Augustus, without encroaching on the general freedom to practise law, conferred on certain pre-eminent jurists the special privilege of giving their opinion *ex auctoritate principis*, i.e. to a certain extent in the name of the emperor; something which would naturally have greatly increased the prestige of these 'Crown'-jurists. But it must be presumed that what Augustus did went much deeper. A strict interpretation of the Pomponius passage cited above leads to this meaning: that the right of 'publicly' giving opinions (*publice respondere*) was to be exclusively reserved to jurists authorized by the princeps. This probably meant in practice that they were the only jurists whose opinions could be produced by litigants in court and were then binding on the court. In this way the possessors of this *ius* (*publice*) *respondendi* bestowed by the princeps obtained an exclusive, direct, and powerful influence on the administration of justice.

We learn in addition from the same passage of Pomponius (§ 48) that the celebrated Massurius Sabinus was, under Tiberius, the first jurist from the equestrian class to receive the *ius respondendi*. We must therefore assume that Augustus admitted only senators to the privilege. But even later the bestowal of the *ius respondendi* on *equites* seems to have been a fairly rare exception; for by far the greater number of all jurists known to us until after the middle of the second century A.D. belonged to the senatorial order, despite the fact that the latter had in the last century of the Republic largely lost its predominant place in jurisprudence to the *equites*. This retrogressive development in the social structure of jurisprudence can only be understood as a probably intentional result of Augustus' imperial policy in creating the *ius respondendi*.

The aim of this policy becomes clear if one realizes that in the late Republic, in spite of the important achievements of the leading jurists, the developments in jurisprudence had led to a certain loss of public confidence in the legal profession. Cicero's complaint (*de off.* 2. 55) that the old glory of jurisprudence had been destroyed in the chaos of the times really means that the extension of the legal profession beyond the senatorial order had brought forth a horde of incompetents, unscrupulous upstarts, and charlatans, whose activity as advisers of litigants and as authors of opinions had brought the practice of law into confusion. Caesar and even the much more conservative Pompey had considered a codification of law in order to cure these grievances. The carrying out of such plans would certainly have given jurisprudence a severe blow, if not its death-wound, since its mode of operation and its function in legal life were closely dependent upon the peculiar structure of the legal system. Augustus attempted the solution of the problem by another route. By giving a small number of pre-eminent jurists exclusive authority to conduct an advisory practice which was both public and with binding effect on the courts, he created a source of guidance for the administration of justice which operated in the same way as do the highest courts in the modern civil law world. He chose these jurists from the senatorial order probably not only as a recollection of the time when jurisprudence had been their monopoly, but also from the consideration that the prestige of the senatorial class, and its peculiar obligation of gratuitously safeguarding the public interest, were essential requisites for the carrying out of the task he had imposed on the bearers of the *ius respondendi*.

And, in fact, the limitation of the *ius respondendi* to a special circle of distinguished jurists who, in addition, were real experts, lent an extraordinary influence to these authorized counsel. As his legal knowledge was usually limited, the private judge whose duty it was in classical procedure to pass judgement was in any case defenceless against the authority of the jurists. He probably scarcely ever departed from the opinion of a jurist with the *ius respondendi*, unless the existence of a second and different opinion forced him to decide the matter for himself. In this way the idea could take root that the *ius respondendi* embodied nothing less than an authority to make law (*iura condere*), so that the force of a statute attached to the unanimous view of the privileged jurists (Gaius, *Inst.* I. 7). This cannot be taken literally for the classical period;[1] but the extraordinary influence exercised by the classical jurists on the legal practice of their time with the help of the *ius respondendi* is certainly accurately described with these words.

The *ius respondendi* did not remain the only link between the

---

[1] The rescript of Hadrian adduced by Gaius probably contained no more than a direction to the judge as to how to behave when faced with two mutually inconsistent opinions.

Principate and jurisprudence. Even at the beginning of the Principate it was taken for granted that a jurist who belonged to the senatorial or equestrian class could, like all his peers, participate in the tasks of administering the world Empire as an official of the emperor; and in the course of time more and more jurists began to do so. From the end of the first century A.D. we find leading posts in the imperial administration being occupied by jurists of senatorial rank and—after the expansion of equestrian offices by Hadrian—by most of the jurists who had come from the equestrian order. A few examples may serve to show how large and many-sided was the sphere of activity which was made accessible in this way. L. Javolenus Priscus, one of the most important jurists of the late first and early second centuries, commanded two legions successively in the service of the emperor, and occupied the position of jurisdictional legate to Britain[1] and that of governor in Upper Germany and in Syria; quite apart from his senatorial career within the framework of the republican constitution, which brought him as far as the consulship and the governorship of the province of Africa. A similarly rich succession of offices was held by the famous P. Salvius Julianus: he was among other things superintendent of the republican state treasury (*praefectus aerarii Saturni*) and of the imperial military exchequer (*praefectus aerarii militaris*), imperial governor of Lower Germany and of northern Spain (*Hispania citerior*) and republican governor of Africa. L. Volusius Maecianus, from the equestrian order, began his career in equestrian officer-commissions, then became an assistant in the administration of public works (*adiutor operum publicorum*), head of the secretariat of Antoninus Pius when princeps-designate, head of the imperial post-office (*praefectus vehiculorum*), thereafter of the imperial libraries, again head of the secretariat (*a libellis*) of Antoninus Pius (now princeps), superintendent of the corn supplies (*praefectus annonae*), and finally governor of Egypt. Of the jurists of the late second and early third centuries, who mostly belonged to the equestrian order, Cervidius Scaevola and Herennius Modestinus turn up as chiefs of police in Rome (*praefectus vigilum*); and Aemilius Papinianus, Julius Paulus, and Domitius Ulpianus as prefects of the praetorian guard (*praefectus praetorio*)—the highest and most influential equestrian office, which, apart from the purely

---

[1] An auxiliary organ of the provincial governor, whose primary function lay in the administration of justice.

military command, already at that time also included the function
of legal adviser to the princeps and that of a highly placed judge.
Many of the other offices just mentioned also possessed important
legal functions: thus not only the provincial governors and their
jurisdictional legates, but also the *praefecti annonae* and *vigilum*,
had a comprehensive competence in the administration of justice;
and the heads of the imperial secretariats assisted the princeps in
drawing up his edicts and legal decisions. Finally, the jurists
exerted a powerful influence on the administration of justice and
on the legal policy of the emperors by virtue of their membership
of the imperial council (*consilium principis*).

We have already encountered the custom of republican legal
practice whereby magistrates and judges had the assistance of an
advisory council in taking decisions. The emperors took over this
custom; we recall, for example, that in an important decision of
legal policy Augustus took the advice of C. Trebatius Testa. But
while up to the time of Hadrian we have only isolated reports of
the drawing of well-known jurists into the *consilium principis*, the
jurists of the late second and early third centuries seem to have
played a very important part in advising the emperor. From
Antoninus Pius onwards there were even permanent and salaried
posts as councillors, which were occupied by jurists of equestrian
rank. Probably the chief duty of these imperial councillors (*consiliarii principis*) was the constant handling of legal cases which
were brought before the princeps's court or which had been brought
up by way of petition. They thus discharged by the emperor's
side the same tasks which fell to the so-called *assessores* in the jurisdictions of the *praefectus praetorio* and other officials, especially
the provincial governors: these *assessores* were salaried auxiliary
officials, though certainly of much lower standing than the imperial
councillors.

2. *The literary works of the classical jurists.* It will be seen from
what has been said that the Roman jurists of the Empire, no less
and perhaps even more than those of the Republic, were practitioners in the application and creation of law. This fact is very well
demonstrated in the peculiar nature of their literary works. In the
first place, with regard both to quantity and to scientific value,
come great collections of opinions delivered by the jurists endowed
with the *ius respondendi* (*responsa*, *digesta*) and related works of an
entirely casuistic nature. Next there are commentaries on the *ius*

civile[1] and on the edicts of the jurisdictional magistrates, in particular of the urban praetor. Less important are the monographs composed particularly in the mid and late classical period which concern isolated legal subjects and the spheres of duty of certain officials. All these works are essentially of a practical nature: they grew out of legal practice and were written for practitioners: and one must not look in them for a speculative or theoretical treatment of the legal order or for a systematic arrangement which goes beyond the simplest comparisons and parallels. In general, it is only in textbooks for beginners (*institutiones*) and similar elementary compositions that we find hints of a more theoretical mode of treatment; and such books play a fairly modest part in the general picture of classical legal literature. At any rate, it is not on them that the fame of Roman jurisprudence rests; for the great strength of the Roman mind lay not in theoretical construction but in the technically accurate mastering of actual individual cases.

In this sphere the classical jurists remained unsurpassed. With sublime sureness of touch they applied the methods of logical reasoning, the technique of the procedural formulas, and the complicated rules and conventions which resulted from the existence side by side of legal institutions old and new, civil and magistral, elastic and strictly formalistic. They avoided vague considerations of equity, moralizing turns of speech, and all stereotyped expressions. They were able to define concisely even the most involved sets of facts or lines of thought, thanks to a language which through centuries of practice had been made flexible in the highest degree, a language whose simple practicality is as distant from the affected laconism of Tacitus as it is from the rhetorical prolixity of Cicero. Often the mere setting-out of the case to be decided is a masterpiece in itself; the decisive legal factors already appear at this stage stripped of inessential details, and thus make a lengthy grounding for the decision superfluous.

The intellectual world of classical jurisprudence is, in its innermost essence, thoroughly Roman, apart from that infusion of Greek method which occurred in late republican times and which naturally continued to be effective thereafter. This is true not only of the jurists of the first century A.D., who almost without exception

---

[1] It was customary to use, as the basis of commentaries on the *ius civile* (since it was not statutorily codified), either the exposition by Q. Mucius Scaevola, or the brief summary by Massurius Sabinus written about the middle of the first century A.D.

came from urban Roman families or from the Italian municipal aristocracy, but also of the jurists of the second and third
centuries who were mostly natives of the provinces. Many of these
were, of course, probably of Italian ancestry: descendants of
Italian colonizing or merchant families who had settled outside
Italy and had achieved wealth and prestige, as is, for example,
known to be the case of the ancestors of the Emperor Hadrian
(*Hist. Aug.*, Hadr. 1). One must count among these Italians born
in the provinces, to mention only the most important name, P.
Salvius Julianus, whose home was at Hadrumetum in the province
of Africa and who belonged to a family evidently so distinguished
that he was able to enter upon a senatorial career. Italian origin can
be clearly proved for the family of another, less well-known jurist
of the same period, P. Pactumeius Clemens from Cirta (the modern
Constantine in Algeria). Others, it is true, probably came from
assimilated provincial families, particularly the leading jurists at
the turn of the second and third centuries, as, for example, Julius
Paulus who bore the family name of the first imperial dynasty or
Domitius Ulpianus, born in Tyre in Phoenicia.[1] But be this as it
may, no foreign spirit can be detected in their writings; and this
is all the more remarkable since the effects of increasing foreign
influence are very noticeable in the non-legal literature of the
Empire. Clearly, the strict traditions of Roman jurisprudence
brought all its practitioners so much under their spell that they
could only operate with its modes of thought.

The working technique of Roman jurisprudence did not leave
much scope for the development of individual characteristics; and
one is in a quandary if asked to indicate the special features even of
such pre-eminent jurists as Julian or Papinian. All classical jurists
employ more or less the same methods on the same subjects, have,
on the whole, the same mode of thinking, and are distinguished
from one another rather through the quality of their work than
through any personal flavour in their style. Even their language is
uniform, leaving little room for individual peculiarities, so that as
a whole it presents a strong contrast with the profusion of tempera-
ments and styles in contemporary non-legal literature.

---

[1] It may be noticed that new citizens regularly bore the family name of the emperor who
had received them into the citizenship. The names Julii, Claudii, Ulpii, Aurelii, which are
found mentioned in documents, especially in the provinces, thus provide evidence for the
gradual extension of the Roman citizenship.

Because the traditional techniques of juristic work had such a strong unifying influence, and the stamp of individual character is scarcely recognizable, we find that during the two and a half centuries of the classical period inner developments in Roman jurisprudence can only be guessed at, from a few and mostly inconspicuous features of the literature. It would be a hard task even for an expert to date with approximate accuracy a large fragment from classical legal literature by relying only on the legal method it incorporated within itself and not on external clues. Accordingly it is chiefly in reliance on facts of *external* legal history that we can divide the classical period into sections. With this reservation we can distinguish in the following pages an early classical period from Augustus up to about the end of the Flavian dynasty)A.D. 96), a mid classical period from Nerva to Marcus Aurelius (A.D. 96–180) and a period of late flowering, principally under the emperors of the Severan dynasty (A.D. 193–235).

3. *The early classical period.* What is characteristic of the early classical period is, above all, the still loose relationship of jurisprudence to the Principate, a relationship basically mediated only by the *ius respondendi*. It was not yet the general rule that the leading jurists also played a prominent part in imperial administration; and although some of them possessed considerable political influence, this rested more on their distinguished origins or their personal relations with the princeps than on any position of power which jurists enjoyed as such. As in republican times, the jurist was still a private person, and his craft was a noble enthusiasm and one which was of service to the common good. With regard to method, too, hardly any difference can be discerned from that of the late republican period: a certain preference for definitions and for conceptual distinctions even in the early classical period probably betrays the still fresh effects of Greek scientific method.

Right at the beginning of the period we meet one of the most significant figures in Roman jurisprudence: M. Antistius Labeo, that contemporary of Augustus whose opposition to the new regime has already been mentioned. While his rival (also already mentioned), C. Ateius Capito, seems to have been a learned but not very productive spirit and probably for this reason is only seldom mentioned in our sources, Labeo left behind numerous and partly very comprehensive works, and through them exercised an influence scarcely paralleled for its deep and long-lasting effects.

This is true in particular of his commentaries on the edicts of the *praetor urbanus* and *praetor peregrinus*, traces of which still turn up repeatedly in the late classical commentaries. The broad culture for which Labeo was noted seems to have extended both to Roman antiquity, which he treated in writings about the law of the Twelve Tables and the law of the *Pontifices*, and to Greek philosophy and rhetoric. His definitions, which often show brilliant accuracy and became signposts for later jurists, are frequently supplemented by etymological explanations, a proof of his familiarity with the methods of contemporary grammar.

Roman tradition associates the rise of the two 'schools' of jurisprudence with the rivalry between Labeo and Capito: the opposition of these schools remained alive long after the early classical period, well into the second century, and indeed for a long time conditioned the whole image of Roman jurisprudence. At the same time it is hardly ever possible to trace the known points of difference between the schools back to Labeo and Capito; and the names of the schools strongly suggest that they did not in fact arise until the next generation. The supporters of one school were called Sabiniani, after the jurist Massurius Sabinus, known to have flourished from the time of Tiberius to that of Nero—or sometimes as Cassiani, after C. Cassius Longinus who reached the consulship in A.D. 30 and died under Vespasian—and the members of the other school were called Proculiani, after Proculus, a contemporary of Sabinus and Cassius.

The two 'schools' were not teaching institutions, although there is no doubt that the education of young lawyers took place largely if not entirely within the framework of the 'school' community. They were unions of jurists, trained or in the course of training, and each school cultivated a definite traditional number of didactic opinions. It seems that they possessed a certain organization, at least some kind of leadership, to which at any given time the most prominent members belonged for life; and in this respect they resemble the Greek philosophy schools. But while the latter were distinct from one another through deep contrasts of basic outlook and of method, we seek in vain in the Roman jurists for some fundamental principle for the opposition of the two schools. Despite the large number of points of difference between the Sabinians and Proculians which we know of, nothing is at stake except concrete individual questions; in their basic scientific attitude and in their method of work the schools seem scarcely to have differed from one another at all. This is, however, not at all surprising, since a division of minds based on principle could probably only have arisen out of notions of the philosophy or politics of law, and such notions are foreign to the mode of thought of all Roman jurists. Indeed, the methods of outlining and solving problems which were developed by Roman jurisprudence had received, long before the appearance of the disputing schools, so fixed and unambiguous a character that contrasts of opinion based on principle were hardly any longer possible. Thus the disputes between the schools apparently lack any deeper meaning and any important objective foundation. Their rise is probably due primarily to certain social motives already known to us; Roman traditionalism and the inclination to form relationships of loyalty of the most diverse kinds—or in other words, the *pietas* of the pupil towards the person and opinions of his master—were probably the principal motives which bound together many generations of jurists in consciously cultivated school traditions. A certain secondary influence may also have been exerted by the outward model of the Greek learned schools.

The leading jurists of the period after Labeo and Capito have already appeared as the heads of the two legal schools. Massurius Sabinus, compared with the senatorial jurists of his era, came from a modest background[1] and was so poorly off that he had to be supported by his pupils, not achieving the wealth-rating of an *eques* until he was fifty years of age. C. Cassius Longinus, of most distinguished birth, was a descendant of the Caesaricide and also (through his mother) of the great republican jurist Servius Sulpicius Rufus, and a man of great political influence. About the personal life of Proculus we know nothing—indeed we do not even know his family name. Besides these, mention ought to be made of M. Cocceius Nerva, who is said to have been the head of the Proculian school before Proculus and was closely connected with the Emperor Tiberius; his son of the same name also practised as a jurist; his grandson was the Emperor Nerva. The most influential of these jurists was undoubtedly Sabinus. His concise outline of the *ius civile* (*tres libri iuris civilis*) achieved almost the authority of a statute, as being the standard compilation of this

[1] Nevertheless, even he seems to have belonged to a very prominent municipal family (from Verona).

central element of the Roman private law system; even after nearly two centuries it still served as the textual basis for the great commentaries on the civil law by the late classical jurists.

4. *The mid classical period.* This period, which begins around the end of the first century A.D., is marked, outwardly at first, by the increasingly close connection of jurisprudence with the imperial administration. A great new field of practical activity was thus opened to the jurists which certainly influenced their general scientific attitude. In the preserved fragments of mid classical literature a greater emphasis on practice now clearly appears, with an even more decided inclination to a casuistic approach than before. The doctrinaire tendencies which turn up sometimes in Labeo and no doubt also in Sabinus and his contemporaries are not found in the leading jurists of this period; the school dispute was indeed continued for a while by the mid classical jurists, but by the middle of the second century it was evidently a fairly obsolete affair, and not long afterwards all traces of it vanish. The most important form of legal literature was now without doubt the collecting of individual practical decisions from the entire field of private law. Under the titles *responsa* (opinions), *epistulae* (letters, i.e. written legal advice), *quaestiones* (legal questions) or *digesta* (from *digerere*, to analyse, arrange, thus 'ordered decisions') these works contained, besides some statements of principle, a huge abundance of practical individual decisions the treatment of which exhibited the full and mature art of Roman jurisprudence.

Two jurists who deserve at least brief mention here, Titius Aristo and L. Javolenus Priscus, stand at the beginning of the mid classical period: their operations probably belong mostly to the Flavian period but extend beyond the turn of the century into Trajan's reign. While Aristo apparently devoted himself entirely to his large practice as counsel and advocate, Javolenus occupied a long series of state offices. The younger Pliny, a vain and rather shallow littérateur who was a contemporary of Javolenus, once said that he had doubts about Javolenus' sanity (*epist.* 6. 15), perhaps only for the reason that the active nature of the jurist showed no particular respect for the literary trifles of upper-class Roman society. Aristo and Javolenus mostly wrote arrangements of older jurists, such as Labeo, Sabinus, and Cassius.

L. Neratius Priscus, who lived somewhat later than Javolenus, had a similarly full political career; he came from a noble rural family whose home was the little Samnite town of Saepinum, and reached a position of such prestige that Trajan is said to have originally designated him as his successor. In his writings the mid classical preference for treating individual cases already appears quite clearly.

The reign of Hadrian—into which the career of Neratius extends—represents a high point in the history of Roman jurisprudence. The greatest jurists of this age are P. Iuventius Celsus, the son of a legal scholar of the same name who lived in the Flavian era, and is thus called Celsus *filius* for the sake of distinction; and P. Salvius Julianus. Celsus, the senior of these (he was consul for the second time in A.D. 129) had a peculiarly sharp and ingenious mind and his powerfully penetrating language can be fairly clearly picked out from among the monotonous chorus of the Roman classical writers. His temperament occasionally impelled him to make severe criticisms, and his tendency to epigrammatic formulation is noticeable; it is certainly no accident that some of the most famous utterances of Roman jurists came from his mouth, as, for example, the definition of law as *ars boni et aequi* (D. 1. 1. 1. pr.) and the two golden rules for jurists: 'scire leges non hoc est verba earum tenere, sed vim ac potestatem' (D. 1. 3. 17) and 'incivile est nisi tota lege perspecta una aliqua particula eius proposita iudicare vel respondere' (D. 1. 3. 24); so also, to mention another kind of example, the legal proverb *impossibilium nulla obligatio* (D. 50. 17. 185). Celsus' chief work was his *digesta*, a compilation running to thirty-nine books and of preponderantly casuistic content.

As mentioned earlier, P. Salvius Julianus, from Hadrumetum in the province of Africa (though presumably of distinguished Italian family), occupied a long series of senatorial offices under Hadrian, Antoninus Pius, and Marcus Aurelius, and resided for a while in Cologne as governor of Lower Germany; he held the consulship in A.D. 148. He was a pupil of Javolenus and enjoyed such repute even as a young man that Hadrian doubled his salary as quaestor—*propter insignem doctrinam*, the reason expressly given in the inscription to which we owe our knowledge of his career— and entrusted to him the important task of carrying out a final revision of the jurisdictional edicts. Julian's peculiarities are not so conspicuous as those of Celsus; his style is simple and more sober, though of great clarity and elegance. With effortless ease he could set out and decide even the most difficult situations of fact.

He was very much more prolific than Celsus: apart from minor writings he left behind a digest of ninety books whose mighty intellectual richness appears most impressively even in the modest fragments which survive. Julian's influence on his successors was extraordinarily strong: he subjected numerous old disputes to a definitive treatment, and found new solutions for many important questions. Perhaps the fact that the opposition of the two 'schools' vanishes after Julian's lifetime is to be traced back to his pre-eminent authority.[1]

With Ulpius Marcellus we meet the same mode of working— preferably casuistic—as that of Celsus and Julian; like them he composed a comprehensive digest, and belonged to the *consilium* of Antoninus Pius and Marcus Aurelius. Another who worked in the same way is Q. Cervidius Scaevola, of the equestrian order; he was *praefectus vigilum* about A.D. 175, and thereafter perhaps also *praefectus praetorio* and at any rate a councillor of the Emperor Marcus Aurelius. His large advisory practice, based to a considerable extent on legal inquiries from the eastern half of the Empire, produced collections of casuistic material of which indeed he himself seems to have drawn up only the *quaestiones*; while his *digesta* and *responsa* were probably published only long after his death, without any thorough literary arrangement having been carried out.

The main stream of jurisprudence in the mid classical age drew its strength chiefly from advisory practice and developed the law to a high state of refinement by means of the ingenious and original treatment of individual cases. Alongside it, about the middle of the second century A.D., a secondary stream can be discerned which was concerned rather with the ordering and clarifying of the legal material heaped up by the older jurists, and the production of simple, easily grasped general treatises. The chief representatives of this branch of mid classical jurisprudence are Sex. Pomponius and Gaius, about both of whom we know very little; Gaius certainly did not have the *ius respondendi*, and whether Pomponius had it is at least doubtful. Neither seems to have occupied any office of state; it may be presumed that they were engaged principally as teachers of law.

---

[1] It is highly probable that Julian was the originator of the rich casuistic material collected by his pupil Sex. Caecilius Africanus in a work entitled *quaestiones*. Another pupil of Julian, L. Volusius Maecianus was the law-teacher of Marcus Aurelius: he wrote a work on *fideicommissa*.

Pomponius, a perhaps somewhat younger contemporary of Julian, stands along with him at the head of all Roman jurists so far as the volume of his writings is concerned. In three great commentaries—*ad edictum, ad Q. Mucium*, and *ad Sabinum*—he summarized the results of classical jurisprudence up to his own times; of his lesser works we should mention here a short student's manual, the *enchiridium* (ἐγχειρίδιον = handbook) because a fragment of it which survives (*D.* 1. 2. 2) contains a concise account of Roman legal history and thus forms the backbone of our knowledge about the development of Roman legal science.

Gaius, too, composed commentaries, among them the only commentary known to us on the provincial edict, i.e. the edictal text published by the governors in the provinces, which had probably been largely simplified and assimilated to the urban edicts on the occasion of Julian's revision or perhaps even earlier. He also wrote a commentary on the Twelve Tables the modest remains of which have a certain importance for our knowledge of the ancient Roman law. Much more important, however, is the fact that his textbook for beginners, the *Institutiones* arranged in four books, has survived almost in its entirety. This work, written about A.D. 161, was in great favour particularly in the post-classical era because of the simplicity of its exposition of the law, and the late Roman legislators borrowed heavily from it. In this way alone a relatively large proportion of the text has survived, although to a large extent deformed and mixed with extraneous elements. But in addition, thanks to a lucky find of the great historian Niebuhr in 1816, we now also have a real manuscript of the work in a palimpsest from the monastic library of Verona; and more recently fragments of two further manuscripts were found in Egypt of which at least one has filled in certain gaps in the Verona text. Since, moreover, we know classical jurisprudence basically only through the mediation of the Justinianic codification, which is often able to give only a distorted or even falsified picture of the classical law, the independent survival of the *Institutes* of Gaius is of extraordinary value for the historical understanding of Roman law. In particular, our knowledge of ancient Roman and classical civil procedure rests almost entirely on this book.

Gaius is by no means one of the most important figures among the Roman jurists; he can hardly be compared with his great contemporaries Celsus and Julian, and even Pomponius excels him considerably in originality and acuity. His main quality is an agree-able and clear expository method, which is not particularly bur-dened with deeper problems. The fact that the work of Gaius is adduced neither by his contemporaries nor by the later classical writers is very significant of the modest rank which he held in legal science. He is a star of only the third or fourth order in the firma-ment of Roman jurisprudence, but on the other hand—through the accidents of survival—that star which glows nearest us and so glows brightest. It may thus be understood how the unsolved riddles which surround his personality have repeatedly stimulated ingenious guesses. It has, for example, been assumed that the writings handed down under the name of Gaius actually come from the famous early classical jurist Gaius Cassius Longinus and were merely revised in the second century A.D. by an unknown author. It is certainly possible that a work from the age of Cassius is the foundation of the *Institutiones* of Gaius, which contain a good deal that can scarcely have been still living law in the mid second century A.D. But the other works which bear the name of Gaius cannot easily be assigned to the era of Cassius. Another hypothesis (defended by Theodor Mommsen) sees in Gaius a provincial jurist who probably lived in Asia Minor or at least came from there. For this theory reliance is placed partly on occasional utterances of Gaius about legal conditions in the provinces and especially Asia Minor; also on the fact that he composed a com-mentary on the provincial edict; and finally on the circumstance that he is known only under the *praenomen* Gaius, which according to Mommsen corresponded to a widespread Greek custom.[1] But these reasons are not convincing, and we must probably content ourselves with continuing to regard the personality of Gaius as a mystery.

5. *The late classical period.* In the period of the Severan em-perors, the connection of the urban Roman jurists with the Princi-pate and with imperial administration became even closer and more

---

[1] This custom did indeed exist, but no longer by the time of Gaius. In as early a context as the New Testament we find the apostle St. Paul, who was of course a Roman citizen, being described not with his *praenomen* (which is unknown) but with his *cognomen*, as would have been the case in contemporary Rome. The same is true of all Romans men-tioned in the New Testament. The Marci, Gai, and Titi who turn up in it from time to time were not Roman citizens but Greeks or orientals who got their names in the same way as a man from the Palatinate got the name Louis, or one from Hamburg the name Percy or William.

unequivocal than in the mid classical era.[1] The leading jurists now belong almost without exception not to the senatorial order but to that of the *equites*, and occupy high equestrian offices; often indeed the prefectship of the praetorian guard (*praefectus praetorio*) is the crown of their careers, in which office an even greater responsibility was taken for the administration of justice and legal advice to the emperor. Even the great jurists were now regularly of provincial origin, and many of them can be proved to have come from the eastern half of the Empire. In the scientific work of the late classical jurists the forefront is quickly taken by work on the collection and arrangement of the older casuistic material, carrying further the trend which we observed in the mid classical period: a clear sign of the gradual failing of productive strength.

Once again, however, the creative power of Roman jurisprudence found convincing expression in the personality of the earliest and greatest of the late classical writers, Aemilius Papinianus. Nothing certain is known about his origins: the report that he was related by marriage to Septimius Severus is neither unambiguous nor completely reliable, and the belief of many, that his family came from the province of Africa or from Syria, remains a mere presumption: his peculiar style, not always easily comprehensible by reason of the compressed abundance of ideas, is no incontrovertible proof of provincial or African origin. We meet Papinian first as head of the imperial secretariat *a libellis*; from A.D. 203 onwards he was *praefectus praetorio*, and it was while holding this office that he was put to death in 213 for having—according to one version of the story—disapproved of Caracalla's murder of his brother and co-regent Geta. Like the great mid classical writers he wrote chiefly collections of casuistic decisions (*quaestiones* and *responsa*), works in which Roman practical legal expertise once more reached the highest perfection. Surrounded by the halo of martyrdom for justice, and also relatively fresh in people's memory through being chronologically the nearest of the leading figures of classical jurisprudence, Papinian was regarded by the post-classical world as the greatest jurist of all time, and this assessment of him remained common up to modern times. Today, of course, through a deeper insight into the history of Roman jurisprudence, we are inclined to

[1] Alongside the great urban jurists there appeared more clearly in this period, as we know from inscriptions, a substratum of provincial lawyers, a sign of the increasing expansion of Roman law and of the gradual decentralization of Roman culture.

regard the achievements of a Labeo, a Julian, or a Celsus, to say nothing of the great jurists of the late Republic, no less highly than the work of Papinian.

With Iulius Paulus, a pupil of Scaevola, and Domitius Ulpianus from Tyre in Phoenicia, a pupil of Papinian, there finally begins the dominance of the late classical spirit, intent on the collection and clarification of the enormous volume of early and mid classical casuistic material and on the simple exposition of the whole legal system. Ulpian and Paulus both reached the office of *praefectus praetorio* under Alexander Severus; both, by the standards of the high classical period, were important jurists even if not figures as pre-eminent as Julian and Papinian; they by no means lacked practical vision and independent judgement, and the perfect mastery of a gigantic and complicated mass of material which can be seen in their writings deserves admiration. But they can hardly have given any decisive impulses towards the further development of Roman law, unless one regards as progressive the occasionally noticeable beginnings—especially in Paulus—of a dogmatic hardening of the elastic and pliable classical ideas. Like Pomponius and Gaius, Paulus and Ulpian composed chiefly commentaries of broad plan in which the *ius civile* (on foot of Sabinus' account) and the *ius honorarium* (on foot of the praetorian and aedilician edicts) were treated with the greatest possible completeness. Here Ulpian, who was somewhat junior, did his best to exceed in comprehensiveness the works of his older rival: Paulus composed seventy-eight books on the praetorian edict, but Ulpian wrote a commentary of eighty-one books; and while Paulus' commentary on Sabinus ran to only sixteen books, Ulpian's was still incomplete at fifty-one. However, the more independent spirit of the two was probably Paulus, and it is certainly no accident that among his writings there are two fairly comprehensive works in the style of high-classical casuistics (*quaestiones* and *responsa*). Among those of Ulpian, on the other hand, apart from the gigantic commentaries it is the monographic treatments of individual legal topics and the elementary textbooks which are most prominent.

A single generation of classical legal writers follows upon the era of Paulus and Ulpian, and one without any really significant figures; only one, a pupil of Ulpian, Herennius Modestinus (*praefectus vigilum* between A.D. 226 and 244), still rises clearly above the mediocrity of his contemporaries. After the middle of the third century the literary productivity of classical jurisprudence is extinguished; there comes now the era of anonymous authors in whose hands the classical inheritance lost its creative abundance and its deeper significance and was remoulded into a simple system of elementary knowledge. Only at the highest point of the administration of Roman justice, in the imperial chancellery, can the traces of classical judgement still be seen towards the end of the third century, in the rescripts of Diocletian.

The reasons for the steep decline of classical jurisprudence lie in the political and cultural conditions of the third century A.D., and they will be discussed later when these conditions are being considered in outline.

IV. *The law of the jurists*

Of all the forces which helped to shape Roman law jurisprudence was unquestionably by far the most powerful. If one looks at its creative effectiveness in the broadest sense one recognizes that probably hardly any innovation in the whole course of Roman legal development came into being without its participation.

The interpretative art of the old lawyer-priests had adapted the law of the Twelve Tables to the requirements of a more advanced age; behind the new formations of praetorian practice, and probably also behind the republican popular legislation on private and procedural law, stood the expert advice of the jurists; and in a similar way, under the Principate, the legislation of the Senate and the ever more prominent imperial law were stimulated and moulded by the classical jurists. But the Justinianic codification, too, the last great juristic achievement of the Roman spirit, betrays throughout the dominant influence of contemporary legal learning.

At the same time, only those legal norms can strictly be called 'jurists' law' which were created by the jurists not through the mediation of the jurisdictional magistrates or the legislature, but directly by means of their advisory activity and literary works. These norms bear neither in form nor in content any special mark of their origin. Like the innovations of the *pontifices*, they appear mostly as mere interpretation of the law already in force; and because of the extreme fluidity of the boundaries between a genuine interpretation remaining within the limits of already existing law, and a creative development, by jurisprudence, of the legal system based upon the norms already there, it is often very difficult to say where the underlying *ius civile* or *ius honorarium* ends and the 'jurists' law' begins. For this reason it is easily understandable that the Romans themselves did not contrast any independent category of jurists' law with the *ius civile* or the *ius honorarium*, although on the other hand they expressly mentioned the 'authority of those learned in the law' as being one of the sources of law (*auctoritas prudentium*, Pap. *D.* 1. 1. 7. pr.; see also Gaius, *Inst.* 1. 7). They counted the jurists' law rather as part of the *ius civile*, a view which probably was thoroughly rational at the end of the Republic, but hardly corresponded any longer to the conditions of the classical, particularly the mid and late classical period. The independent development of magistral law had by this time come to an end, and the further growth of this branch of law lay now just as much in the hands of jurists as did that of the *ius civile*, so that the jurists' law of the classical period was equally closely connected with both fields. And since the jurists neither dealt with the *ius civile* without constantly having regard to the *ius honorarium*, nor, conversely, set out the *ius honorarium* without its basis in the *ius civile*, a gradual fusion of both bodies of law began, in which the fusing element was to a certain extent represented by the 'jurists' law' which was concerned with both. Already in the last classical authors this process of fusion can be seen beginning, but it was not completed until post-classical times. By then the old structural contrasts of classical law were no longer understood and therefore the whole mass of material handed down through classical legal literature, whether *ius civile* or *ius honorarium*, was now regarded as a uniform 'jurists' law' (*ius*, in contrast to *leges*, late imperial statutes).

8

IMPERIAL LAW

1. *Popular and senatorial legislation under the Principate*

WITHIN the framework of the Principate constitution the emperor enjoyed—at least in the formal sense—no legislative powers. The official sovereignty remained as before with the republican organs of state, and Augustus rejected, as being inconsistent with the republican system, the extraordinary powers which were repeatedly offered him for the reform of law and morals (the *cura legum et morum*, see the Monumentum Ancyranum, 1. 6); his reformatory legislation was put through in the strictly legitimate form of *plebiscita*. In this way, under Augustus, a considerable number of fundamental and, for the most part, very extensive popular statutes were passed affecting the constitution of the courts and the law of procedure (*leges Iuliae iudiciorum publicorum* and *privatorum*), criminal law, and private law. Under the succeeding emperors, too, up to and including Claudius, other popular statutes of lesser significance were passed. Thereafter popular legislation disappeared and senatorial legislation took its place.

Like so many changes in Roman legal life, this one too took place, not by way of an express regulation, but tacitly, through the force of circumstances. Popular legislation was never abolished, it merely vanished away because it had become obsolete; and the statutory force of the Senate's decrees needed no special recognition, as there were precedents for it which went back to republican times. Of course, a decree of the Senate was in theory no more than a direction to a magistrate consulting it, a direction by which necessary political or administrative measures were arranged but by which no norms were laid down that were generally binding and valid for all future time. But the Senate of the late Republic occasionally exceeded these limits of its competence and passed decrees on topics which ought really to have been regulated by a popular statute. This explains why the *senatus consultum* is occasionally mentioned as a source of law alongside the popular statute as early as the time of Cicero (see, e.g., Cic. *top.* 5. 28). At first this idea was evidently disputed (see Gaius, *Inst.* 1. 4); but it gained ground quickly under the Principate, particularly as Augustus did all he could to raise the Senate's prestige and to make it once more the real centre of the republican constitution. For a time the Senate and the popular assembly were active in legislating side by side, and in this period the more ceremonious form of the popular statute was usually reserved for the more important measures. The statutory force of the Senate's decrees was thus presumably already fairly generally recognized by the time the popular legislature ceased to function. In their outward form the *senatus consulta* of the second century A.D. are still mere directions to magistrates; a clear indication that no express transfer of legislative power to the Senate ever took place.

In the course of the first two centuries A.D. a not inconsiderable number of *senatus consulta* were responsible for changing the Roman law of inheritance and also isolated areas of the law of persons and of obligations.[1] Just as popular statutes were called after the proposing magistrates, so too the *senatus consulta* of the Empire were commonly (though not officially) entitled after that magistrate or emperor whose proposal had been the occasion of the Senate's decision (e.g. *senatus consultum Iuventianum* after P. Iuventius Celsus, consul in A.D. 129).

As has been said earlier, the Senate's freedom of decision laboured right from the beginning of the Principate under the absolute power of the emperor, so that the *senatus consulta* became increasingly little more than declarations of the imperial will. As early as the second half of the second century, therefore, the custom began of citing not the actual *senatus consultum* but the imperial address (*oratio principis*) read out at the Senate session; and this was the

---

[1] In the law of inheritance the Senate's legislation brought innovations in the field of the statutory order of inheritance, which in spite of praetorian reforms still rested largely on the Twelve Tables (introduction of succession between mother and child through the *SC Tertullianum*, under Hadrian, and *Orfitianum*, A.D. 178). In addition, the law of bequests was reformed by several *senatus consulta* (*SCa Neronianum* and *Trebellianum* under Nero, *Pegasianum* under Vespasian, and *Iuventianum* under Hadrian). Significant in the law of obligations is, for example, the *SC Vellaeanum* (A.D. 46?) which made credit transactions with women voidable if they had been entered into not in their own interest but in someone else's, and the *SC Macedonianum* (A.D. 47), a prohibition on giving loans to persons still under the power of their *paterfamilias* (*filii familias*). Frequently, too, new crimes were created by resolutions of the Senate, though in most cases these were inspired by criminal statutes of the republican and Augustan eras.

first step in a development which ended in post-classical times with the *senatus consultum* becoming an imperial decree in the formal sense.

11. *Creation of law by the princeps*

Actual legislation remained throughout the Principate at least nominally in the hands of the republican organs and was only in-directly controlled by the princeps. But there existed also from the beginning a number of other forms in which the princeps was active, inconspicuously but none the less effectively, as an inde-pendent creator of new legal rules. All these forms were connected to a greater or lesser degree with the model of magistral creation of law but the standards were at all times quite different; for the power of the princeps, in practice almost unlimited in scope and lifelong in duration, lent his ordinances a degree of authority which was never possessed by the measures of the annual republican magistrates. Thus it is not surprising that the measures decreed by the princeps (*constitutiones principis*) are mentioned as sources of law, as early as the revision of the edict under Hadrian, alongside popular and senatorial legislation, and that legal theory expressly attributed statutory force (*legis vigorem*) to them by, at the latest, the middle of the second century A.D. (Gaius, *Inst.* 1. 5; Ulp. *D.* 1. 4. 1). This concession of the force of law to the imperial *con-stitutiones* was justified by a theory which constantly recurs in the history of authoritarian systems of government, namely that the emperor received his power from the Roman people through the *lex de imperio*, and that his decrees therefore rested at least in-directly on the popular will.

Of the various forms of imperial creation of law that which most closely corresponds to the magistral model is the imperial *edictum*. Enjoying, as he did, magistral or quasi-magistral powers (in par-ticular the tribunician power and the *imperium proconsulare*) the princeps also arrogated to himself the right of issuing edicts (*ius edicendi*). Since these powers were lifelong, the imperial edicts remained in force during the whole reign of their authors; and while the edicts of the republican annual magistrates always lost their validity on the expiry of their period of office, it appears that those of the princeps continued in force even after his reign unless specifically rescinded by his successor. The edict was the usual form for all communications addressed directly to the public, and for this reason the content of the imperial edicts known to us is very heterogeneous. They deal with questions of private law, criminal law, the constitution of the courts, affairs of provincial administration, the legal conditions surrounding aqueducts and state-owned land, privileges, the bestowal of citizenship; even the famous *constitutio Antoniniana* of Caracalla, through which Roman citizenship was granted to the great bulk of the population of the provinces, was an edict. The emperors, however, never issued jurisdictional edicts like those of the praetors, aediles, and provincial governors; and in general the importance of the imperial edicts in the development of Roman private law is not especially great. No doubt the chief reason for this is that the emperors preferred fundamental changes in this area to be carried out through the republican legislative organs.

By contrast to the *edicta*, which were addressed to the general public, *mandata* were internal directions of the princeps to the officials in his service. Originally no doubt addressed personally to each individual official, they soon acquired a traditional character and, to the extent to which they applied to the same or related official fields, largely the same wording. Surviving citations show that they included, besides general principles about behaviour in office, also a considerable number of individual provisions on matters of substantive law and procedure, particularly in the field of criminal law. In spite of their formally internal character, their contents were regarded as generally binding law, so that private citizens, too, could have recourse to them.

Statutory validity was also assumed for the decisions contained in the emperor's correspondence (*rescripta*). According to their outward form there are two types to be distinguished here: the imperial letter (*epistula*) and the marginal decision given by the princeps (*subscriptio*). The more binding form, the *epistula*, was used chiefly in relations with officials, provincial communities, provincial assemblies, and, in general, with all the more important persons and bodies; and in it the princeps maintained the epistolary style usual between private persons, so that a clear distinction between his private and official correspondence is really not possible.[1] Petitions (*libelli*) from people of lesser standing, on the other hand, were dealt with by *subscriptio*; this consisted of a

[1] This is particularly evident in the surviving correspondence of the Emperor Trajan with the younger Pliny during the latter's governorship in the province of Bithynia.

decision written in under the petition, which was then not sent to
the petitioner but was brought to his attention by being exposed
publicly.

The legal content of the rescripts was naturally even more varied
than that of the *edicta*. They became particularly important for
the development of private law after it became usual in the second
century—even among private persons—to petition the emperor
for a decision in a doubtful question of law. The rescripts which
were issued on such petitions were not judgements, because they
were always based on the supposition that the state of facts alleged
by the petitioner was correct, and left it to the judge's competence
to establish whether this supposition was justified; if it was, then
the judge was bound by the imperial decision, and this decision,
contained in a rescript, created thus a binding precedent for future
cases. Basically, this imperial rescript-practice, which assumed an
extraordinary compass in the third century, rested on the same
principle as the advisory activity of the jurists endowed with the
ius respondendi; the only difference being that it was no longer the
jurist authorized by the emperor but the emperor himself who gave
the legal advice sought. The development of the rescript-practice
was carried out in close co-operation with the legal profession,
whose leading representatives participated in it as officials or
advisers of the emperor and were frequently (even if probably not
always) the actual authors of the imperial decisions. But the free
and independent advisory activity of the jurists lost more and more
ground through the competition of the highest power in the State,
and, probably as early as the first half of the third century, the
jurists found themselves able to take part in the development of
law only as officials of the emperor. This was a fatal blow to Roman
jurisprudence, and in the rise of the imperial rescript-practice we
may therefore see one of the chief reasons for the rapid decline of
late classical legal science. The Principate, to which the legal profession had once owed such extraordinary advancement, now
crushed it with its overwhelming power and extended its unlimited
dominance to the field of the creation of law.

Even by the second half of the second century A.D. the jurists
had begun to cite the imperial rescripts in great quantity and even
to build up collections of them. It is true that of the oldest work of
this kind known to us, the collection of *constitutiones* in twenty
books made by Papirius Justus, only a few fragments remain in

the Digest of Justinian. The main bulk of the rescripts known to us survive in the *Codex Justinianus* and come from collections of the period of Diocletian; in addition, isolated rescripts survive in inscriptions or in papyri.

Finally, alongside the rescripts, the *decreta* of the emperors also gained a very considerable importance as a source of law. By contrast with the rescripts, they are in fact genuine judicial decisions pronounced after an oral proceeding before the emperor's court. Something has already been said of the development of this court and of the importance which it finally achieved. The practice of the imperial court was fundamental to the development of the law, above all in those cases in which other courts felt unable, in view of the legal provisions in force, to do justice to a morally right claim of a party; here the supra-legal power of the princeps made possible a creative decision which could free the situation from the bonds of the existing law. If a highly developed legal culture ever contained a truly 'kingly' judge, then that judge was the Roman princeps, above all in those decades of the second century A.D. in which figures of the rank of Hadrian, Antoninus Pius, and Marcus Aurelius, advised by the greatest jurists of antiquity but still often following their own instinct in making decisions, administered justice with the greatest care and with an earnest concern for truth and justice.[1]

111. *Imperial law*

In the creative legal practice of the Roman emperors we find that the pattern of development of magistral jurisdiction is once more repeated: a new stratum of freer and more equitable legal norms is formed, and the barriers of old formal requirements and traditional principles are overthrown. The influence of imperial law was admittedly not so deep and revolutionary as was that of the jurisdiction of the late republican magistrates; it was basically marginal. While the kernel of the previous legal order was further developed only in isolated (though sometimes very important)

---

[1] A picture of proceedings before the imperial court is best given (apart from isolated reports in classical legal literature, e.g. *D.* 4. 2. 13 = *D.* 48. 7. 7, and descriptions in the letters of the younger Pliny. 4. 22; 6. 22; 6. 31) by the unfortunately incomplete record of a court proceeding before Caracalla in an inscription from Dmeir in Syria: see most recently Kunkel, *Festschrift Lewald* (1953), 81 ff. (with text and bibliography). *Decreta* of the emperors which are important for legal development are frequently adduced by the classical jurists.

points, there arose, above all in the law of inheritance and on foot of imperial innovations, a quite independent group of new legal norms, the law of *fideicommissa*: this was then further developed by jurisprudence and also in part by senatorial legislation. Again, imperial law, by contrast with the edictal *ius honorarium* of the republican magistrates, for a long time lacked any over-all unity, scattered as it was over a broad field and dressed in the very various forms of imperial legal creations. For this reason, and also because the efficacy of popular statutes was attributed to the imperial constitutions, imperial law was regarded not as an independent element in the legal system but, like the jurists' law, as part of the *ius civile*: an interpretation which did not do full justice to its historical origins. It was not until the late Empire that any contrast was drawn between imperial legislation—a fast-growing corpus now united in great collections—as simple statutory law (*leges*) and the law of the writings of the classical jurists.

Part Three

THE LAW OF THE
LATE ROMAN EMPIRE

9

THE STATE AND SOCIETY IN THE LATE EMPIRE

1. *Historical basis*

BY the beginning of the third century A.D. the Roman state bore in many respects an essentially different character from that of the time of Augustus and his immediate successors. By a gradual development the *imperium* of the city state of Rome had given way to a uniform world Empire in which the legal positions of ruling and subject people were no longer distinguished. The republican system which Augustus had carefully restored was now no more than a venerable and weather-beaten façade; the magistracies and the Senate had sunk into political insignificance. The Principate was thought of as a necessary institution and from the time of Septimius Severus (A.D. 193) displayed more or less openly the character of an absolute monarchy founded on military power, whose administrative machinery had consolidated itself and extended its sphere of operation even further. As we have noted earlier, the Roman element was still dominant in the state and its cultural life; but its most important representatives now came from the provinces, not from Italy, and a large proportion of them were of foreign blood. Even the Roman Senate now consisted to a considerable degree of provincials, and, among these, members from the eastern half of the Empire became ever more numerous. The economic preponderance of Italy had already disappeared; Rome itself was no longer a centre of economic power but merely a centre of enormous consumption.

The period of internal peace which had lasted for nearly two and a half centuries, from Augustus up to the time of the Severan emperors, had not in fact resulted in a lasting strengthening of the Empire. After a great resurgence there had been a static period, and then a perceptible falling-off in vitality in all departments of life. Too many sections of the community had adopted a comfortable existence supported by unearned income and were living on the labour of slaves and of rural tenants; economic development halted, intellectual vigour degenerated, cultural life began to bear the marks of sterile senility. We can see how the revenue of the Empire at the end of the second century was able to bear the costs of the administration and of the expensive mercenary army only with great difficulty; so that extraordinary burdens imposed on the state through wars and natural catastrophes, above all in the reign of Marcus Aurelius, were a serious blow to its well-being. At about the same time the finances of numerous communities, both in Italy and in the provinces, were so disorganized that the emperors were obliged to interfere in municipal self-government by the appointment of special state officers (*curatores rei publicae*). With this there is closely connected a phenomenon which also becomes perceptible for the first time in the course of the late second century and became of the greatest importance in later social and political development: the gradual transformation of honorary municipal offices and councils into *compulsory* offices in the interest of the state's fiscal administration. Just as in the Republic, a large part of the taxes for which the provincials were liable was collected not directly from the population but from the different municipalities, who were responsible for getting the money. When with the universal economic decline the financial situation of many cities became difficult, the Empire was obliged to impose a personal liability on the organs of the city administrations for the payment of the taxes. This liability to the revenue authorities, together with the heavy expenditure for the benefit of the community which was expected of municipal magistrates, threatened the well-being of the upper stratum of provincial society, and made the honorary municipal offices, once the goal of the ambition and local patriotism of wealthy citizens, seem in time less desirable. As the number of candidates able to discharge these tasks became smaller, so the burdens falling on the individual magistrate became heavier, and accordingly the state had to interfere more ruthlessly with measures of compulsion. Even children under age were forced into the city councils for the sole purpose of making them liable for the financial interests of the state. In this way what had been an office of honour (*honos*) became an oppressive office of compulsion (*munus*, λειτουργία), and self-government in the innumerable city-communities in the Empire began to decay.

These and similar phenomena mark the first beginnings of the great crisis from which the Empire finally emerged in the last stage of its history with a greatly changed social and political system. The high point of this period of crisis lies in the second half of the third century, an age of grave catastrophes and of political and economic anarchy. The army, which was now composed of the least civilized elements in the population of the Empire, set itself up as sole lord in the state and raised up emperors from its own ranks; incessant military revolts allowed no ordered government to emerge; the Empire was attacked from all sides by neighbouring peoples who laid waste huge stretches of its territory. The rural population suffered very heavily under the extraordinary levying of taxes in kind for the supply of the army (*annona*), the burden of quartering the soldiers and the requisitioning of means of transport; often they attempted to avoid this intolerable oppression by simply running away, so that large tracts of fertile land fell into desolation. Industrial production and trade languished; lack of money and of precious metal caused the emperors to debase the coinage again and again, measures which in their turn produced increases in prices, the complete confusion of the money system and, to a large degree, a return to a primitive natural economy. In many parts of the Empire the oppressed population rebelled and separatist movements developed. In these circumstances it was inevitable that everything which had outlived its usefulness should collapse, and that every element which in the quiet days of the Principate had been growing only gradually and inconspicuously should now openly show its face. This explains how it was that Diocletian, under whose reign (A.D. 284–305) more stable conditions first reappeared, became in fact the founder of a new political order, although his attitude was fundamentally conservative.

11. *The late Roman state*

This new order, set up by Diocletian and consciously developed in the new direction by Constantine the Great (A.D. 306–37) was an unconcealed and unlimited monarchy with a bureaucratic administration and characterized by a ruthless limitation of personal freedom in the interests of the state. The republican façade of the Principate had disappeared; so had the predominance of Rome and of Italy in the Empire. The Empire was now a cosmopolitan structure with a dual, Greco-Roman culture in which the

preponderant element tended more and more to be Greek. Diocletian resided mostly in Nicomedia in Asia Minor, Constantine
founded the second imperial capital, Constantinople, in the east,
and even the western emperors now chose as their seat not Rome,
but Treves, Milan, or Ravenna. The organs of the Roman city-
state constitution had no longer the least political importance. Of
the old Roman magistracies the consulate was a mere decoration
for deserving worthies (as indeed it had already been in the Principate). The lesser offices, to the extent to which they still existed at
all, played no part except in the narrow sphere of the city of Rome
itself; and even here they had lost all real administrative functions,
including the administration of justice, to the *praefectus urbi* nominated by the emperor. The Senate certainly still possessed a certain
aura of dignity, but no longer had the slightest influence: its
members merely formed the highest rank of imperial subjects to
which the heads of the imperial army and bureaucracy belonged,
together with some representatives of the urban Roman aristocracy; the former predominated even more exclusively in Constantine's newly created Senate in the eastern capital.

   The population of the Empire (apart from the slaves, whose
numbers were falling) was no longer divided, as under the Principate, into Roman citizens and non-citizens whose legal position
depended on the political standing of their home communities, but
into vocational groups separated from one another by ever more
insurmountable barriers. On each of these groups special and
mostly very oppressive burdens were imposed, and the state did
not allow anyone to avoid these burdens by transferring to a more
favourable group; indeed, children were as a rule obliged to remain
in the group to which their fathers had belonged. Thus, for example,
in order to control the decline in agriculture produced by the flight
of the small farmer population from the land, the heavily oppressed
tenants of state and private lands (*coloni*) were transformed into
half-free serfs hereditarily bound to the soil (*glebae adscripti*:
adscripticii). The artisans who even under the Principate had been
partly organized in guilds and burdened with compulsory production for the benefit of the state, often became hereditarily bound
workers in industries owned or supervised by the state. A particularly burdensome hereditary position was held by the councillor
members of the urban aristocracies (*curiales*); they were liable for
the collection of all taxes imposed on the urban territory. Some

groups were privileged: the army (in which foreign mercenaries from outside the Empire, mostly of German origin, played an increasing part), the bureaucracy, and (in Christian times) the clergy.

The iron compulsion of the state and its requirements which conditioned late Roman society in this way was the result of the economic decline, which grew more and more acute after the beginning of the third century, and the fall in population which accompanied it; and this compulsion was thought to be the only way of maintaining the gigantic machinery of the Empire in a decaying world. But this system was not altogether without forerunners in the preceding periods of antiquity; indeed its roots go back to the organization of certain states in the Hellenistic era, in particular that of the Ptolemaic kingdom in Egypt. The administrative methods which were developed there and which were directed to the extraction of the greatest possible revenues had never been abandoned under Roman domination. But whereas under the Principate they had remained restricted basically to their countries of origin and thus to those sections of the Empire's population which had been accustomed to them for centuries, they were now applied to the whole Empire and all its inhabitants. Perhaps it is in this fact that one sees most clearly how the late Roman régime represented in certain respects a victory of the Hellenistic-Oriental world over the west and over the Roman way of life.

Even in the position of the late Roman emperors and the shape of their bureaucratic apparatus Hellenistic and oriental influences are clearly in evidence. The emperor, who in the period of the early Principate had, at least in the capital city, mostly worn the Roman citizen's dress with the purple stripes of the senator, tended in the second and third centuries to dress with ever-increasing splendour; and now he appeared in public only in a gold-embroidered purple robe. He wore the diadem, a cloth band set with pearls, the old badge of oriental kingly dignity. A most elaborate court ceremonial regulated every movement in his presence and, in particular, prescribed that anyone who approached him must throw himself on the ground, as had once been the custom in the court of Darius or Xerxes. All of this is an expression of the fact that the emperor was now no longer merely the first citizen of the Roman community, but the unlimited ruler before whom all inhabitants of the Empire, without distinction, had to bend the knee. Thus modern historical scholarship has coined the expression 'Dominate' (from *dominus*, 'lord') for this late Roman form of the imperial office, intended to indicate an essential distinction from the Principate. To this Hellenistic-Oriental kingly dignity there corresponds also the worship of the living emperor as a god. This cult had been tolerated even under Augustus in the east of the Empire, but restrained as far as possible in Rome itself and in the Romanized west because it completely contradicted the ideology of the Principate, and this attitude was maintained with greater or lesser determination at least by the majority of the succeeding emperors. In the third century these inhibitions disappeared, and under Diocletian the religious worship of the living emperor belonged to the official essence of the emperorship. Later, of course, it was undermined by Christianity; but the epithets 'divine' (*divinus*) and 'sacred' (*sacer*) for everything connected with the emperor's person remained lasting elements of late Roman official jargon.

The administration of the Empire, unlike that of the Principate, was almost completely separated from the military command, and was attended to by a huge bureaucracy with numerous gradations of rank and a precisely determined system of promotion. Under the military emperors of the third century the military profession had obtained a particularly favoured position, and the junior posts in the civil service had originally been filled largely by demobilized junior officers and common soldiers. Thus the late Roman bureaucracy, although it had in fact no further connection with the army, claimed all the privileges of the military state as well as the description *militia* ('military service') for its office; it even maintained the fiction of belonging to 'regiments' of the field army (*legiones*) and 'battalions' of the frontier troops (*cohortes*). Just as the income of the Roman state now rested chiefly on contributions in kind (*annona*), which had grown out of the irregular requisitions of the third century and had been reorganized by Diocletian, so the salaries of the officials now consisted no longer of money but of payments in kind. In view of the currency difficulties which still existed in the fourth century, this was actually the most secure way of calculating something which would remain stable in value; but in practice, however, the payments were soon revalued in money terms (*adaeratio*). A widespread system of 'gifts', which was most oppressive for the population, increased the income of many officials and contributed greatly to the moral degradation of the bureaucracy—just as did the officially recognized buying and selling of most offices. This degradation showed itself in corruptibility, in extortions, and every kind of vexation committed on the defenceless people. Attempts were indeed made to put down this corruption by means of a subtle system of informers; but often all that was achieved was a new round of corruption, since the superintendents sent out by the central administration (called *frumentarii* until Diocletian, later *agentes in rebus*) naturally used their powers to gain personal advantages for themselves.

The highest civil officials were the *praefecti praetorio* of whom there were now four, two each in the western and eastern halves of the Empire. They were to a large extent representatives of the emperor, particularly in the administration of justice; in addition they administered the collection of taxes in kind and thus the most important part of the imperial finances; but they no longer had any military authority. Since a fixed part of the territory of the Empire was assigned to each of them, they really did not belong any longer to the central administration but were rather the heads of the local administration, which was organized under them into vicariates and numerous provinces (much reduced in size compared with the earlier provincial division). The *praefecti* as well as the *vicarii* and the provincial governors were assisted by large secretariats (*officia*), the chiefs of which were simultaneously entrusted by the central government with the task of watching their superiors. The heads of the actual central government were: the chief of the imperial secretariats (*magister officiorum*) under whose superintendence the various offices (now called *scrinia*, 'cabinets') were divided, for the carrying on of imperial correspondence in the same way as under the principate; the imperial treasurer (*comes sacrarum largitionum*, so called because it was his job to pay out the imperial donations to soldiers and officials which were usual on certain occasions); the head of the administration of the imperial estates (*comes rerum privatarum*); and the *quaestor sacri palatii*, a sort of Minister of Justice. These four departmental chiefs also belonged to the emperor's council of state (*consistorium*) which had developed out of the *consilium principis* of the early Empire; this *consistorium* consisted, apart from these officials, of full-time councillors (*comites consistoriani*). Its main function was that of an imperial court of justice, and, from the mid fourth century, it usually did its business in the emperor's absence, though its decisions required his confirmation. But, in genuinely oriental fashion, one of the highest and most influential imperial offices was that of the emperor's chief chamberlain (*praepositus sacri cubiculi*, literally, superintendent of the emperor's bedchamber) who was in charge of the imperial household and who was, as a rule, a eunuch.

A peculiarity of the late Roman constitution of great importance for the destiny of the Empire and which we have not yet mentioned was the division of the imperial authority among several emperors: a division not in the sense of joint reigns, as had repeatedly been the case in the Principate but one with geographically distinct spheres of operation and with far-reaching independence. The author of this institution was Diocletian, whose purpose was in this way to intensify imperial government as well as to avert troubles about succession. His remarkable system, according to which the eastern and western halves of the empire each had a principal emperor (*Augustus*) and a subsidiary emperor (*Caesar*) and the latter was supposed to be the successor of the former and then in his turn to choose a junior colleague, in fact did not survive its creator. But the division of the empire thus introduced, into a Latin west and a Greek east, became in the end permanent, after some interruptions, because both halves of the Empire now found themselves in internal opposition to one another. Cultural and economic development took very different courses in the two parts of the Empire. In the east the Greek element quickly achieved absolute dominance, while the west remained Latin in language and civilization. In the eastern half industry and commerce still flourished quite strongly while the west was sinking back further and further into primitive conditions. In the east the system of the state-controlled economy of compulsion was able to assert itself more or less successfully, in spite of certain feudalistic tendencies and of the loss of power and the difficulties which the authority of the state underwent through the increasing influence of the church; in the west, on the other hand, the system largely failed through the power of the great landowners, who for the most part held the leading posts of imperial government in their hands and for that very reason were easily able to avoid the oppression of the state. Thus the destinies of the two halves of the Empire parted from one another: the western fell immediately a prey to the Germans who were invading it in ever greater hordes; the eastern continued in existence, in the form of the Byzantine state, for a full millennium, up to the frontiers of modern times.

III. *The administration of justice*

Next to the collection of taxes, the administration of justice was probably the most important function of the civil authorities in the late Roman Empire. After the last traces of the jury-courts of the republican and Augustan eras and of the civil jurisdiction of the praetor had died out in the course of the third century, all civil and criminal proceedings came under the official *cognitio*, a procedural system which, in the unitary course which it took as well as in the official character of its judges, displays a much closer similarity to a modern system of justice than do the procedural forms of the later Republic or the early Empire. The judges of first instance in Rome and Constantinople (and within a radius of 100 miles around these cities) were the *praefecti urbi*, and in the provinces the governors (*praesides*).[1] All of these were entitled to entrust the hearing of a case to a subordinate judge (*iudex pedaneus*), whose decision could be appealed against to the judge who had delegated him. The judgement of a provincial governor, too, was always subject to appeal; the aggrieved party could go either to the *vicarius* or to the *praefectus praetorio*. A further appeal from the *vicarius* to the emperor's own court was possible; but the decisions of the *praefectus praetorio*, who administered justice in the name of the emperor himself (*vice sacra*) could not be appealed against.[2] Appeal from the judgements of the *praefecti urbis* was allowed only in very special conditions (which varied greatly from time to time) and was then taken always to the emperor.

On the civil side, the formulae had lost their meaning with the disappearance of the old procedure divided between praetor and *iudex*. They may have survived for a while in connection with the appointment of subordinate judges; but the sons of Constantine expressly forbade their use, on the ground that the verbal hair-splitting felt to be associated with them prejudiced the parties in litigation (*C.* 2. 57. 1; 342 A.D.). This may be true of practice in

---

[1] The magistrates of the municipalities continued to possess jurisdiction only where matters of small value were in dispute. Alongside them there existed, in the later Dominate, a sort of peacemaker jurisdiction, that of the *defensor civitatis*, an official whose job it was to protect humble people against the powerful (the *decuriones* or the governor).

[2] The same thing is admittedly said of the *vicarii* and the *praefecti urbis*, whose judgements, none the less, were not immune to appeal.

the fourth century, because practitioners were no longer able to manage correctly the legal concepts and the ingenious formula-technique of the classical period.[1] Actions were now instituted by means of a document, in which the cause of action was supposed to be stated, though this requirement was apparently often neglected. The defendant replied with another document (*libellus contradictorius*). If he failed to turn up for the oral hearing in court, and ignored a further summons, judgement by default finally issued against him. The court proceedings were incorporated in an exhaustive record, the spoken judgement was delivered to the parties in writing, and the execution of the judgement was carried out by an official (*exsecutor*). The parties were obliged to make payments in respect of all official acts done by the court's staff. A certain number of recognized advocates were attached to every court (with the exception of the emperor's own court); they were called *advocati*, but also *togati*, because when they appeared in court they had to wear the ancient garment of the Roman citizen —the *toga*—which had long since dropped out of ordinary use. These advocates no doubt had always had a training in rhetoric, but not necessarily always in law; the study of law in a law-school such as that of Berytos, as a preparation for the career of advocate, does not seem to have become usual until the mid fourth century, and then only in the eastern part of the Empire. The Emperor Leo decreed in 460 that admission to the profession of advocate should require the sworn certificate of a law-teacher attesting the applicant's knowledge of the law, but this rule may have applied only to those wishing to practise in the court of the *praefectus praetorio*, to whom the *constitutio* in question (C. 2. 7. 11) was addressed. Certainly the fact that eleven advocates from the court of the *praefectus praetorio Orientis* in Constantinople were recruited for the production of Justinian's Digest suggests that a considerable proportion of the bar there must have enjoyed the reputation of outstanding legal expertise; and it was from the advocates' profession, too, that *iudices pedanei* and also the assessors of the judges were customarily drawn. Since an assessor was frequently more familiar with both the law and the practice of the courts than the

---

[1] When the divided procedure disappeared, the conception of *litis contestatio* at first disappeared along with it. When the expression was used in later times, it was taken to mean the beginning of the substantive oral hearing, after any procedural objections (e.g. to the capacity of one of the parties to litigate, or to the competence of the court) had been dealt with.

judge himself, he probably exerted in many cases a decisive influence on the judgement.

In spite of its character as an offspring of central state authority, the administration of justice in the late Empire was not, in essence, an arbitrary system. In civil proceedings and probably even in criminal indictments it is probable that the parties themselves still mainly controlled both the content and the course of the trial. In addition, the possibilities of appeal—which in some respects might be thought excessive—offered a procedural guarantee of an objectively correct decision. At the same time, litigation was expensive; court fees and advocates' fees had to be paid; an appeal taken at the distant seat of the *vicarius* or perhaps before the *praefectus praetorio* or the emperor himself was something which certainly none but the well-off could afford. The encroachments of bureaucracy into the sphere of procedure, and the usually very lengthy times permitted for the various steps in litigation made the latter long-drawn-out and troublesome. It seems that corruption was not exceptional, above all in the courts of the governors, who were relatively badly paid. For all these reasons it is easy to imagine that the arbitral jurisdiction of the bishops became popular; it had begun to compete with the administration of the state's justice, and had been the subject of frequent imperial legislation from the time of Constantine.

10

LEGAL DEVELOPMENT IN THE LATE
EMPIRE UP TO JUSTINIAN

1. *Post-classical jurisprudence*

1. *The fall of classical jurisprudence*. In the context of the political
and cultural changes which determined the appearance of the late
Roman state and its society may be placed the fall of classical jurisprudence, which, as has been seen, was completed about the middle
of the third century A.D. One of its causes we have already seen in
another connection: the rise of the imperial rescript-practice, above
all under the Severan emperors, gradually choked the free advisory
practice of the jurists and thus destroyed the principal basis of an
independent jurisprudence. It is true that the service of the state
with its practical opportunities for legal work still remained open
to the jurists, and the rescripts of the period of Diocletian prove
in fact that, at least within the central imperial government, the
tradition of classical legal science was preserved up to the threshold
of the fourth century. But the position of the jurists in the state
service in the rough and uncultured times of the military emperors
and later under the absolute régime of the Dominate was no longer
the same as it had been under Hadrian, the Antonines, or even the
Severan emperors. The jurist was no longer the adviser who dealt
with the monarch almost on an equal footing, but was merely the
unfree tool of the imperial will. Even more significant than this
change in the outward position of the jurist was, probably, the
inner break with the traditions of the classical period: the
Roman element had finally played out its leading role in political
life, the constitutional and procedural bases of classical law were
obsolete and hardly any longer even comprehensible, and for
this reason the whole structure of the classical norms, with all its
subtle distinctions rooted in history, was no longer a living thing.
If, finally, one reflects on the general falling off in intellectual
power which took place in the third century in all spheres of
cultural life, then one can understand that the creative period

of Roman jurisprudence came to an end with the crisis of the Principate.

For a period of about 200 years, i.e. up to the second half of the fifth century, the fortunes of legal science are submerged in anonymous obscurity. Reports on the work and circumstances of jurists become extremely scanty. It is only seldom that we meet even a single name, and these names alone tell us nothing, as we can usually connect with them no idea of the personality and work behind them. Whatever we possess of the literary production of post-classical jurisprudence is—with few exceptions—either unnamed or is concealed under the names of late classical authors; not until the critical research of the last fifty years was the real origin of this second group of post-classical writings recognized. Only recently has it been possible to construct a credible chronological arrangement of the remains of post-classical legal literature. After many false starts, recent scholarship has achieved results in the study of the textual history of Roman legal sources and the inner development of post-classical law which make it possible to give at least an outline account of the history of jurisprudence between the end of the classical age and the codifications of Justinian. This period falls into three parts (sections 2-4, below). The first includes the jurisprudence of the later third century and of the time of Diocletian and Constantine. The age of vulgar law lasts in the western empire until the end of antiquity and runs into the legal life of the Germanic kingdoms on Roman soil. In the east, however, it is replaced by a renaissance of classical law in the law-schools of the fifth century, and the last section of our account of post-classical legal science will be devoted to this return to classical law.

2. *The later third century and the era of Diocletian and Constantine* (*till the mid fourth century*). The legal science of this time was, as we now know, in close touch with the literary heritage of the classical writers, especially the late classical writers of the early third century. In the law-schools which flourished at that time, above all in Rome, the great commentaries of Paulus and Ulpian, for example, were carefully studied and interpreted. But they were no longer fully understood in the spirit of the classical tradition because the requisites for such an understanding no longer existed. The school method tended to be dogmatic and to prefer easily managed formulations and simplified statements of reasons. But even in the science of the schools of the late second century—as

reflected in the *Institutes* of Gaius—something similar can be seen, notwithstanding that it was contemporaneous with the living tradition of classical jurisprudence. These tendencies obviously became even stronger in post-classical times.

The work of the early post-classical school-jurists issued in the continued manuscript publication of the works of the classical authors. It is probable that in the era of Diocletian and Constantine new editions, for instance, of Ulpian's commentary on the edict were brought out, editions revised in the spirit of contemporary science by the schools, and that for this reason the 'Ulpian' fragments in Justinian's Digest not infrequently represent not the original text of the classical jurist but rather a version informed by post-classical thinking. The falsifications discovered by so-called 'interpolation-research' in the Justinianic reproduction of classical legal writings were originally attributed to Justinian's codifiers, and later also to the eastern law-schools of the fifth century. Today, however, modern scholarship tends to presume that many of them crept in in the course of the third century, or, at latest, in the period of Diocletian and Constantine.[1]

Apart from this work of interpretation of the great classical writings, the early post-classical school-jurisprudence produced chiefly short elementary works, in part revisions of classical text-books, in part compilations from great classical works. These mostly circulated under the names of classical authors[2] and were long regarded as the genuine works of Paulus, Ulpian, or Gaius; and only modern research has succeeded in attributing them with greater or lesser certainty to the post-classical period. This class of writings includes, for example, the so-called *regulae Ulpiani* (also called *tituli ex corpore Ulpiani*), which, however, show a much closer relationship with the *Institutes* of Gaius than with the surviving remains of Ulpian's works; they have survived independently

---

[1] This supposition can be proved in the admittedly very rare cases in which we find the same legal text not only in the Digest of Justinian but also in one of the early classical collections (the *Fragmenta Vaticana* or the *Collatio legum Mosaicarum et Romanarum*), and both texts exhibit identical falsifications.

[2] An exception to this is represented by the *iuris epitomae* (excerpts of which are found in the Digest), a respectable work which bears the name of its real author, Hermogenianus —presumably the same man as the author of the *Codex Hermogenianus*, but possibly, on the other hand, to be identified with a *praefectus praetorio* of the same name who is mentioned in the *Acts of the Martyrs* of St. Sabinus and who would thus have lived under Diocletian. See Liebs, 'Hermogenians *iuris epitomae*', in *Abhandlungen der Göttinger Akademie der Wissenschaften*, Phil.-hist. Klasse, 1964.

of the Justinianic codification, although only in a fragmentary condition and in the form of an abbreviated revision, in a manuscript of the Vatican library. In the same way we possess another text, independent of Justinian and handed down chiefly through the Visigothic codification,[1] of the so-called *Pauli sententiae*; this is an elementary book formed from late classical legal writings (probably not only of Paulus), the basic elements of which were probably first composed in the third century but repeatedly changed in the following centuries by abbreviations and additions. An early postclassical revision of the *Institutes* of Gaius (to name a third example of these elementary writings) was probably also the *res cottidianae* ('everyday law') or *aurea* ('golden rules') which circulated as an original writing of Gaius, of which we possess admittedly only some fragments in the Digest of Justinian. In these fragments can be seen a considerable progression—compared with the original work of Gaius—in the direction of dogmatic exposition of legal materials.

From these elementary outlines must be distinguished another group of literary works belonging to this period: works which openly purported to be selections from the works of the classical writers and from imperial legislation. Here the excerpts are not arranged into a cohesive text, but each of them is described by a reference to the name of the author and the original source. The same technique is used in composing most of the codifications of the fifth or sixth centuries, in particular Justinian's Digest and Codex, of which these works may be regarded as the first and private forerunners. Apart from two collections of *constitutiones* from the reign of Diocletian which will be discussed later, we know two other works of this type, which besides some imperial laws contain chiefly excerpts from late classical legal literature; and both exist in texts independent of Justinian's codifications. The collection of excerpts from Papinian, Paulus, Ulpian, and imperial legislation, which is preserved in a fragmentary condition in a manuscript in the Vatican library and is thus known under the title *fragmenta Vaticana*, must—so far as we can judge from the available fragments—have been a work planned on a large scale, in size perhaps

---

[1] A sheet of parchment which came into the possession of the University Library at Leiden in 1954 contains an important and previously unknown piece of the *Pauli sententiae*, whose contents concern criminal law (on the *repetundae* procedure and on the *crimen laesae maiestatis*); there is an edition with an exhaustive commentary by various authors in *Studia Gaiana*, iv, Leiden, 1956.

not very inferior to Justinian's Digest. Presumably its principal purpose was to replace the rare, expensive, and clumsy original classical works available for legal instruction (which of course was also one of the main objects of Justinian's Digest). Still, it may have also been used by practitioners for whom the adduction of classical originals was probably often even more difficult than for the schools. Similar ends were no doubt served by the Roman law kernel of a further collection, the so-called *Collatio legum Mosaicarum et Romanarum*. In the form in which it has come down to us—a text which was probably compiled very much later, not before the last decades of the fourth century—this little work, which calls itself *Lex Dei quam praecipit Dominus ad Moysen*, bears admittedly another and very peculiar character. In order to demonstrate the basic agreement of Roman law with the ordinances of the Bible, the excerpts from Gaius, Papinian, Paulus, Ulpian, Modestinus, and the imperial constitutions (of which the most recent were inserted afterwards into the body of the work) are confronted with provisions from the Mosaic law. The later reviser of the work thus wished either to contribute to the propaganda of the Christian (hardly of the Jewish) faith, or perhaps, on the other hand, to justify the law of the pagan jurists and emperors by the standards of the Christian state religion.

3. *The dominance of vulgar law*. Later in the fourth century the level of jurisprudence seems to have declined rapidly. Acquaintance with the great late classical works was obviously to a great extent lost. Of the classical writings all that was still known was probably generally only the *Institutes* of Gaius, but even these were soon felt to be too long and too difficult and were therefore shortened and paraphrased. In addition attention was paid to the imperial constitutions and the elementary works of the early post-classical age, above all to the *Sententiae* of Paulus, which were shortened and adapted, by additions, to the conditions of the age. Although through the mediation of this elementary literature a glimmer of classical legal art may still have penetrated to the schools of the late fourth and early fifth centuries, the practice of law lost almost all contact with the subtly thought-out ideas and principles of the great past. In place of the classical law of skill there now appeared a 'vulgar law', the entirely different character of which has been made more accessible to us only through the researches of Ernst Levy. The vulgar law had not only completely lost the classical procedural

foundations; even the conceptual distinctions of the Roman system of contracts had largely vanished; the distinctions between possession, ownership, and real rights over another's property were confounded, and sale had lost its character as a transaction giving rise to obligations and had again become, as in ancient Roman times, a mere basis for the acquisition of ownership. In the lower stratum of Roman legal life such notions, departing as they did from the law of the classical jurists, may have long been widespread; for the circle of men who had mastered the complicated rules of classical legal art was at all times relatively small, and wherever their influence did not reach—above all in the provinces but no doubt to some extent even in Italy and in Rome—shallower and less complicated legal concepts may have been common even in the classical period. But now this vulgarized legal thinking overshadowed all else in legal life. Already under Constantine, who allowed the classicizing attitude of the rescript-practice of Diocletian to be abruptly abandoned, the body of ideas belonging to vulgar law had begun to penetrate imperial legislation (which for this reason is one of the most important sources for research into vulgar law). In the juristic writings of post-classical times, which were after all basically a school-literature and leaned more or less heavily on classical tradition, we do not find the thought-forms of vulgar law until very much later. They appear in the west-Roman works of the fifth century, above all in the commentaries on the *Sententiae* of Paulus and of the post-classical collections of constitutions, which along with these sources themselves were included in the Roman code of the Visigoth king Alaric II. This so-called Visigothic *interpretatio* contains few traces of the spirit of classical law.

It is not only the Visigothic Roman code that bears the mark of vulgar law. The other codifications in the Germanic kingdoms of the migratory period—even those which were intended only for the Germanic population of these states—are clearly rooted in the same set of notions, which, only recently, new knowledge of the development of vulgar law has recognized as ultimately of Roman origin. The question of Roman influence on the Germanic law of the early Middle Ages must now be posed anew as a result of this research on late Roman vulgar law.

The legislation of the eastern half of the Empire was also influenced in the late fourth and fifth centuries by the forms of thought of vulgar law. It is probably safe to assume something

similar for legal practice, in which, admittedly, local law, principally Greek customary law, continued in existence over a large
area. This native law, as has been seen, had in these places never
been fully supplanted by Roman law. Since vulgar law and Hellenistic law were in many ways structurally related it is often difficult
to draw a clear distinction between these two components of eastern
legal life.

4. *The school-jurisprudence of the eastern Empire.* It is thus all the
more surprising that in the science of the schools of the eastern half
of the Empire a return to classical law was achieved. The chief agent
in this development was the law-school in Berytos in Phoenicia
(Beirut). This city, in which Augustus had settled the veterans of
two legions, had since then been a Roman citizen-colony and lived
as such according to Roman law in the midst of its Hellenistic-
Oriental surroundings. By the middle of the third century according
to report, Roman law could be studied there; and a constitution of
Diocletian preserved in Justinian's Codex (*C.* 10. 50. 1) granted the
request of a number of young people, who were staying there for
the purpose of learning law, to be exempted from the compulsory
services (*munera*) in their home community. We have, however, no
precise knowledge of studies at Beirut until the fifth century,
when we even learn the names of a number of professors. At
this period the law school at Beirut had become a formal faculty
of jurists with a fixed curriculum arranged in annual courses,
the subject of which was the study of the imperial constitutions
and of classical legal literature. A second law-school in the
same style was officially founded in 425 in the eastern capital,
Constantinople.[1]

The working method of these east Roman Law schools is very
reminiscent of the Italian universities of the high Middle Ages
which, 700 years later, introduced a second revival of Roman law,
this time one much more widespread in its effects. The teaching
was based directly on the classical texts and on the collections
of constitutions, the contents of which were taken and explained
step by step. The literary works of the east-Roman law-teachers,
of which we possess admittedly only very scanty remains from

---

[1] In other places also in the eastern Empire legal instruction was given but it was evidently instruction of a primitive kind: Justinian expressly prohibited (Const. *Omnem* 7)
the 'law-schools' of Alexandria and Caesarea, where he had discovered that 'bungling
teachers taught their pupils an emasculated science'.

pre-Justinianic times, corresponded to this exegetical method.[1] The more abundantly preserved works of the Justinianic and post-Justinianic jurists allow certain inferences to be made about the literary forms of their forerunners: commentaries on the classical works and concise statements of contents (ἴνδικες, 'summaries') were composed, perhaps also collections of sources on individual problems and other monographical treatises. The gathering of parallel passages and the discovery and explanation of contradictions in the classical texts presumably played as important a role as in medieval jurisprudence.

Compared with classical jurisprudence the learning of the East Romans admittedly seems unreal and dead: they were neither practitioners nor original thinkers, and they remained entangled in rigid belief in the authority of an intellectual world belonging to the great past. Even the lesser spirits of the classical age stood head and shoulders above them, not perhaps in acquired knowledge but certainly in independence, in judgement, and in practical outlook. But in spite of all this the jurists of Beirut and Constantinople have one great merit: it was they who first found the way from the shallows of the preceding centuries back to the study and understanding of the classical authors; without their activity it may be presumed that just as little of the spirit of classical jurisprudence would have found its way into the Justinianic codifications as into the codes of the western Empire.

The observer who takes classical jurisprudence as his starting-point and its intellectual vigour as his standard will find it hard to assess correctly the service rendered by post-classical jurisprudence.

---

[1] It is probably from the sphere of the Beirut law-school that the *Scholia sinaitica* come (so called because preserved in a manuscript belonging to the monastery on Mt. Sinai). This is a fragment of a Greek commentary on Ulpian's *Libri ad Sabinum*, the author of which displays a relatively wide acquaintance with late classical literature and with the imperial constitutions. A further very short and mutilated piece of what may be the same commentary on this work of Ulpian has been found on a papyrus sheet (Pap. Ryl. iii. 475). The opinions of the law-teachers of the fifth century, finally, are also occasionally cited in the earliest commentaries on Justinian's codification. The Greek original of the so-called Syrio-Roman code, apparently composed in the eastern Empire towards the end of the fifth century, was on a lower level; we possess only revisions of it in Syriac, Armenian, and Arabic. The content is not (as was long believed) a mixture of Roman and Greek-Oriental legal norms, but is Roman law throughout, which because of multiple translation into other languages is in part no longer easily recognizable as such. Probably the original was a commentary on a collection of imperial constitutions of similar character to the Visigothic *interpretatio*. It could hardly have been composed in Beirut, and is more likely to have been composed in one of the other eastern law-schools of lesser standing.

As has been seen, the jurisprudence of the late Empire did not possess genuinely creative strength at any stage of its development. Nevertheless its work, spread over centuries, was of great importance for legal history, and each of its periods made a contribution of its own to the world mission of Roman law. The inability of the late third and early fourth centuries to understand properly the basis and character of classical thought led to certain simplifications; these actually made the work of the classical authors more comprehensible and manageable for later ages, because they concealed to some extent the complications of the classical system and its connection with certain historical circumstances. The complete collapse of classical legal art which is seen in vulgar law caused the decomposition of the classical material to the point where it was suitable for use as a cultural fertilizer for the development of Germanic law in the early Middle Ages. Finally, the classicism of the east-Roman jurists of the fifth century had the effect of saving the work of the classical authors from oblivion and of preserving its effectiveness through the Justinianic codification up to the present day.

The question often posed from different points of view, to what extent the post-classical jurists imported non-Roman notions into the classical heritage, is still disputed. Even if one regards it as not impossible for influences in particular from the Greek-Oriental sphere to have operated, one must be careful not to over-estimate the possible effect of these influences. For it is precisely the eastern law-schools, by reason of their geographical position most often thought to have been open to such influences, which with their classical bias seem to a great extent to have resisted them. And early post-classical jurisprudence, which was perhaps more heavily conditioned by the ideas and practice of its own time, still had its centre of gravity in the western Empire and was thus further removed geographically from those presumed sources of foreign influence.

11. *The legislation of the late Empire*

These influences (together with their limits) can be seen more clearly in the imperial codifications of the late Empire, which, so far at any rate as bulk is concerned, represent the most important factor in post-classical legal development. In the field of legislation, as everywhere else, the post-classical Empire had thrown away the republican camouflage which had characterized the Principate. The emperors now issued statutes in the formal sense; and this imperial legislation is the only kind known to the late Empire. It is only in certain distinctions of nomenclature and of the mode of publication that the relationship with the basically different forms of law-making in the Principate can be recognized. What was once the proposal of the princeps for the passing of a senatorial resolution (the imperial *oratio*) now became an imperial statute which was merely promulgated in the Senate. The designation *leges edictales* for such statutes as had been published either directly by the emperor or through an official charged by him with that task is reminiscent of the edicts of the Principate, which in their turn, as has been seen, had their starting-point in the *ius edicendi* of the republican magistrates; but there remained in these late imperial laws no trace of the peculiar nature of these edicts. The only distinction which had material significance in the late Empire was that between those utterances of the emperor which laid down generally binding norms (*leges generales*) and the decisions of actual individual cases (*rescripta*) which no longer had a general binding force, as they had had in the period up to Diocletian (cf. Arcadius *C.Th.* 1. 2. 11; A.D. 398). Even this distinction became blurred by the fact that the emperors sometimes combined declarations of principle with the decision of individual cases; and to this extent rescripts did again have statutory force, at least in the law of the fifth and sixth centuries.

In the great collections of constitutions of the late Empire (which will shortly be discussed) a huge mass of post-classical imperial constitutions is preserved—though certainly only a fraction of the total number actually issued. Among the surviving constitutions of Diocletian the most conspicuous are the rescripts, conservative in nature, concerned with private law, which rest on the principles of classical law. From Constantine onwards, however, the dominant element is the *leges generales*, some of which contain bold innovations; but their centre of gravity lies entirely in the field of administration, of economic and social policy, and of criminal law. Still, they also effected numerous changes in certain areas of private law, particularly family law: changes which are to be explained partly by reference to Greek-Oriental influences, partly to specifically Christian ones. The extent of these influences is admittedly not yet fully clear in every case. But this much is certain, that apart perhaps from family law they did not cause any very deep interference with the substance of the inherited Roman law.

As has already been said, the primitive legal notions of vulgar law predominate in the constitutions from Constantine onwards. Together with a pompous and cliché-ridden garrulity they make up a style which the modern reader—and particularly the lawyer trained, according to the classical Roman model, in brevity and precision—finds repellent. From the point of view of its content, also, post-classical imperial legislation, with its uninhibited concentration on revenue, its lack of consistency in its legal and political philosophy, and its indiscriminate and immoderate threats of punishment seems to us a product of a legal culture in decay.

111. *Laws of citation and collections of constitutions*

The 'jurists' law' (*ius*) contained in classical legal literature, with its infinitely rich and diversified casuistics, and the imperial legislation (*leges*) constantly increasing in bulk and generally no less casuistical in character, formed—in theory—the books of law of the post-classical period. But in fact both source-fields were certainly accessible to most judges and advocates only to a very imperfect extent. Even the commentaries of the late classical jurists which provided a fairly complete conspectus of *ius* were probably to be had only in a few places; and imperial legislation at first lacked any system of official compilation or distribution. If one had entry to the imperial archives, one might examine or copy them there; but a large number of people probably only had access to those constitutions which had been treated or collected in the private writings of the jurists. Quite apart from such technical difficulties attaching to the use of this material, it was also no longer possible for any individual to master the entire range of these sources. Even the law-schools began in early post-classical times, as has been seen, to fail when confronted with this task, and had increasing recourse to elementary books and collections of excerpts. The level of practice no doubt fell back even more rapidly to the primitive stage of vulgar law.

Nevertheless, the content of the classical jurists' writings was valid law and could be applied in a case at any time. According to a practice at all times widespread in the ancient world, it was the business of the advocates to demonstrate to the judge those legal norms which were favourable to the parties they represented; and thus a resourceful advocate could adduce at any time citations from legal literature or from imperial constitutions and could demand that the judge should respect the rules they contained. The judge was probably seldom in a position to test the genuineness of the texts cited; and if both parties relied on mutually contradictory sources, then he had the embarrassing duty of deciding which of the two opinions to follow.

It is only against the background of such conditions that a group of fourth- and fifth-century laws become comprehensible, laws which are usually called collectively 'laws of citation'.[1] They contain provisions about which jurists' writings might be adduced before a court, and how their relative testimony should be evaluated. The two older laws of this type decide merely individual questions which had apparently become disputed in practice: the first of them, of the year A.D. 321 (*C.Th.* 1. 4. 1) deprived of validity the critical notes on the *responsa* and *quaestiones* of Papinian, which had been handed down under the names of Paulus and Ulpian; only Papinian's own opinion was thus permitted to be cited in court. The second, also issued by Constantine (in the following year: *C.Th.* 1. 4. 2), ratified the authority of all the writings of Paulus, in particular the *sententiae* which were in circulation under his name (but which, as has been seen, were written not by him but by a post-classical author). About a century later there appeared the most comprehensive of the laws of citation, a constitution of Theodosius II and Valentinian III (A.D. 426: *C.Th.* 1. 4. 3), which defined the group of jurists who might be cited in court as authority on the *ius* and simultaneously introduced a sort of 'voting' system for them. Thus, all the writings of the leading late classical jurists Papinian, Paulus, Ulpian, and Modestinus as well as those of Gaius (who as the author of the much-used *Institutiones* was, in the eyes of the later Empire, one of the great jurists) were to have validity in court; in addition, the writings of the older jurists cited by these, but only if their utterances could be reliably proved by the comparison of several manuscripts. If it turned out that the authorities thus admitted in a legal question were divided, then the majority of them was to be followed: if the voices were equal in number on each side, then Papinian's view was to be decisive. At the end of the constitution the validity of the *sententiae* of Paulus is again

---

[1] Laws of similar character turn up also in the Middle Ages and in modern times: cf. the fine study by Teipel, *Z. Sav.-Stiftung*, 72. 254 ff.

confirmed, and in a manner which seems to mean that this post-classical elementary work would be decisive wherever cited as against all other authorities. And indeed it can hardly be imagined that in the early fifth century the great late classical works still played a very important part in the practice of the courts. The *Sententiae* of Paulus on the other hand, with their manageable and easily understandable brevity, seem to have been generally used in the fifth century; this view is supported by the fact that it was the *interpretatio* written on this work which was later received into the Roman law of the Visigoths.

A few years after this strange law Theodosius II formed the ambitious plan of creating a code out of the immense mass of both *ius* and *leges* which would 'leave no room for errors or obscurity and, published under the imperial name, would show every man what he must do and what he must avoid'. But the commission appointed by the emperor for this purpose evidently produced nothing. A second commission called into being six years later completed in two years a work which, originally intended as a mere preliminary to the planned code, was a collection of the imperial constitutions since Constantine.

This work, the *Codex Theodosianus*, represents the continuation of two private constitution-collections which were made under Diocletian. The older of these, the *Codex Gregorianus*, contained constitutions from Hadrian up to Diocletian; the later and less extensive one, the *Codex Hermogenianus*, merely constitutions of Diocletian. The authors of both collections, Gregorius and Hermogenianus, were evidently able to use the imperial archives—presumably they were officials of the central government—and thus brought together an abundant collection of constitutions which they produced in their original text. Only small fragments survive directly from both of these works, but the entire handing-down of imperial constitutions prior to Constantine in the codes of Justinian and of the Germanic kings of the West goes back to them.

Much more complete, although not without lacunae, is the state in which the *Codex Theodosianus* survives, handed down in part directly, in part through the mediation of the Visigothic Roman code. Although it is merely a continuation of the older private collections just mentioned, it nevertheless represents, as a product of state-directed codification, a new type among the Roman sources of law; it is the beginning of the series of late Roman codifications.

First published on 15 February 428 in the eastern Empire, the *Codex Theodosianus* was subsequently accepted by the west Roman Emperor Valentinian III for the area over which he ruled, and it came into force for the whole Empire on 1 January 439. This extensive work falls into sixteen books, and each book in turn has a number of titles (*tituli*) of which each is devoted to a definite subject and contains the relevant constitutions in chronological order.[1] The arrangement of the titles is connected as far as possible with the structure of the great casuistical works of the classical period (*digesta* and the like), but the immediate models were evidently the *codices Gregorianus* and *Hermogenianus*; in the case of the former, at any rate, a corresponding arrangement of material can be proved from the surviving remains.

The imperial constitutions issued after the *Codex Theodosianus* were repeatedly made the subject of collections both in the eastern and in the western Empire. While the eastern collections were supplanted by the Justinianic codification into which they were worked, and thus have disappeared, those of the western Empire have survived (*Novellae Posttheodosianae*). They contain constitutions of the years A.D. 438–58.

IV. *Codification of Roman law in the Germanic kingdoms on western Roman soil*

Not much more than a generation after the publication of the *Codex Theodosianus* the western Roman Empire came to an end. At the end of the fifth century the whole west of the Empire was in the hands of Germanic warrior kings, who even if they recognized the sovereignty of the (eastern) Roman emperor *de iure*, still exerted a *de facto* rule, based on their absolute power, over the masses of their own peoples as well as over the indigenous Roman or Romanized population. The two population-elements remained in general separate in the law they used: the Germans lived in principle according to their own Germanic tribal law, the Romans according to Roman law.[2] Thus the principle of the *personal* application of

---

[1] Citations are made with the abbreviation *C.Th.* and the numbers of book, title, and constitution. *C.Th.* 7. 8. 15 is thus the fifteenth constitution in the eighth title of the seventh book. Constitutions of some length are also subdivided in modern editions into paragraphs, the numbers of which are then given at the end of the citation, e.g. *C.Th.* 12. 6. 32. 2.

[2] This has recently been disputed by Spanish scholars (Garcia Gallo, d'Ors) so far as concerns the Visigothic empire. But see on this point Levy, *Zeitschrift der Savigny-Stiftung*, 79. 479 ff.

laws, which had once been the starting-point of Roman legal development and which was perfectly familiar also to the Germans, came to have a new practical importance on Roman soil. This legal situation was unsatisfactory for the Roman element of the population. The difficulties associated with the application of its statutory and jurists' law remained, and indeed increased through the further decline in intellectual power in the Germanic states, which were sealed off from the main Empire and were sinking back into primitive economic conditions. Thus the need for a concise and lucid synopsis of Roman law must have been particularly keenly felt in this late period. This explains what at first seems a surprising fact, that even after the end of Roman rule official restatements of Roman law were drawn up in the west. The surviving works of this kind admittedly all come from a relatively limited area, namely from the Visigothic kingdom, the centre of which then lay in south-west Gaul (south of the Loire), and from the Burgundian kingdom on the Rhône.

It was in the Visigothic kingdom and not, as was long believed, in the Italy of the eastern Goths that probably the oldest of these restatements of law, the so-called *Edictum Theoderici*, was drawn up. Its name probably refers not to the eastern Gothic king Theoderic the Great, but to the western Gothic ruler Theoderic II, during whose reign (453–66) the western Roman Empire still existed and the imperial power in Gaul was represented by the *praefectus praetorio Galliarum*. The *edictum Theoderici* seems in fact to have been issued not by the west Gothic king himself, but by a holder of this prefectship, Magnus of Narbo, c. 458–9. This is altogether credible, for up to the dissolution of the western Empire the Visigoths, however great their practical position of strength may have been, were in the eye of the law mere foreign mercenaries (*foederati*) who had been allowed to settle on Roman soil; their king had in principle no sovereign rights. These conditions probably also explain how it is that the *edictum Theoderici*, unlike the laws which will be discussed later, claimed validity not only for the Roman population but for the Goths as well. Its content is Roman law; the material for its 155 short chapters is mainly formed from the imperial constitutions of the three *codices Gregorianus*, *Hermogenianus*, and *Theodosianus* and from the *sententiae* of Paulus. Instead of the original wording of these sources, however, a vulgarized paraphrase is frequently used, presumably in part that *interpretatio* which we meet later in the *lex Romana Visigotorum* (see below) and which we have already got to know as a characteristic product of west Roman jurisprudence of the fifth century.

A further extensive statement of law from the Visigothic kingdom, which is preserved only in a fragmentary condition, was drawn up about the year 475 under the successor of Theoderic II, King Eurich, and is thus called the *Codex Euricianus*. It was intended for the Goths but not for the Roman population as well.[1] It is without doubt the work of Roman jurists, and its contents are largely not Germanic legal material, but Roman vulgar law, which is handled with remarkable independence. Not only the later codes of the Visigothic kings rest on the *Codex Euricianus*; it can be proved to have influenced also the laws of the Frankish, Burgundian, Alemannic, and Bajuvaric tribes, and thus to have played an important part as a medium for the transmission of Roman vulgar law to the Germanic world of the early Middle Ages.

In the year A.D. 506, just before the collapse of Visigothic rule in southern France, King Alaric II had a law code for his Roman subjects composed and published: the *lex Romana Visigotorum* (also called the *breviarium Alarici*). This undertaking was carried out under pressure of the fear of war with the Franks. It was an attempt to consolidate at the eleventh hour the understanding with the Roman population and with the Catholic church which represented it, and in this way to provide the Goths, who as Arian heretics were in a difficult situation *vis-à-vis* the Catholic king of the Franks, with a more favourable position for meeting the unavoidable show-down.[2] Quickly and carelessly a sequence was drawn up of whatever sources of Roman law were at that time familiar to the teachers and practitioners of southern Gaul: the *Codex Theodosianus*, greatly abridged, together with post-Theodosian *novellae*; a version of the *Institutes* of Gaius reduced to two books and departing from the original text in many places; an extract from the *sententiae* of Paulus; some constitutions from the *Codices Gregorianus* and *Hermogenianus*; and, at the end, a single short *responsum* of Papinian. Except for the version of Gaius, the text of the code is accompanied by an *interpretatio* which provides at times

---

[1] The Spanish authors mentioned in the previous note take a different view.

[2] See as to this political background of the *lex Romana Visigotorum* E. F. Bruck, *Über römisches Recht im Rahmen der Kulturgeschichte* (1954), 146 ff.

a summary of contents, at times an exhaustive paraphrase of the text, and which also contains references. These references, however, are partly to sources which are not included in the code, and from this it may be inferred that the *interpretatio* was not composed by the Visigothic lawgivers themselves but was taken over from an older private work. As has been seen, it had probably already been used in the preparation of the *Edictum Theoderici*; thus it must originally have been composed not later than soon after the middle of the fifth century.

The *lex Romana Visigotorum*, although thin and crude as a work of legislation, none the less played an important part in the legal history of south-western Europe in the Middle Ages. In Visigothic Spain it became, along with the *Codex Euricianus*, one of the foundations of the code promulgated by king Recesvind about the mid seventh century for Romans and Goths alike. In southern France it remained in force for about 500 years after the end of Visigothic rule; indeed it extended also to Burgundian territory and to Provence, which at the time of its original composition had belonged to Ostrogothic Italy. Not until the knowledge and cultivation of the Justinianic codifications penetrated in the thirteenth century from Italy into southern France was the *lex Romana Visigotorum* supplanted by these greatest and most important of the late Roman codifications.

In the Burgundian kingdom, too, a code for the Roman population was promulgated shortly before the Frankish conquest (A.D. 532), under conditions similar to those in force when the Visigothic Roman code was drawn up. This *lex Romana Burgundionum*, which probably belongs to the reign of King Gundobad who died in 516, is based on the same materials as the *lex Romana Visigotorum*: it, too, rests on the *Codices Gregorianus*, *Hermogenianus*, and *Theodosianus*, on the *sententiae* of Paulus and the *Institutes* of Gaius. But these sources are, in this code, not simply placed side by side, but are amalgamated into a unified text which differs in wording from its originals and which rests to a large extent on the same or similar *interpretationes* as accompany the text of the Visigothic Roman law. The Burgundian code is for this reason more coloured by vulgar law and is much less informative on older Roman law than the *lex Romana Visigotorum*; nor did it gain any great importance for the legal history of the Middle Ages.

11

THE JUSTINIANIC CODIFICATIONS

1. *Political and legal background*

IN the eastern Empire, as has been seen, the law school of Beirut, joined at the beginning of the fifth century by that of Constantinople, had reopened the way to the great works of classical legal literature, a way which had been blocked up to then by post-classical developments. The commentaries of Ulpian and Paulus, together with the *responsa* and *quaestiones* of the late second and early third centuries, and above all the writings of Papinian, were again read and understood. In the same way legal practice was probably not limited to what in the west was becoming an increasingly exclusive use of elementary works, but began again to make more active use of late classical writings. Unlike those elementary works which contained a fairly manageable number of apodeictic principles and decisions which could be used when needed even by lawyers of low intellectual standing, the later classical writings contained an infinite abundance of cases and problems and, above all, innumerable disputes and contradictions. It is thus easily credible that the reanimation of classical law in the eastern Empire, though it might raise the level of judicial activity, was none the less bound to exacerbate the difficulties of the practitioners already referred to, and to make especially urgent a legislative limitation and simplification of the whole body of inherited legal material. Of course such a work of legislation in the eastern Empire could be carried out only on the broad foundation of the sources which had been made available through the activity of the law-schools. These considerations suffice to explain to some extent both the emergence of the Justinianic codification and the monumental dimensions which it displayed by comparison with corresponding works in the western Empire.

The personality of Justinian, the special character and the political and cultural tendencies of his reign also played a part. Justinian, born in 482 and succeeding to the throne in 527 after a period of inner weakness in the eastern Empire, was, measured by the standards of the age, a great ruler; a man of vigour and high purpose. He felt himself called to the task of renewing the old glory of the *Imperium Romanum*. It is as various aspects of his dedication to this task that we must understand his foreign policy, which led to the reconquest of North Africa, Italy, and even a small part of Spain, his architectural activity all over the Empire and particularly in Constantinople, his ecclesiastical policy, aimed at the ending of dogmatic divisions and at the subordination of the church to the Emperor, and finally, too, his work of codifying the law. This codification was planned in the same large and generous spirit as his cathedral of Sancta Sophia, and its execution began soon after his accession to the monarchy.

11. *Composition of the codifications*

We are informed about the course of the work of codification by a series of Justinian's constitutions by which the undertaking was ordained, the collaborators were summoned, the direction which their activity was to take was laid down and, finally, the completed parts of the codifications were published. These constitutions are prefixed to the individual parts of the whole work, and, like papal bulls, are usually cited by their initial words (e.g. the *constitutio Imperatoriam*; *constitutio Tanta* or *Δέδωκεν*, the former denoting the Latin, the latter the Greek version of this constitution published in two languages). What we learn from them are admittedly rather the external dates of the codification; they contain only very general and perhaps not always reliable information about the procedure inside the codifying commission and about the methods by which a selection from the abundance of classical legal literature and imperial constitutions was made and by which the material thus obtained was handled. The boastful rhetoric of the postclassical constitutions in general and of the Justinianic constitutions in particular ought in any case to counsel a careful utilization of many of these statements. Modern research tries in another way, namely by analytical treatment of the codification itself, to achieve accurate insights into the working methods of the codification commissions.

Among the men whom Justinian used for the execution of his codifying work—we call them compilers because they 'plundered' (*compilare*) the classical texts and the imperial constitutions for the

codification—the principal was Tribonianus.[1] Unfortunately we
know very little about the personality of this man, for the words of
praise heaped on him by Justinian at every opportunity tell us
nothing. At the beginning, i.e. in the years 528 and 529, as *magister
officiorum* (superintendent of the imperial secretariats) he was only
a collaborator, and by no means the head of the commission which
was making a new collection of constitutions, but he distinguished
himself so greatly in this work that he was given the office of minister
for justice (*quaestor sacri palatii*) and thereafter also the chairmanship of the codification work. However, he must evidently be
credited not only with the chairmanship but also with the planning
of the later parts of the codification. The emperor's decision,
apparently not made until the completion of the collection of constitutions (the first *Codex Justinianus*), to have a selection also made
from classical legal literature—in other words the great plan of the
Digest—was probably inspired by him. Even the choice of collaborators in this immense task was placed by Justinian in Tribonian's hands. Obviously it was under his influence that a significant
change took place in the composition of the legislative commissions
which were working out the individual parts of the Justinianic
codifications. While at the beginning it was almost exclusively the
heads of the imperial central government who were brought in, in
the later parts of the work teachers of law (*antecessores*) from the
two schools of Beirut and Constantinople participated decisively;
these were joined also by advocates from the courts of the capital
city. Presumably it is this change of compilers which explains how
the codification took on an even more monumental character than
had originally been planned, and how the centre of gravity of the
whole—contrary to the constitutional conditions of the time—
moved from the collection of imperial constitutions to that of the
jurists' law. We possess samples of the juristic competence of the
two law-teachers most closely engaged, Theophilus from Constantinople and Dorotheus from Beirut, in the form of fragments
from commentaries which they later wrote on the Justinianic codification; and Justinian tells us in connection with a third, the professor Anatolius from Beirut, that his father and grandfather had

---

[1] We know him only under this single name; the Roman system of triple names had
been more and more supplanted by the system of single names from the third century
onwards. Only the Emperor Justinian himself still carries in the preface to his codifications
a family name of the old Roman style: Flavius.

been famous lawyers (Const. *Tanta* 9). Eudoxius, the grandfather of Anatolius, is indeed known to us as one of the law-teachers who flourished in Beirut about A.D. 500. We know nothing but the names of the other compilers.

We must now follow the course taken by the codification. It began in the year 528. On 13 February in this year Justinian summoned by the Constitutio *Haec* a ten-man commission consisting of high officials of the central government, among them Tribonian, and Theophilus the law professor from Constantinople, who at that time was also a member of the imperial privy council (*comes sacri consistorii*), and charged them with the task of drawing up a new collection of imperial laws from the *Codices Gregorianus*, *Hermogenianus*, and *Theodosianus* as well as from the constitutions subsequently issued. Obsolete laws were to be kept out, contradictions were to be banished, and the texts were to be limited to what was of practical importance. The work was completed within the space of a year; it was published on 7 April 529 by the Constitutio *Summa* and came into statutory force on 16 April. On this day the older *codices* and all other imperial constitutions which had not been included in this new *Codex Justinianus* went out of force, except for those which were the subject of special privileges. Since the *Codex Justinianus* of 529 underwent a new edition in the course of the further work of codification, it remained in statutory force for only a few years, and has not survived; we possess only a fragment of an index of contents from it on an Egyptian papyrus.

The Constitutio *Deo auctore* of 15 December 530 then introduced the mighty work of collecting the jurists' law. Tribonian was made chairman and given full powers in the choice of his collaborators; he co-opted the *magister officiorum*, who at that time also held the post of *comes sacrarum largitionum* (chancellor of the exchequer), two professors each from Beirut and Constantinople, and eleven advocates from the court of the *praefectus praetorio Orientis*. Planned originally to take ten years, this gigantic undertaking was pushed ahead by Tribonian's eagerness and by the constant interest of the emperor so quickly that the finished result was published a bare three years later, on 16 December 533, by the Constitutio Δέδωκεν (in the Latin version, the Constitutio *Tanta*). The work was divided into fifty books, which in their turn were divided into titles, and it received, after the model of the great casuistical works of the high classical revival, the name *Digesta*—also the Greek name *Pandectae* (πᾶν δέχεσθαι, to take in everything): this title is also found in classical legal literature.[1] On 30 December 533 the Digest came into force. The original writings of the classical jurists henceforth disappeared from the law-schools and from the court practice of the eastern Empire.

Even before the publication of the Digest an official textbook for beginners in the study of law had been completed and published, the Constitutio *Imperatorium* of 21 November 533. It was formed out of the *Institutes* of Gaius and some other elementary writings of the classical and post-classical period, and, like these, bore the title *Institutiones*. Its authors were the two law-teachers Theophilus and Dorotheus, and Tribonian also presided over the work. Although intended primarily for legal instruction, this book too was given statutory force, at the same time as the Digest. Like the *Institutes* of Gaius the new official textbook was arranged in four books, which, however, were subdivided into titles, unlike Gaius' work.[2]

In the composition of the Digest many individual questions had been met with which had been disputed among the classical jurists, and also legal provisions and points of view which were felt to be obsolete or unjust. Many of these offending elements were got out of the way by the compilers by simple exclusions, additions, or other changes. Other questions it was thought necessary to decide by special laws; and thus, in the course of the work on the Digest, numerous reforming constitutions of Justinian were issued. Other decisions of this kind had been promulgated in the interval between the publication of the Codex of 529 and the commencement

---

[1] Citations are made today with the abbreviation *D*. (or *Dig*.) and the numbers of book, title, fragment, and paragraph. Fragments (also called *leges*) are the individual excerpts from legal literature. At their beginning there stands always the name of the author in question, and the work and book from which the excerpt has been taken (this is the so-called *inscriptio*). The division into paragraphs, which does not take place if the fragment is very short, was first used in the Middle Ages; it merely serves to make the longer fragments easier to survey. The first paragraph is always called the *principium* ('beginning'; abbreviated to *pr*.); § 1 is thus really the following or second paragraph. *D*. 19 1. 45. 2 thus means: the 'second' (really the third) paragraph in the 45th fragment of the first title in book 19 of Justinian's Digest. According to the *inscriptio* of the fragment, this passage comes from the 5th book of the *quaestiones* of Paulus. Books 30, 31, and 32 are not divided into titles. It is better to think of them as making up collectively the title on legacies (*de legatis et fideicommissis*).

[2] Abbreviation: *I*. (or *Inst*.). The titles are arranged in paragraphs just as are the Digest fragments.—*I*. 1. 6 pr. thus means: the beginning (first paragraph) of the sixth title of book 1 of the Institutes of Justinian.

of work on the Digest, and had been collected together, presumably in the summer of 530, into the so-called *Quinquaginta decisiones*, which has not survived. The next task was to work these reforming laws into the *Codex* of 529 and in general to adapt the *Codex*, which was the oldest element in the whole codification, to the position which the law had meanwhile reached. Tribonian, together with the Beirut professor Dorotheus and three advocates, completed this task so quickly that the refashioned *Codex Justinianus* (*codex repetitae praelectionis*) was published on 16 November 534 and came into force on 29 December of that year. It is divided into twelve books, which in turn are divided into titles. The titles, as in the other parts of the codification, deal always with specific legal topics and contain the relevant constitutions in chronological order.[1] The oldest constitution in the Codex comes from Hadrian (A.D. 117–38); the most recent had been issued in the year 534, and thus directly before the publication of the *codex repetitae praelectionis*.

Codex, Digest, and Institutes formed, according to the will of the legislating sovereign, a unified codification, which, it must be said, lacked a name, for the description *Corpus Iuris Civilis* (*corpus iuris Justiniani*) belong to modern times.[2] There were supposed to be neither contradictions nor confusions in it. Every legislator tends to believe this of his work, but hardly any has entertained such illusions about the perfection of his work as did Justinian and his compilers. Considering the casuistic nature and the monstrous dimensions of the materials they had to handle, and the speed with which the gigantic undertaking was completed, numerous weaknesses were unavoidable. Even where Justinian carried out planned reforms, traces of the older state of the law often remained in more or less hidden corners. Wherever the Justinianic codification was in force as law, legal science felt obliged to explain away the innumerable contradictions, a technique known as 'Pandektenharmonistik'. But present-day research in legal history uses these contradictions as welcome starting-points for the recovery of pre-Justinianic legal development and particularly the law of the classical period.

---

[1] Abbreviation: *C.* (or *Cod.*); to distinguish it more clearly from the older codes, especially the *C.Th.*, it is also called *C.J.* (*Codex Justiniani*). The individual constitutions begin with an *inscriptio* with the name of the emperor and the names of the persons to whom the constitution is addressed, and end mostly with a dating according to consuls. Citation as in the Digest.

[2] It is first met with as the title of a complete edition of the Justinianic codification in 1583 (edition of Dionysius Godofredus).

III. *The Digest*

The richest and most massive part of the Justinianic codification, the Digest, requires closer consideration. It is, as has already been indicated, the principal source of our knowledge of the classical period of Roman law. If we merely possessed what remains of classical jurisprudence outside the Digest, we would have only a very elementary idea of classical law, and practically no idea at all of the scientific achievement of the great classical jurists. The Justinianic codification even included some fragments of republican jurists from Q. Mucius Scaevola onward. Thus the Digest offers us, although in varying degrees of clarity, a cross-section of the entire development of Roman jurisprudence from the last century before Christ up to the end of the classical period. So much of the enormous strength of this jurisprudence remains in it as a living thing that renewed study of the Digest over the course of many centuries has repeatedly led to a fresh blooming of juristic thought. Only a few works of the world's literature have shown such enduring strength; and if one reflects on this, then the creation of the Digest must, in spite of all its defects, seem a great and significant event in the history of the world.

1. *The compiling of the Digest: the* Massentheorie *of Bluhme and the hypothesis of 'pre-Digests'.* It is a problem how such a work could come into being in a space of only three years. A list preserved in the Florentine MS. of the Digest shows the juristic writings used by the compilers, mentioning over 200 works (of which admittedly not all are represented in the Digest), and Justinian himself reports (Const. *Tanta* 1) that it was necessary to work through nearly 2,000 books (*libri*: in the sense of the ancient method of dividing into books) containing more than 3 million lines. Even a conservative estimate based on these hints suggests a volume of material at least fifteen or twenty times greater than the volume of the Digest itself. What was the compilers' method in boiling down this gigantic mass of material? Is it at all conceivable that they themselves actually read and selected excerpts from all the classical works?

An answer was given to the first of these questions as early as the year 1818 by Friedrich Bluhme,[1] which since then has successfully stood up to every critical test and may therefore be regarded as a

---

[1] *Zeitschrift für geschichtliche Rechtswissenschaft*, iv. 257 ff.

proven theory. He observed that, within the individual Digest titles, excerpts from distinct groups of classical writings tended to stand side by side. The kernel of the first group was formed by the late classical commentaries on the *ius civile*, the *libri ad Sabinum* of Ulpian and Paulus: this group was therefore called the 'Sabinus-group (*Sabinusmasse*). A second group of excerpts, the so-called 'Edict-group' (*Ediktsmasse*), centred on the commentaries on the edict by the mid and late classical authors. A third group was built on the collections of *responsa* and *quaestiones* made by Papinian, Paulus, and Ulpian; here the Papinian fragments usually come first, so that this group of excerpts is called the 'Papinian-group' (*Papiniansmasse*). In several Digest titles there appears, finally, a small fourth group of fragments as well, drawn from works of various kinds, the so-called 'Appendix-group' (*Appendixmasse*). These conclusions (which can only be broadly outlined here) led Bluhme to suppose that the Digest commission was divided into subcommittees, each of which had to work through a definite part of classical legal literature—one of the three main groups; and that at the end the selections of excerpts produced by the three sub-committees were not worked into one another within the individual titles, but were placed one after the other as they stood. The 'Appendix-group', however, evidently comes from a number of juristic writings which were discovered in the course of the work of compilation and were then subsequently included.

Using Bluhme's observations as a starting-point, two English scholars have recently attempted to discover the method of procedure used by these three subcommittees in dealing with the groups of material assigned to them.[1] A close investigation of the sequence of fragments inside the various groups led them to the following conclusions: first, that the main work was done by six of the seventeen members of the commission, namely (they suppose) by Tribonian himself, by the *magister officiorum* Constantinus, and the four professors of law. The three subcommittees each consisted of two of these six men, and the remaining eleven (all advocates) were called on as and when they might be needed; in particular, whenever excerpts were required from several works which—like the commentaries of the mid and late classical periods —contained much the same material and so could more profitably be read simultaneously by several people who would subject them

[1] A. M. Honoré and A. Rodger, *Zeitschr. Sav.-Stift.* 87 (1970), 246 ff.

to constant comparison with one another. Then, in order to secure an even tempo in the progress of the work, the books needing excerption were divided in equal numbers and distributed little by little to the two standing members of each subcommittee. Each of these would work by himself on his own allotted quantity; and it seems (apart perhaps from certain general directives) to have been a matter for his own judgement what he would decide to excerpt and what to leave out. A working method like this, dominated by the idea of getting ahead rapidly, would be bound to produce a very uneven result, given natural differences in diligence and thoroughness between the different persons involved. But it would explain how it was possible to get through the enormous volume of legal literature on which the commission had to work; and would also explain the irregularities in the sequence of the different 'groups', and of the excerpts within the groups, which Bluhme and later scholars observed.

If the results of this ingenious investigation are correct, they put an end to the doubts, repeatedly expressed since the turn of the century, about the correctness of Justinian's assertion that his commission itself read through all available classical works and excerpted from them all that was essential and usable. But of course they also put an end to any basis for the theory that there must have been 'pre-Digests' in existence already before Justinian's codification, i.e. a work or a series of works in which the material of the Digest had already been more or less completely put together for the use of the law-schools of the eastern Empire.[1] However, it still remains a likely supposition that the members of the Justinianic commission, and in particular the professors of law among them, were influenced both in their choice of fragments and perhaps also in their arrangement of them by what the law-schools had already done in commentaries. But having regard to our scanty knowledge of the literary productions of these law-schools, it will scarcely be possible to prove this in detail.

[1] The most radical 'pre-Digest' theory was developed by H. Peters, who tried to prove that the oldest of the Greek digest-commentaries (see below) did not relate originally to Justinian's Digest at all, but to another, older collection, very similar to Justinian's, which was then merely revised and extended by the colleagues of Tribonian ('Die oströmischen Digestenkommentare und die Entstehung der Digesten'; the essay appeared in 1913 in the *Sitzungsberichte der Sächsischen Akademie der Wissenschaften*, Phil.-hist. Klasse, 65. 1). Peters's thesis won much notice at the time, but in general was not accepted. Still, even in later times it was being assumed that small collections of excerpts, of earlier date than Justinian's Digest, formed the source of individual parts of that work.

2. *The Justinianic interpolations and critical research for genuineness.* Justinian himself tells us (Const. *Tanta* 10) that his codifying commission carried out numerous changes of great importance in the text of the classical material they were dealing with, in order to adapt it to contemporary requirements and to the purposes of the codification ('. . . multa et maxima sunt, quae propter utilitatem rerum transformata sunt'). The great jurists of the humanist age, above all the Frenchman Jacobus Cuiacius (1522–90) and the Savoyard Anton Faber (1557–1624), made efforts to uncover these 'interpolations' (insertions, falsifications) of the compilers and thus to make the pure law of the classical period once more accessible. Admittedly, wherever the Justinianic codification was studied predominantly as an immediate source of practical law (as was the case for centuries in Germany), not much attention was paid to the interpolations, since for the practice of law it was Justinian's text alone which was of significance, and not the wording of the classical originals upon which it was based, and which was in any case capable only of hypothetical reconstruction. Thus it is certainly no accident that interest in *Interpolationenforschung* (search for interpolations) did not become lively in Germany until, with the emergence of the *Bürgerliches Gesetzbuch* (German civil code), the *Corpus iuris civilis* lost its practical importance. At about the same time research in Italy also began to take this direction; and this hunt for interpolations then quickly became central to all scientific work on Roman law. It was carried on with the help of philological and legal criteria in a more or less radical manner, and often seemed to be self-perpetuating; there is no doubt that in this way many excessive claims were made. A very considerable proportion, probably indeed the majority, of the innumerable allegations of interpolation made since the end of the last century[1] has been shown after critical analysis to be untenable or at least highly questionable; many others, apparently credible in themselves, do not justify the historical conclusions for which they have been used as evidence. Still, despite all exaggerations and mistakes, this dedication to the search for interpolations was not misconceived; it was responsible

---

[1] The allegations of interpolation made up to the end of the 1920s are collected in the *Index Interpolationum*. It is intended to carry the *Index* up to the year 1955; and in the meanwhile it has been extended so as to take in the *Codex Justinianus* as well (see next footnote). Interpolations suggested from 1956 onwards, as well as other exegetical contributions on individual passages in the Roman legal sources, are collated in the Italian periodical *IVRA*.

for overcoming the predominant nineteenth-century scholarly approach, which was too conceptual, given to systematizing and hostile to historical reality, and for gaining new, historically sound perspectives and methods. More than a few of the results gained by the help of interpolation-research have proved their worth; and the question of genuineness must still be posed in any investigation directed to establishing the ideas of the classical jurists from the Justinianic (or in general from the post-classical) sources. But the perspective and methods of the study of genuineness have changed considerably over the years: they have become more heavily stratified, more complicated, and more cautious.

While at first the tendency was to attribute nearly all contradictions, confusions, and unevenness discernible in the Digest to interference by the Justinianic codifying commission, it is nowadays supposed that the writings of the classical jurists reached the commission in a form already changed, with omissions, additions, and paraphrases of the kind that occur in those few fragments of late classical works which survive, independently of Justinian's codifications, in the private compilations of the early fourth century (*Fragmenta Vaticana*; *Collatio legum Mosaicarum et Romanarum*). The extent of these changes is disputed, but it is generally agreed that their purpose was, broadly speaking, to paraphrase, illustrate, and expand the thought of the classical author. Justinian's compilers, for their part, carried out changes evidently much more by way of abridgement than by way of making substantive amendments to the classical texts. It is most unlikely that any influences in regard to system, or derived from philosophy or rhetoric, which may have reached them through the law-schools of the eastern Empire had any effect on their work, having regard to the tendency of these schools to stick to classical patterns and having regard also to the extreme barrenness of their work, so far as we can judge it.

In general, the modern tendency is to attach much less importance than formerly to purely formal traces of interference with a text as an indication of substantive amendment of the law. Grammatical and stylistic unevenness, or gaps in the train of argument, formerly regarded as signs of substantive interpolation, can often be more credibly explained as the result of mere abridgements of the text or of defects in the manuscripts available, abridgements or defects which may be of post-Justinianic as well as of pre-Justinianic date. In earlier times, moreover, the search for interpolations was sometimes based on an unjustified and excessive reliance on a supposed purity of style and grammar on the part of the classical authors, and on a standard of classical Latinity approaching that recommended in modern textbooks. The fact is that we are not entitled to imagine that the classical authors, and least of all the late classical authors, went in for antique purism in the language they used, despite the strong individuality of legal speech and despite its close adherence to a tradition, going back to the Republic, of unadorned simplicity and clarity. They were men of their own age and used its vocabulary; and it is certain that they did not anxiously avoid all the grammatical and stylistic liberties and inelegancies that were used by their contemporaries. Moreover, when one considers the colossal volume of legal writing of, say, Paulus or Ulpian, and remembers that they were, in addition, very busy officials, it is natural to assume that, even in the original versions of their work, both train of thought and its expression were bound to suffer occasionally from some degree of carelessness.

Even where substantive signs of interpolation might be assumed, the modern tendency is for research to be much more cautious and much more reserved, the further it has got away from the dogmatism of the nineteenth century. In the early decades of this century effort was directed towards discovering, concealed behind the law as given by Justinian, a more or less uniform classical law; but modern research is directed to a greater degree of discrimination. The objective now is to trace the course of development even within the classical law itself; it is taken more for granted than formerly that there must have been differences of opinion in the midst of classical legal literature, and the task now is to get a more distinct notion of the methods and the range of classical legal thought. We already know, as a result of this line of research, that a great deal of what a former generation considered foreign to classical thinking, and the result of Justinianic interpolation or post-classical law-school theory, in fact must be attributed, in whole or at any rate in the main, to the classical period.[1]

[1] Interpolations are found also in the imperial constitutions of the Codex. Here Justinian even interpolated his own constitutions in order to adapt the earlier ones to the advances made by his legislation. The Institutes, too, contain Justinianic additions between the passages which were copied more or less word for word from classical and post-classical models.

IV. *The Novels*

The completion of the great codification by the publication of the *Codex repetitae praelectionis* in 534 did not mean the end of Justinian's legislative reforms. On the contrary, the emperor subsequently interfered with the legal system by means of numerous and in fact fairly extensive individual laws, and made complete innovations in important areas of private law, chiefly in the law of the family and of inheritance. An official collection of these supplementary laws (*leges novellae*) was planned by Justinian at the time of the publication of the Codex of 534, but was not carried out. On the other hand several private collections were made.

Most of the *novellae* of Justinian were composed in Greek. Greek had always been the language of business in the eastern Empire, and even the Roman government there mostly used Latin only in the internal contacts among the highest departments. But in the time of Justinian the ability to speak and write Latin began to decline noticeably in the upper imperial government agencies. Only the circumstance that it was usual in the law-schools and probably also in the practice of the higher courts to use classical texts and constitutions in their original Latin can explain how Justinian's great codification held fast to Latin. A break was now made with this tradition. The small number of *novellae* which had been published in Latin were directed to the Latin-speaking provinces on the fringe of the Empire, or concerned the internal course of business of the central government, or related to certain older constitutions which had been composed in Latin. A few *novellae* were published bilingually.

Apart from special collections of imperial ecclesiastical laws we possess four assortments of Justinianic *novellae*. The oldest of these is an abridged Latin version of 124 laws from the years 535-55, composed in the reign of Justinian himself by one Julian, who was a teacher of law in Constantinople (the so-called *Epitome Juliani*). It was probably intended for use in reconquered Italy, and it was known there throughout the Middle Ages. On the other hand, a second Latin collection of 134 *novellae* did not turn up until 1100 in the law-school of Bologna. Since it was thought at that time that it contained the original text of the novels, it was called the *Authenticum*. In fact, however, it contains only the Latin novels in their original text and the Greek novels in a faulty Latin translation. This

collection was made in the sixth century in the law-school of Constantinople, at that time still bilingual. But the collection which (at
least originally) really did contain the original text of all the novels
—the Greek ones in Greek, the Latin ones in Latin—did not become known in the west until after the fall of the eastern Empire,
when Greek scholars and manuscripts came to Italy and decisively
advanced the study of Greek as well as the general development of
humanism. The manuscripts of the collection which reached Italy
at that time reproduced, it is true, only the novels which had been
published in Greek; the Latin ones, which had long been not understood in Byzantium, were left out or replaced by Greek summaries.
For this reason this collection is called the Greek novel-collection.
When it was still complete it contained 168 novels, among which,
apart from Justinian's novels, some constitutions of his successors
Justinus II and Tiberius II are included, while some further texts
are not imperial constitutions at all but decrees of *praefecti praetorio*.
The contents of the collection prove that it cannot have been
completed before the reign of Tiberius II (572–82). Its place of
origin was Constantinople. Finally, one of the manuscripts of the
Greek novel-collection contains by way of appendix thirteen novels
of Justinian under the title *Edicta Justiniani*.[1]

---

[1] The standard modern edition of Schoell and Kroll gives all the 168 novels of the Greek
novel-collection in the original text, and, for the Greek novels, also gives (so far as it exists)
the Latin version of the *Authenticum*, together with a modern Latin translation. The
Edicta Justiniani and other scattered constitutions of Justinian are added by way of an
appendix. The novels are numbered from 1 to 168. The customary abbreviation is *Nov.*
They are divided into chapters (in the case of extensive novels) and paragraphs.

EPILOGUE

ROMAN LAW AFTER JUSTINIAN

1. *In the east*

WITH the fall of the last emperor in the Roman west in 476 antiquity came to an end and the Middle Ages began (according to the traditional division of periods in the world's history). In truth, however, there was a long transitional period which began, almost unnoticeably, much earlier, and ended just as gradually and very much later. Long before the end of the western Empire the decline of Roman culture had begun; and the christianizing of the Empire, social and economic developments, and the continuous stream of immigrant Germanic peoples had already laid the foundations from which the early medieval world would rise. On the other hand, long after the disappearance of the Roman emperor of the west, Roman administration and Roman law remained alive, although in an increasingly primitive shape. The imperial idea, too, survived the emperors; the concept of the *Imperium Romanum* remained so powerful that even after centuries it was still able to impose its mark on the state system of the western world and in the long run to influence the course of European history.

The traditions of antiquity continued to operate in the east more strongly and less interruptedly. Here the Empire did not survive merely as an idea, but continued in existence up to the end of the Middle Ages. Roman law, therefore, remained valid not, as in the west, through the force of inertia, but as part of a living political system. But the spread of Islam opened a new epoch in the east, and in the east Roman Empire, too, in spite of all continuity of state, law, and cultural tradition, changes ensued which led from antiquity into a new era. Just as in the west, the sixth century, that of Justinian, lay in the period of transition. Justinian himself, who wished to restore the *Imperium Romanum*, was in reality one of the founders of the Byzantine state, both un-Roman and in many respects no longer part of the ancient world and with an individual culture of its own. His imperial foreign policy had

no lasting effects. In his architectural activity, his ecclesiastical
policy, and in the inner political developments of his reign—the
dedication to an intensified absolutism after the so-called Nike
riots—can be clearly seen, in a long historical perspective, features
which are un-Roman and which point towards the Byzantine future.
These features are not entirely lacking in his legislation: we notice
the final abandonment of the Latin language and the clear break
with the traditions of Roman law in many of his reforms, especially
in the Novels. Of course, the codifying work of Justinian essentially looks to the past; not for nothing has the plan of the code
been called romantic, and his often-displayed love of falling back
on very old sources and principles of Roman law archaistic. One
might imagine, for the sake of comparison, a modern code of civil
law being drawn up today containing citations from the *Sachsen-
spiegel*, most of which comes from the legal literature of the period
of the Thirty Years War, and giving only a relatively modest number of fairly specialized statutes from the nineteenth and twentieth
centuries. Such a consideration not only makes clear to us how
quickly the world has changed, in the few centuries which separate
our age from the Middle Ages, in comparison with the rate of
development in antiquity; it also makes the backward-looking
attitude of late antiquity, and in particular of the age of Justinian,
stand out in sharp relief.

One may ask oneself what effect such a work may have had on
the legal practice of the eastern Empire, Greek-speaking and committed to Greek-Oriental legal ideas as it was: a work which synopsized, though within limits so wide as to be scarcely manageable,
the more or less unfamiliar legal culture of six centuries. The
Latin language alone must have made its use extraordinarily difficult, although here translations could have helped. But the content
of the law could only be enforced where advocates and judges
functioned who had become familiar with its concepts and with its
casuistic labyrinth through years of study at one of the two great
law-schools. Such jurists were certainly not to be found everywhere
that cases were decided and contracts formulated. For this reason
it is not surprising that while we can trace the influence of Justinian's
codification in many details of the Egyptian papryi of the sixth
century yet, seen as a whole, we find in them a fairly uninterrupted
continuation of the inherited Greco-Egyptian legal world. In the
face of this new code native law asserted itself here too. One ought

not, accordingly, to imagine the influence of the Justinianic code
in legal practice as being omnipotent; probably it was effective up
to a point only in the courts of the capital, the courts of the superior
provincial authorities and perhaps also those of the large provincial
cities. At the same time it formed, as was always intended, the basis
of legal study in the law academies, among which in later times that
of Constantinople was the most important and is the only one about
whose functioning we have any exact knowledge. Here there developed a vigorous literary activity of which extensive remains
have survived.

Just as Frederick the Great was to do 1,200 years later (in 1749)
when he published the draft of the *Corpus iuris Fridericiani*, Justinian had forbidden all commentary on his code under the threat
of punishment as for forgery, so that the innumerable disputes in
older Roman law, which he thought he had done away with, could
not be revived. He had allowed only literal translations into Greek
(κατὰ πόδα, following 'in the footsteps' of the original Latin text)
and collections of parallel passages (παράτιτλα). But even in his
lifetime this prohibition was evidently transgressed. There appeared, along with literal translations, also synopses and explana-
tory statements of contents (ἴνδικες, indices: though they are also
called *Summae* after the pattern of analogous writings in western
Europe of the Middle Ages) and comments in the form of footnotes
(παραγραφαί), and later also monographic treatises on individual
topics. Our knowledge of this post-Justinianic legal literature
comes chiefly through a much later work of codification, the Basilica,
and through the commentaries connected with it.

The Basilica (βασιλικά = the imperial law)[1] is a Greek adaptation of the Justinianic codification, made under Leo the Wise
(886–911); in it the Digest fragments relevant to a particular subject are grouped in a single title with the constitutions from the
Codex and with the Novels and with the parts of the Institutes
relating to the same subject; the whole work is arranged in sixty
books. In putting this work together, use was made not of the
original Latin texts (which at that time hardly anyone would still
have understood) but of Greek *summae* from the early Byzantine
epoch. The Digest fragments found in the Basilica are taken from
a *summa* by an author whose name even then was no longer known
and whom the Byzantines themselves therefore called Anonymus.

---

[1] The Byzantine emperor carried once more the old Greek name for a king: βασιλεύς.

The Codex elements were taken mainly from a *summa* composed
by one Thalelaeus immediately after the publication of this part
of the Justinianic compilation. The passages from the Institutes
came from a Greek paraphrase of which we have an almost complete version surviving independently of the Basilica.[1] It was only
in the case of the Novels that the original (Greek) text was used.

Thus the text of the Basilica itself consists mainly of works of
the early Byzantine school of legal learning. Further tracts from
the writings of this school were joined together with the Basilica
text in the shape of a 'chain-commentary' ($\kappa\alpha\tau\eta\nu\eta$), familiar also
in Byzantine theology: each Basilica passage was explained by
means of a chain of excerpts from works written by way of commentary to the Digest or the Codex either under Justinian, or
shortly after his time.[2] By contrast with the Basilica text, these 'old
scholia' contain not only a brief note in Greek of the content of
the Justinianic originals, but also explanations and references of
several different kinds. For this reason their importance for the
understanding of the Justinianic codification is considerable; and
since two of the authors of these scholia—Dorotheus and Theophilus—were actually themselves members of the codifying commission, and so must have known the law of the immediately
preceding period, we meet in them, here and there, traces of pre-
Justinianic legal rules.

Side by side with the older scholia originally composed on the
Digest and Codex, the Basilica commentary contains also later
comments written on the Basilica text itself; some of them are as
late as the thirteenth century. Thus the whole apparatus of scholia
on the Basilica represents a cross-section of the entire history of
Byzantine jurisprudence. Its standard was always uneven; we find
some poor intelligences in the early period, and some ingenious
minds at work in the later period; but, all in all, their performance
does not match that of the medieval jurists of western Europe.

---

[1] The standard edition is that of C. Ferrini, *Institutionum Graeca paraphrasis Theophilo
antecessori vulgo tributa* (2 vols. 1884 and 1897). The attribution to Theophilus, colleague of
Tribonian (also in the composition of the Institutes) is disputed by many scholars, Ferrini
in particular.

[2] According to the treatise of H. Peters mentioned above, Anonymus himself had
attached to his Digest *summa* a 'chain' from the works of the Justinianic and immediately
post-Justinianic period, and this 'chain' was then transferred to the Basilica text, itself
formed from the *summa* of Anonymus. This hypothesis has been attacked by H. J. Scheltema
and defended by F. Pringsheim; the probabilities are against its correctness. Further
details on relevant literature are given below in the Bibliographical Appendix.

They were exclusively dedicated to the exegesis of the Justinianic codification, and were far removed from the legal practice of their own day, and its needs. Their understanding of the Justinianic texts was often imperfect; and creative thinking was rare among them.

In the western Empire the unimpeded simplification and harmonization of the law characterized the scanty Roman systems of the Visigoths and Burgundians; in the east this development was slowed up, but not stopped, by the work of the law-schools and by Justinian's great codifying plan. That it dominated legal practice can be seen, above all, from the primitive law-books from the epoch of the Isaurian emperors of the eighth century. It seems very doubtful whether the return to the law of Justinian, signalized in the composition of the Basilica, had any deep influence on practice. At any rate, a continuing tendency towards simplification, and the ironing out of all subtleties, is visible also in the legal literature following on the Basilica.

At the end of this epoch there stands a manual of the whole law in six books (ἑξάβιβλος), composed about the year 1345 by a certain Constantine Harmenopulos, a judge in Salonica; and in this atrophied form Justinian's law survived the era of the Turks. As a consequence, Roman law was in force even in modern Greece until 1941 when a civil code was introduced, heavily influenced by German civilian science, but also associated with the native traditions of Roman law.

11. *In the west*

In western Europe, as has been seen, west Roman vulgar law prevailed throughout the early Middle Ages, mainly based on the *lex Romana Visigotorum*. Only in Italy was the Justinianic code introduced after the fall of the east Gothic Empire, through a law of Justinian of the year 554, the so-called *Sanctio pragmatica Pro petitione Vigilii*; Codex, Institutes, and Novels (these in the form of the *Epitome Juliani*) remained known here; but hardly any positive trace can be found in the early Middle Ages of a knowledge of the Digest. Even in Italy jurisprudence declined to the lowest level conceivable. Modern scholarship has tried in vain to prove the existence in Italy of a continuous Roman law tradition of some standing.

All the more astonishing, therefore, is the powerful revival of the study of the law in Italy at the end of the eleventh century. There is no doubt that it is connected with the discovery of the Digest;[1] and through the Digest all the greatness and strength of Roman jurisprudence was again bestowed on western Europe. All that was needed was the ability to master this profound and difficult work, and for several reasons this ability did in fact exist at the end of the eleventh century. The intellectual boom associated with the early economic prosperity of the cities of Italy on the eve of the crusades, the training in logic which was furthered by scholastic theology, and the existence of a respectable school of Lombardic law in northern Italy, helped to make it possible. But together with such factors the intellectual achievement of a single man was, as far as we can see, of decisive importance. Irnerius of Bologna, originally presumably a teacher of rhetoric, penetrated so deeply into the spirit of Roman law in his study of the Digest that he learned to understand and master the work. With Irnerius is associated the glorious development of the law-school of Bologna, the oldest university in western Europe along with the theological school in Paris. It was joined in the course of the twelfth and thirteenth centuries by a number of similar schools in other cities of northern and central Italy and of southern France.

Irnerius and his successors up to the thirteenth century used the exegetical method as the east-Roman law-teachers had done before them: they explained in their lectures the text of the *Corpus Iuris*, title by title and sentence by sentence. The literary form corresponding to this method of instruction, and typical therefore of the oldest jurists of medieval western Europe, is the gloss, an explanation contained in a brief note based on individual words of the text. The original instance of a gloss is a mere explanation of a word (thus the name γλῶσσα: a word foreign to general usage and therefore needing explanation). The jurists of the Middle Ages behaved in fact just like a schoolboy of today who, in reading Cicero or Horace, writes in the meanings of words which he has had to look up either above the line (an interlinear gloss) or in the margin (a marginal

---

[1] The manuscript (no longer surviving) on which the Italian manuscripts of the high and late Middle Ages are based, the so-called Codex S(ecundus) was probably written about the middle of the eleventh century in southern Italy. The celebrated Florentine manuscript must also have been in that area at that time, as the writer of S used it, along with another manuscript, as his original. One tradition (up to now fairly generally disbelieved) has it that the Florentine manuscript was stolen by the Pisans in Amalfi (gulf of Salerno) and brought to Pisa in 1135, whence it came to Florence in 1406.

gloss). The natural consequence was that legal explanations also tended to be given. References to other passages, which either said the same thing as the passage under consideration or something inconsistent with it, were given and attempts were made to explain the inconsistencies and generally to expose the conceptual and logical background of the texts. Through the continuous glossing of the individual parts of the Justinianic code there arose whole apparatuses of glosses; and the network of these notes which covered the margin of the medieval manuscripts of the *Corpus Iuris* created everywhere the cross-connections which the student needed to survey and understand this gigantic mass of material, clarified conceptual relationships, and uncovered contradictions— though only in order to explain them away at once. For as the Bible was to the theologians so was the *Corpus Iuris* to the jurists of the Middle Ages. It was the repository of all wisdom: all contradictions could be only apparent, and it must be possible in some way to resolve them. The feats of memory alone performed by these jurists are astonishing; they were able without much loss of time to run down a Digest passage cited merely by title-heading and by its first words. No less great was their ingenuity, which often points out even to the modern scholar the way to a correct interpretation. We call these scholars Glossators after their standard literary form, though of course they also wrote works of other kinds: concise synopses of contents (*summae*) like the ἴνδικες of the Byzantines; explanations of conceptual distinctions (*distinctiones*), collections of controversies (*dissensiones dominorum*)[1] monographic treatments of single legal topics, in particular of the law of procedure, and so on.

By the middle of the thirteenth century the work of the preceding generations of glossators had been compiled by the Bologna law-teacher Accursius in a gloss-apparatus to the whole *Corpus Iuris*. This immediately achieved a canonical authority and drove the older gloss-apparatuses out of use; from then on it was published along with the text in all manuscripts (and in the older printed versions) of the *Corpus Iuris*. This so-called *glossa ordinaria* is proof that the basic task of penetrating and mastering the Justinianic code had been successfully accomplished.

Meanwhile the *Corpus Iuris* had entered into the practical legal life of Italy. Here its norms, which had grown out of the conditions

---

[1] *Domini* were the law-teachers of the time of the glossators.

of antiquity, were confronted by an entirely different environment. Questions repeatedly cropped up which could not be answered directly from the *Corpus Iuris*. Thus the Italian jurists from the end of the thirteenth century onwards found themselves facing new problems: they had to adapt the law of the Justinianic code to the needs and conditions of their own time. By means of the interpretative methods of formal logic, by limitations and extensions, by subtle distinctions and ingenious analogies, they succeeded in doing so. For a work of this kind the short gloss was no longer the appropriate literary form, and its place was now taken by broadly planned commentaries on the Justinianic law-books, commentaries which were particularly exhaustive in the areas where it was necessary to deduce new principles for legal practice. The argumentation was often more closely based on the Accursian gloss than on the Justinianic text. Commentaries of this kind, which achieved an authority as great as that of the Accursian gloss itself, were composed chiefly by Bartolus de Saxoferrato (1314-57) and his pupil Baldus de Ubaldis (1327-1400). The usual modern term for this later development of medieval Italian jurisprudence is the Commentator-school, as distinct from the glossators.[1] In the generations after Bartolus and Baldus, however, the literary emphasis was increasingly on legal opinions (*consilia*) instead of commentaries, of which only a few were now composed (thus F. Wieacker prefers to use the term *Konsiliatoren*). These opinions, specifically concerned with the solution of practical legal cases, went considerably beyond the commentaries in their adaptation and transformation of Roman law. The humanists of the sixteenth century and later writers exclusively interested in pure Roman law thought little of the work of the commentators; they could see in them no understanding of Roman legal norms in an historical sense, and found their expository method tasteless because of its prolixity and its tendency to overflow with quotations. Today, however, it is realized that the commentators, for all their laborious erudition, were creative jurists who served both their own age and the future by developing, from the scanty clues in the Roman sources, leading principles for the formation of new areas of law. Thus, for example, they laid the foundations of private international law, of commercial law, and of the legal doctrine of money.

[1] The term which used to be common—'post-glossators'—wrongly described the commentators as being merely insignificant followers of the glossators.

The influence of the commentators reached far beyond the borders of Italy. At the time of the glossators huge crowds of students from Germany, France, Spain, and other countries had come to the Italian universities, and now the commentators became to an ever greater extent the legal instructors of Europe. In the schools which had sprung up everywhere in Europe in the course of the late Middle Ages—which at first had a well-marked theological character and thus cultivated mainly canon law—there grew up from the fifteenth century onwards seminaries of the commentators' science. This science thus became very rapidly, almost at one blow, the basis of a common European legal culture. In it—and thus in the Roman law which was applied in practice and adapted to the needs of the times—may be found the roots of the modern legal life of the peoples of continental Europe, and of many nations beyond who borrowed their legal system at one time or another from Europe or else formed it on the model of the European tradition. It is chiefly thanks, too, to this science (apart from later cross-connections) that the jurists of every land, despite the peculiar development of their own native legal systems, can more or less understand each other up to the present day on the common basis of Roman legal concepts, just as Spaniards and Italians understood each other's tongue because both are based on Latin. The Anglo-Saxon area remained excluded from this great legal family because England, which in the twelfth century—the time of the early flowering of the Glossator-school—had come under the first influences of Roman law, later consciously closed itself to these influences. Here by the end of the thirteenth century a native legal profession had grown up, organized as a guild which rejected foreign law and its methods. It was this English legal profession which from its own traditions lent Anglo-Saxon law those features which distinguish it today so sharply from the legal world of the Continent: features which nevertheless for all their individual nature still often remind one surprisingly of the structure of classical Roman law.[1]

The extension of the commentators' science and of Roman law over Europe is represented only partially by the so-called 'Reception' of Roman law in Germany. It deserves attention only because of the relatively large extent to which, in the Reception, positive norms of Roman law acquired practical validity. As a consequence of the political fragmentation of Germany, German law of the late

[1] See, on these similarities, H. Peter, *Römisches Recht und englisches Recht* (1969).

Middle Ages was fissured into innumerable local legal systems; and these could not offer the same resistance to foreign law as other more solidly established laws, such as the Germanic customary law (*coutumes*), systematically collected by the Crown, which continued in force in northern France. While, therefore, in other places it was not so much the concrete individual rules which gained acceptance as the juristic methods developed by the commentators in their work on Roman law, in Germany the native legal rules, already withered through their isolation and fragmentation, were often swept away by the encroaching flood of foreign law. In this way Germany became a stronghold of Roman law. Only in places such as Saxony where there were fairly big areas of more or less uniform character did German law hold out better. It was from places of this kind that in later times certain areas of law—chiefly in the field of family law and the law of things—were reconquered by the intellectual world of national German law.

The subject of the Reception was, as has already been indicated, the law of the Justinianic code, in the peculiar form which the commentators had given it. In addition it included—chiefly in the field of the law of procedure—the canon law which was based on ecclesiastical legal sources and had grown out of Roman, Germanic, and specifically Christian elements,[1] and finally the Lombardic feudal law[2] which was taught at the Italian universities. In this fairly variegated mixture of legal norms the kernel was formed by what was Roman, although this Roman element underwent considerable change. The period of the Reception stretches mainly over the late fifteenth and the sixteenth centuries: but according to the political and legal fragmentation of Germany, it took place at different times and in different ways in different areas. The Reception movement, already active in several places, received a powerful impetus from the composition of the highest court of the Holy Roman Empire, the *Reichskammergericht*, newly reformed in 1495. This court was half composed of *Doctores iuris*—jurists trained in Roman law—and was directed to pass judgement according to the common laws of the Empire, i.e. according to the legal

---

[1] Synopsized in the *Corpus Iuris Canonici*, which, like Justinian's code, consisted of several parts of different kinds; it was not the result of a uniform and systematical operation of codification, but had grown up in the course of the centuries (twelfth to fourteenth).

[2] Since the time of the glossators the sources of the Lombardic feudal law, the *libri feudorum*, including also laws of medieval German emperors, had been incorporated in these Justinianic novels as *decima collatio novellarum*.

norms of the commentators just described. The local princes, too, created learned supreme courts on the model of the *Reichskammergericht*, and through their jurisdiction the Reception was in a certain sense propagated from above. At the same time the foreign law was adduced by litigants to the courts in which lay judges still sat, because litigants had begun to employ learned advocates. The courts were thus also obliged to use the services of learned jurists: in the cities, the city advocates or *syndici*, who had formerly been used only for representation before foreign courts or in diplomatic service; in the country, the prince's officials or the professors of a nearby faculty of law. Litigants often addressed themselves from the beginning to the prince's officers as arbitrators, and avoided the lay courts altogether. In addition to all this, from about the seventies of the fifteenth century Roman legal rules had been introduced in many places by legislation of the local princes and of the cities.

The significance of the radical break with former legal life represented by this development was not fully recognized by people at the time. For the Holy Roman Empire of the German nation counted as the continuation of the ancient Roman Empire, and therefore the law of the *Corpus Iuris* of Justinian counted as its hereditary law, while people were inclined to look on native German law as the product of a secondary and partly unfortunate development. The complaints often met with in the historical sources of the Reception period are therefore directed more against the learned jurists and their incomprehensible methods than against the foreign law itself. But even the learned lawyer was favourably judged by the age of humanism; indeed humanism and the spread of learned jurisprudence were only individual elements of one and the same phenomenon: the growth of a worldly learning, drawn from the models of classical antiquity, which replaced the medieval culture dominated by the traditions of the church and more or less reserved to the clergy.

Although in this way humanism in a sense helped to smooth the way for the spread of learned jurisprudence and of Roman law, on the other hand it was sharply opposed to the prevailing methods of this science in the theory and practice of law. The civilized connoisseurs of the ancient classics found both the bombastic language and the unhistorical, hair-splitting scholastic interpretative method of the commentators and their pupils disagreeable. It was inevitable that people began to treat Roman legal sources, as they treated Cicero and Livy, as mere evidence for ancient culture, without bothering much about their practical validity or about the confused mass of controversy and often very subtle constructions with which the centuries-long work of the medieval jurists had obliterated the clear lines of these sources.

At the beginning of this period of humanistic treatment of Roman law (the so-called elegant jurisprudence) stand the Italian Andreas Alciatus (1492–1540) and the German lawyer Ulrich Zasius (1461–1535), who was a professor and town clerk in Freiburg in Breisgau. Apart from the latter, the new German jurisprudence contributed a certain amount to the achievements of humanistic jurisprudence. Thus the first edition of the Greek novels of Justinian (as part of a general edition of the *Corpus Iuris* which appeared between 1529 and 1531 in Nürnberg) comes from Gregorius Haloander (Gregor Meltzer) from Zwickau. But in the long run the humanistic trend could not assert itself either in Italy, where the tradition of the commentators was all-powerful, or in Germany, where all forces were occupied by the practical tasks of the Reception. Thus its real home became France, where Alciatus had sometimes taught. It was chiefly at the new school at Bourges that humanistic jurisprudence came to its highest flowering. In the sixteenth century a series of men taught here whose work is admired even today and is gratefully exploited by modern research: above all Jacobus Cuiacius (Jacques Cujas, 1522–90), who combined juristic and philological ingenuity with all-embracing knowledge of the ancient sources, and Hugo Donellus (Doneau, 1527–91) the most important systematizer of Roman law before Savigny. But the flowering of humanistic jurisprudence in France did not last long. A large number of the best men of this cast of mind adhered to the Reformation, and these were obliged to emigrate at the outbreak of the great persecution of the Huguenots in 1573. Thus Donellus died as professor at the Nürnberg university of Altdorf after he (like other French humanists) had taught for a time at Heidelberg. The French emigrants created a lasting humanistic tradition only in the Netherlands; in this rich country, which offered a more favourable place for the cultivation of the arts and sciences than the Germany impoverished by the Thirty Years War, 'elegant jurisprudence' lived on into the eighteenth century and continued to produce important work.

In this book, the proper subject of which is ancient Roman law, there is no room to discuss how Roman law developed further in Germany and other lands; the details of how it came to terms with inherited national law, with practical requirements and with the natural law ideas of the period of the Enlightenment; and how from this conflict the foundations of the modern European legal systems developed. It would indeed be impossible to enter upon the manifold radiations of the political thought of the Romans— communicated by the humanism of the sixteenth and the classicism of the late eighteenth and early nineteenth centuries—which have influenced modern political development. The history of these influences, which are partly of an external character but partly also penetrated into the structure of political life, has only been written in isolated fragments. But it is worth indicating how research into ancient Roman law has been intensified since the turn of the eighteenth century. The starting-point—and, for more than a century, the central point—of this movement was Germany, and the mind from which it sprang was that of Friedrich Carl von Savigny (1779-1861).

Just as elegant jurisprudence was rooted in the humanistic movement, so too Savigny's 'historical school of law' grew out of the intellectual development of his time: out of the revolutionary changes which overcame the rationalist, unhistorical mode of thought of the Enlightenment and opened up new regions of the world of the human spirit. Classicism and romanticism in German poetry, classicizing love for antiquity and romantic enthusiasm for medieval art and culture, the foundation of the modern science of antiquity and the rise of Germanic philology, are the contradictory consequences of this revolution—appearing partly simultaneously, partly successively. In the personality of Savigny both classicism and romanticism were living things. To the rationalist love of experimenting shown by the Enlightenment and in particular by the French revolution, he opposed a doctrine influenced by romanticism: a conservative view of the state and of law, that law develops gradually and almost unnoticeably out of the secretly working *Volksgeist* (national spirit) and is stamped with ever greater clarity by the essential characteristics of the nation. One-sided though his view is, Savigny discovered law as an historical phenomenon and raised it to the status of a subject of historical research in the highest sense. Classical feeling produced Savigny's delight in the 'noble

lines' of Roman law, a delight which made him devote his life to
this foreign system and not to that of his own country. This classical sense of form—but also the pressure towards systematization
exerted by the natural law doctrine which he had overcome—
helped to generate his great creative powers, shown in his legal
masterpiece on the law of possession, written at the age of twenty-
four, and no less in the great work of his old age, the *System des
heutigen römischen Rechts.*

The basic movements which dominated the development of
Roman jurisprudence in nineteenth-century Germany go back to
Savigny: and for a long time it was the systematic movement which
predominated over the historical. Roman law, which until 1 January 1900 had direct validity in large parts of Germany, stood, both
in teaching and in practice, in the centre of civil law thought.
Permeated by ever-stronger dogmatism, the scientific exposition
of 'pure' Roman law put up almost the same claim to be a universally valid law of reason as the unhistorical law of nature had
once done in the eighteenth century. Through its influence on
practice it produced in many fields a 'late Reception' of Roman
legal principles. It gave its peculiar character to the *Bürgerliches
Gesetzbuch* (German Civil Code), which put an end to the direct
validity of Roman law; not only the greater part of its contents but
also its spirit is Roman, at least in the sense in which the nineteenth century understood Roman law. Thus it was reasonable
that, decades after the introduction of the German Civil Code,
lectures on Roman private law served as an introduction to the
study of private law generally.

The modern view sees Roman law as above all an essential part
of the history of our legal culture. Attention is focused on it not,
as in the nineteenth century, as a closed logical system but in order
to understand its historical development. Its continuous existence
throughout two millennia (counting the later life of Roman law)
reveals in a unique way the historical essence of law in general, the
change of meaning which its norms have experienced through
changes in environment, and the gradual working-out of timeless
values in our legal culture. Such a view presupposes not only an
understanding of the historical development of law as such, but
also the interpretation of it in relation to the political, social, economic, and spiritual environment, in close contact with neighbouring sciences. The study of Roman law in this sense owes a

great debt to Theodor Mommsen (1817-1903). Basically a lawyer trained in the jurisprudence of the nineteenth century in the clear conception and systematic association of what it had learned to understand, he was able by his comprehensive mastery of the whole Roman tradition to place all branches of the science of Roman antiquity on new foundations and to point out their common tasks.

BIBLIOGRAPHICAL APPENDIX

ANCIENT SOURCES AND MODERN LITERATURE

General

HARDLY ever in the history of mankind has the entire life of a people been so completely dominated by political and legal ideas as was that of the Romans. For this reason almost all the surviving source-material provides important evidence for the building up of Roman legal history.

This source-material[1] is of either a literary or an archaeological nature. The literary material consists of the works of the ancient writers which were for the most part preserved, studied, and copied in the monastic libraries of the Middle Ages, or sometimes remained in some forgotten corner until they were rediscovered during the Renaissance or even later. Modern finds in Egypt have given us new fragments of ancient literature, though admittedly, since Egypt belonged to the Greek part of the Roman Empire, these are preponderantly works in the Greek language. Archaeological material consists of the monuments of Roman art, the inscriptions on bronze or stone, found wherever Roman culture once reigned; also the abundant documents of daily life in papyri, wooden tablets, and parchments which have survived intact, especially in the dry desert sand on the edge of the Nile basin, but also in the lava covering Pompeii and Herculaneum. After a series of accidental finds, these have been revealed by systematic excavations since the end of the nineteenth century. The basic structure of our knowledge of Roman legal history (as of ancient culture generally) is formed by the literary source-material; the archaeological sources supplement it to a varying extent, depending on the subject-matter. In spite of the abundance of what actually remains we possess only a small fraction of the evidence about Roman legal life which once existed; and what we do possess is very unevenly distributed over the different chronological and geographical sections of Roman antiquity. Thus our knowledge must remain to a large extent piecemeal, and it can only be improved by the most careful evaluation of every new discovery, however insignificant, and by the constant reassessment of what we already know.

Among the literary sources the most important for the purposes of legal history are naturally the specifically legal sources, i.e. the late Roman codifications and the remains of the writings of the Roman jurists (most of these are contained in the codifications). This part of the

[1] For details see H. Bengtson, *Einführung in die alte Geschichte*, 6th edn., 1969.

source-material has been dealt with in some detail in the course of this outline; and, to the extent to which supplementary remarks on modern editions and modern investigations are necessary, these are given in the following pages in the notes on the respective sections of the main text.

Roman non-legal literature is of especial importance for our account of the development of the Roman state. Here the real basis of our knowledge lies in the works of the Roman historians (and of the Greek historians who deal with Roman history) and the Roman antiquarians, together with the political speeches and theoretical writings of Cicero; though all these works are also of great importance for legal history in the narrower sense. In the latter field we also use the forensic speeches of Cicero, Roman technical literature on surveying and on agriculture, and even many poetical works, so that, for example, the comedies of Plautus are an important source for the legal life of the end of the third and the beginning of the second centuries B.C., and there are passages in the satires of Horace to which the ingenuity of the legal historian has been repeatedly applied. These brief references by no means exhaust the literary sources. Rhetorical writings and epistolary literature, the works of the Fathers of the Christian Church, the *Natural History* of Pliny, and several other writings have helped us to piece together the history of Roman law.

The most interesting part of the archaeological source-material is, for the legal historian, the statutes, *senatusconsulta*, edicts, etc., preserved in inscriptions, together with the legal documents of daily life —the contracts, testaments, procedural records, corporations' rules, and so on—sources which allow us to see how Roman law looked in actual practice when divorced from the jurists' dissections of concepts. Research has provided an abundance of new insights from these sources since the end of the last century. The Latin inscriptions from all parts of the Roman Empire are collected according to geographical origin in the enormous *Corpus Inscriptionum Latinarum* (*CIL*) organized by Theodor Mommsen and published by the Berlin Academy of Sciences; the inscriptions dating from the Republic form a special collection in the first volume of the work, and are also collected by A. Degrassi, in *Inscriptiones Latinae liberae rei publicae* (2 vols., 1957 and 1963). There are, besides, special collections for certain parts of the Roman Empire, in particular for the African provinces. The new edition of all the inscriptions found in Italy (*Inscriptiones Italiae*) which has been undertaken by Italian scholars has not yet got very far. For inscriptions in the Greek language, of which not a few are of importance for Roman legal history, there exists a collection corresponding to the *CIL*, though still incomplete, the *Inscriptiones Graecae* (*IG*); those of relevance to Roman conditions will be found in *Inscriptiones Graecae ad res Romanas pertinentes*, edited by R. Cagnat and others (*IGR*); planned as four volumes, but only three appeared (1922-7). A broadly based selection of the most important Latin inscriptions (about 10,000) is contained in the work of H. Dessau, *Inscriptiones Latinae selectae* (3 vols., 1892-1916). Much narrower is the selection in the following specialized collections for the purposes of legal history: C. G. Bruns, *Fontes iuris Romani antiqui*, 7th edn. (with volume of illustrations and index) by O. Gradenwitz, 1909 (reprinted 1958); P. F. Girard, *Textes de droit romain*, 6th edn., by F. Senn, 1937, 7th edn., vol. i, 1967; S. Riccobono, J. Baviera, C. Ferrini, J. Furlani, V. Arangio-Ruiz, *Fontes iuris anteiustiniani* (3 vols., 2nd edn., 1940-3). A collection of the state contracts of antiquity preserved in literary or epigraphic sources is being published by the Kommission für alte Geschichte und Epigraphik (*Staatsverträge des Altertums*: so far, vols. ii and iii (covering the period 700-200 B.C.) have appeared (1962 and 1969)). The last two contain also literary sources of law. Selected papyri will be found in the second volume of the authoritative work of L. Mitteis and U. Wilcken, *Grundzüge und Chrestomathie der Papyruskunde* (1912), and also in P. M. Meyer, *Juristische Papyri* (1920). Research work must naturally fall back repeatedly on original editions, some very comprehensive, which cannot be mentioned here. A list of the editions which have so far appeared, together with a register of the abbreviations usual in citations, can be found in M. David and B. A. van Groningen, *Papyrological Primer* (4th edn., 1965), pp. 6* ff. The importance which ancient art, too, can have in legal history research may be seen from two treatises by the Hungarian historian A. Alföldi, 'Die Ausgestaltung des monarchischen Zeremoniells am römischen Kaiserhof' and 'Insignien und Tracht der römischen Kaiser' (*Mitteilungen des Deutschen Archäologischen Instituts, Römische Abteilung*, 49, 1934, 1 ff., and 50, 1935, 1 ff.; reprinted in 1970 under the title of *Die monarchische Repräsentation im römischen Kaiserreiche*), in which pictorial representations from the Empire (and particularly the designs on coins) together with the literary sources yield important results for the understanding of the development of the Roman monarchy. Another example of the value of images on coins when dealing with problems of constitutional history is provided by K. Kraft, 'Der goldene Kranz Caesars und der Kampf um die Entlarvung des "Tyrannen"' (*Jahrbuch für Numismatik und Geldgeschichte*, 3-4, 1952-3).

In modern times, Roman legal history—in many countries an ordinary part of legal training—has been the subject of many manuals and textbooks. Of the German works[1] the most comprehensive is the unfinished book of O. Karlowa (2 large volumes, 1885-1901), which includes also the history of private law. The Roman legal history of B. Kübler (1925) is very solid and clear, though not free from overloading. The extremely

---

[1] Unless otherwise indicated, the titles of the works cited in this paragraph are all the same: *Römische Rechtsgeschichte*.

brief and concentrated outline by the eminent Romanist and civilian H. Siber (1925) is composed with such conceptual sharpness that the element of gradual historical development is somewhat obscured. A particularly mature and balanced account is the treatise of C. G. Bruns, revised in a masterly fashion by O. Lenel, 'Geschichte und Quellen des römischen Rechts' in Holtzendorff and Kohler's *Enzyklopädie der Rechts-wissenschaft*, i (7th edn., 1915, pp. 303 ff.). Excellent of its kind, distinguished by its breadth of perspective and its careful regard for modern research, is the *Grundzüge der römischen Rechtsgeschichte* of E. Weiss (1936). The outline by H. Kreller offers in its second edition (1948) a brief description of the historical development of Roman law, which considers certain parts of substantive law, particularly the law of persons and family and inheritance law, and gives a systematic conspectus of these doctrines of Roman legal science which are important for modern law (i.e. principally the law of things and that of obligations). The excellent textbook of M. Kaser (1950) is related to the present work in scope and in purpose, but is more comprehensive. The short textbook of G. Dulckeit (5th edn., revised by F. Schwarz, 1970), which is also good and frequently takes an individual line, emphasizes constitutional history. A. Söllner's brief introduction to the subject (1970) is illustrated by citations of sources. The material for a Roman legal history is also contained—although curiously arranged—in the comprehensive, graphic, and often very penetrating work of U. von Lübtow, *Das römische Volk, sein Staat und sein Recht* (1955).

There are some excellent Italian accounts of Roman legal history;[1] thus the works of P. Bonfante (2 vols., 4th edn., 1934, reprinted with appendix on literature in 1959); P. de Francisci (unfinished; 2 vols., 1st and 2nd edns., 1938- -; 3rd vol., part i, 1936); and especially the ingenious book of V. Arangio-Ruiz (7th edn., 1957). To these classic works of Italian Romanistic studies there should be added a large number of more recent accounts, e.g. those of A. Guarino (4th edn., 1969); G. Grosso (5th edn., 1965); and P. Frezza (2nd revised edn., 1968). The modern French manuals of legal history (*Histoire des institutions*) comply with the usual course of French legal study by not confining themselves to Rome, but embracing the entire legal history of antiquity and including also French legal history. A particularly thorough treatment of Roman legal history, with strong emphasis on its social foundations and with extensive bibliographical references, is that of J. Gaudemet, *Institutions de l'antiquité* (1967). The subject of Roman legal history is also dealt with in the solid and comprehensive English work of H. F. Jolowicz, *Historical Introduction to the Study of Roman Law* (2nd edn., by Barry Nicholas, 1972). A shorter account of Roman legal

[1] These Italian treatises are all entitled, unless otherwise indicated, *Storia del diritto romano*.

history in English was written by H. J. Wolff, *Roman Law, An Historical Introduction* (1951).

A book of special character is that of F. Wieacker, *Vom römischen Recht* (2nd edn., 1961); it contains a whole series of essays—complete in themselves, thoughtful and stimulating—about the most important factors of Roman legal development; reference will be made to it in the following pages. A book of a different kind is that of F. Schulz, *Prinzipien des römischen Rechts* (1934, reprinted 1954; published in English under the title *Principles of Roman Law*, Oxford, 1936: reprinted 1956). In it, central ideas and peculiarities of method which marked the essence of classical Roman law are worked out, not by following the historical development but rather by a static, conceptual method; this important book belongs therefore in the context of 'internal' rather than 'external' legal history in the sense of the present work. Related to it in the goal pursued, but entirely different in execution, is the celebrated book of R. von Jhering, *Der Geist des römischen Rechts auf den verschiedenen Stufen seiner Entwicklung* (3 vols.; it appeared first in 1852, and the last reprint of the most recent editions was in 1921-4). Although obsolete in the light of modern research, as well as in its historical approach, the ingenious and vivid account which it contains is still effective. A work written from the perspective of the social historian is the stimulating and fascinating book by J. A. Crook, *Law and Life of Rome* (1967).

The modern interpretation of Roman constitutional law, particularly that of the Republic, still rests, despite many newer insights, largely on the epoch-making treatise of Theodor Mommsen, *Römisches Staatsrecht* (vols. i and ii in the 3rd edn., vol. iii. 1 in the 1st edn., 1887-8, reprinted 1952; there is a short outline of the *Römisches Staatsrecht* in Binding's *Handbuch der deutschen Rechtswissenschaft*, i. 3, 2nd edn., 1907). With the acuity of the dogmatic jurist, Mommsen deduced from widely scattered sources the conceptual world of Roman constitutional law, and worked it into an extraordinary systematic structure. In doing so he did less than justice to many aspects of Roman constitutional life; and in order to keep his fascinating systematization in perspective we should also have recourse to a work much less dominated by the notion of system, L. Lange's *Römische Altertümer* (3 vols., 3rd edn., 1876-9). Other treatments of Roman constitutional law from the eighties of the last century are overshadowed by Mommsen's supreme work, and do not need to be individually mentioned here. It is not until recent decades that general treatments of Roman constitutional law have been again undertaken on the grand scale. These newer works attempt not only to collate the conclusions reached in the last two generations and scattered in numerous monographic works by historians and lawyers, but also to set up a more historical view as against the dogmatic system of Mommsen. Here the posthumous work of H. Siber, *Römisches Verfassungsrecht* (1952), in spite of numerous corrections on individual points (which are in part the results of important monographs by Siber), remains nevertheless fairly close to Mommsen's basic notions; in particular Siber, like Mommsen, consciously excludes all sociological and ideological elements of political development from his account of constitutional law. Entirely different is the method of F. de Martino in his broadly planned *Storia della costituzione romana* (5 vols., 1951-67; the volume containing the index has not yet appeared; vol. i reprinted in 1958, vol. ii in 1960); written from a Marxist point of view, this work lays special emphasis on social and economic elements in Roman constitutional history. These elements are also taken into account by A. Burdese, *Manuale di diritto pubblico romano* (1966), a shorter treatment, without references to sources or bibliography, but which is a respectable and balanced synthesis, dealing also with criminal law and procedure. Intended for a wider readership and written from an historical rather than from a legal perspective are the excellent synoptical works of L. Homo, *Les institutions politiques romaines* (last edn., 1950) and Ernst Meyer, *Römischer Staat und Staatsgedanke* (1948; 3rd edn., 1964).

A supplement to Mommsen's *Staatsrecht*, concentrating on the technique of administration, is J. Marquardt's *Römische Staatsverwaltung* (3 vols. in the 2nd and 3rd edns., 1884-5; reprinted 1952). This work has been largely rendered obsolete by various specialized treatises, but it has not yet been completely superseded.

Theodor Mommsen also wrote the standard work on Roman criminal law ('Römisches Strafrecht', in Binding's *Handbuch*, i. 4, 1899; reprinted 1955). Despite essential advances in research there is no modern general treatment that really takes its place. J. L. Strachan-Davidson's *Problems of Roman Criminal Law* (2 vols., 1912) arose from a critical examination of Mommsen, but is basically dependent on him. Similarly W. Kunkel's 'Untersuchungen zur Entwicklung des römischen Kriminalverfahrens in vorsullanischer Zeit' (*Abhandlungen der Bayerischen Akademie der Wissenschaften*, Neue Folge, 56, 1962) is also restricted to the criminal procedure of the Republic, though it attempts, on the basis of modern specialized literature, to draw a very different picture of its development from that in Mommsen's account. For more specialized literature see below, the notes on §§ 2. 11 and 4.

Of the innumerable textbooks and manuals on Roman private law only a few of the newer works in German can be mentioned here: the comprehensive treatise by M. Kaser in the *Handbuch der Altertumswissenschaft* (2 vols., 1953-9; new edition in course of preparation) and the *Kurzlehrbuch* ('Nutshell') by the same author (6th edn., 1968); between the two in point of length is P. Jörs and W. Kunkel, *Römisches Recht* (3rd edn., 1949), which contains also an account of the history of the sources of law, together with an outline by L. Wenger of the law of civil procedure. The principal English work on Roman private law is that of W. W. Buckland, *A Textbook of Roman Law* (3rd edn., by P. Stein, 1964); more concise and readable works for beginners are those of B. Nicholas, *An Introduction to Roman Law*, 1962; and F. Schulz, *Classical Roman Law*, 1951.

The history of the sources of Roman law is dealt with in the monumental work of L. Wenger, *Die Quellen des römischen Rechts* (1953), a repository of knowledge for many problems, particularly those lying on the margins of Roman legal history. For some important fields, however, and particularly for the history of legal science (dealt with in a rather niggardly way by Wenger) one must still use also (in addition to the special treatises to be mentioned later) the 'Geschichte der Quellen und Literatur des römischen Rechts' by P. Krüger (in Binding's *Handbuch*, i. 2, 2nd edn., 1912), a model of clarity and thoroughness. Similarly, in *Geschichte der Quellen des römischen Rechts* (4th edn., 1919) Theodor Kipp offers a reliable guide, concise, substantial, and independent. But both books have become obsolete to some extent as a result of modern research and the discovery of new sources.

For a proper understanding of the Roman state and Roman law the student must constantly turn back to the general historical works. For this reason at least a few of the more important accounts of Roman history must be mentioned here. Unequalled in artistic power and in the richness of its perspectives, even though influenced by the views of the nineteenth century and by its author's own political ideals, is Theodor Mommsen's *Römische Geschichte* (volumes i–iii appeared first in 1854–6; volume iv, which was to contain the history of the Principate period, is lacking; volume v, with a wonderful survey of the social, economic, and cultural conditions of the Empire under the Principate appeared in 1885; there were many reprints, also an abridged edition in a single volume; and an English translation, *The History of Rome* (4 vols., latest edn., London, 1913)). German historical writing never again achieved such distinction. The most modern short synopis, with comprehensive bibliography, is that of H. Bengtson, *Grundriß der römischen Geschichte mit Quellenkunde I* (up to A.D. 284; 1967), in I. von Müller's *Handbuch der klassischen Altertumswissenschaft*). An account intended for a wider readership is E. Kornemann's *Römische Geschichte* (Kröner's pocket edition, 2 vols., 5th edn., 1963). Also for the general reader, and very short, though most impressive in its descriptions and explanations of decisive political events is the *Römische Geschichte* of A. Heuß (2nd edn., 1964); the last chapter contains an excellent survey of the present state of research. Only two volumes of a broadly planned *Römische Geschichte* by F. Altheim (going up to 338 B.C.) have so far appeared (1951 and 1953). There are two scientific works of significance in Italian, which, however, deal only with early Roman history: E. Pais, *Storia critica di*

Roma durante i primi cinque secoli (4 vols., 1913–20), containing radical criticism of the early Roman sources, and G. de Sanctis, *Storia dei romani* (4 vols., 1907–64, 2nd edn., 1956, unfinished) which is more conservative in its critical attitude. A brief French account, valuable particularly because of its references to the central points of modern research, is A. Piganiol's *Histoire de Rome* (4th edn., 1954). The most comprehensive modern account of Roman history is to be found in the great *Cambridge Ancient History*, a joint work by several authors which deals with Roman history up to A.D. 324 in volumes 7–12 (1928–39). A similar French undertaking, the *Histoire ancienne*, contains partial accounts of Roman history by E. Pais, G. Bloch, L. Homo, and M. Besnier. The *Istoria drevnevo mira* by the great Russian historian M. Rostovtzeff (see below) has been translated into English (*A History of the Ancient World*, 2nd edn., London, 1945) and contains a brief account of Roman history.

The economic history of the Roman Empire, finally, is of the greatest importance for the understanding both of political development and of private law. It has been decisively advanced in modern times by the systematic exploitation of all the sources, including the finds of excavations. The most important work in this field, reminiscent of Mommsen in its forceful mastery of the material and its largeness of perspective, is M. Rostovtzeff, *Social and Economic History of the Roman Empire* (1926, reprinted 1953). An economic history of antiquity (*Wirtschaftsgeschichte des Altertums*) with a great abundance of material is the two-volume work of F. Heichelheim (1938; English edition under the title *An Ancient Economic History*, vol. i, 1958; ii, 1964). Finally, there is *An Economic Survey of Ancient Rome*, a joint work by the Americans T. Frank and his collaborators; it gives a detailed account of the economic development of the various parts of the Empire (1933–40, 6 vols.).

Although this brief bibliographical review permits only occasional references to essays appearing in periodicals, it is no harm to mention at least the leading periodicals in which contributions on Roman legal history regularly appear. The Italian periodicals *Bullettino dell'Istituto di diritto romano 'Vittorio Scialoja'* (cited in older works with the abbreviation *Bull.*, nowadays mostly *BIDR*), *IVRA*, and *Labeo*, together with the *Revue internationale des droits de l'antiquité* published in Belgium, are devoted entirely to Roman law and the other legal systems of antiquity. The same is true—despite the more comprehensive-sounding title— of *Studia et documenta historiae et iuris* (*SDHI*) published by the Papal 'Institutum utriusque iuris'. Other periodicals, such as the *Tijdschrift voor Rechtsgeschiedenis* (*Tijdschr.* or *TS*) published by Dutch and Belgian scholars, and the French *Revue historique de droit français et étranger*, embrace also medieval and modern legal history (particularly that of their own countries). Of the three parallel divisions of the *Zeitschrift der*

Savigny-Stiftung für Rechtsgeschichte (*SZ* or *ZSSt*) the 'Romanistische Abteilung' is devoted to the history of Roman law from the earliest to modern times, and to the other legal systems of antiquity. All these periodicals contain, as well as essays of varying size, reviews of newly published books. A very wide-ranging and complete list of all newly published works on ancient legal history—including essays in periodicals, reviews, and obituary notices—will be found each year in *IVRA*, while *Studia et documenta* contains from time to time a list of published source-material and of research in the special areas of legal papyri and of epigraphy. An Italian publication called *Index*, with the sub-title *International Survey of Roman Law*, which appeared for the first time in 1970, contains essays, numerous reviews, and also reports on new publications on Roman law in different countries.

Formerly it was not uncommon for articles on legal history to be published in periodicals which were primarily devoted to modern law (e.g. the German *Archiv für die zivilistische Praxis*, the Italian *Archivio giuridico*, or the English *Law Quarterly Review*), but this has almost entirely ceased, as a consequence of sharper divisions between the different branches of legal study and the increased number of periodicals specializing in legal history. An exception is *The Irish Jurist* (new series begun in 1966) which regularly contains about an equal volume of articles on both modern and historical jurisprudence.

The large number of periodicals in other spheres of the study of antiquity which are of importance to the legal historian (ancient history, classical philology, comparative philology, Byzantine studies, archaeology, papyrology, epigraphy) cannot be listed here, but will be found very completely listed in Bengtson's *Einführung in die alte Geschichte* (6th edn., 1969).

On § 1 (The city state as the starting-point of Roman legal development)

The early period of Rome is one of the most difficult for historical research because of the fragmentary and unreliable nature of the ancient sources (first recognized fully by B. G. Niebuhr, 1776–1831). Even the oldest Roman historiography (the so-called annalistic literature), which began in the second century B.C. and of which only small fragments survive, was clearly based on a very scanty knowledge of real events and conditions before the fourth century. It filled the gaps with legends, which then emerged for the first time into an apparently historical context, and more and more with arbitrary inventions the purpose of which was often the glorification of certain noble families. These were concocted from known historical happenings or even from the conditions of the writer's own times. It was from these annals that, in their turn, the historians of the Augustan period (Livy, Diodorus, Dionysius of Halicarnassus, and others) drew for their own writings; and they are our literary sources for the early period of Roman history. The point at which we may claim greater reliability for the sources, and the extent to which credible reports are contained even in the predominantly legendary accounts, are very disputed questions. On the whole the legal and historical research of the last few decades has tended to find the Roman sources rather more acceptable than did the radical criticism of an earlier generation. In particular, the most important of these sources, the list of consuls from the beginning of the Republic onwards (the *fasti consulares*), again enjoys widespread confidence.

Nevertheless we must rely largely on inferences from later conditions particularly for our knowledge of the early Roman social and political system; the rigid traditionalism of the Romans offers at least some guarantee for the correctness of this procedure. Valuable clues may be found too in linguistic history, and a careful comparative treatment of other early commonwealths and legal systems can help. The archaeological finds, which have become increasingly important in the last few decades for purely historical research (though they have also raised more problems than they have solved), are not so important for the legal historian, especially as epigraphic evidence from this period survives only in a few very isolated instances.

In P. de Francisci's *Primordia civitatis* (*Studia et documenta*, 2, 1959; see critiques by U. Coli, *Studi Senesi*, 71, part 3, 1959, and W. Kunkel, *Zeitschrift der Savigny-Stiftung*,[1] 77 (1960), 345 ff.) the beginnings of the Roman commonwealth are dealt with in great detail and with an admirable mastery of the whole field. The general accounts of Roman constitutional law and of Roman history mentioned above are also useful. To these may be added the following works, which deal only with the history of the Roman early period or of the Republic: J. Beloch, *Römische Geschichte bis zu den punischen Kriegen* (1926), a work of this important historian's old age, probably not quite in the same class as his great treatment of Greek history, and often very radical in his criticism of the sources, but still one of the most important contributions to early Roman history; A. Alföldi, *Early Rome and the Latins* (1965), with new and to a great extent very persuasive theories on the relationship of Rome with the Latins and on the early development of the *ager Romanus* and of the area of the Roman jurisdiction. The most recent German account of Roman history in republican times is that of J. Vogt, *Römische Geschichte*, i, *Die römische Republik* (4th edn., 1959); see also the stimulating works of F. Altheim—which need, however, to be critically read— *Epochen der römischen Geschichte* (1934), and *Rom und Italien* (2 vols., not dated). The monographic literature on early Roman constitutional history is too extensive to be adequately surveyed here; it can be found in the general treatises of Siber and de Martino; and, for the earliest

[1] All citations of this periodical refer to its Roman law division (*Romanistische Abteilung*).

times, very fully in de Francisci's *Primordia civitatis*. An outstanding
critical review of the most important problems of the early history of
the Roman state is given by A. Momigliano, *Journal of Roman Studies*,
55 (1963), 95 ff.

The following is a small selection of works of a more general character.
On the early Roman state, J. Beloch, *Der italische Bund* (1880), and
Römische Geschichte, pp. 144 ff.; Alföldi, *Early Rome*, 296 ff. R. E. A.
Palmer's *Archaic Community of the Romans* (1970) deals mainly with the
curiate constitution and reaches daring conclusions on the internal history of Rome up to 367 B.C. On the (local) *tribus*-division and its development and political significance, see L. Ross Taylor, *The Voting Districts
of the Roman Republic* (1960). The same author has produced a thorough
and graphic account, in *Roman Voting Assemblies* (1966), of the composition and procedure of the Roman popular assemblies (though restricted
to the period after the Second Punic War). On the patricians and the
senatorial aristocracy: A. Alföldi, 'Der frührömische Reiteradel und seine
Ehrenabzeichen' (1952), with new views as to the origin of the patrician
class; F. Münzer, *Römische Adelsparteien* (1920), a work which reached
important conclusions on the development of the senatorial nobility in
the mid and late Republic. On the kingship: U. Coli, 'Regnum' (*Studia
et Documenta Historiae et Iuris*, 17, 1951, 1 ff.); W. Kunkel in 'Ius et
Lex' (*Festgabe für M. Gutzwiller* (1959), pp. 3 ff.). Basic material on the
magistracy and on magistral power: L. Wenger, *Hausgewalt und Staats-
gewalt im römischen Altertum* (1924); F. Leifer, *Die Einheit des Gewalt-
gedankens im römischen Staatsrecht* (1914) and *Studien zum antiken
Ämterwesen I* ('Zur Vorgeschichte des römischen Führeramts', 1931);
A. Magdelain, *Recherches sur l'imperium* (1968). The treatise of A. Heuß
(which has attracted much notice in modern literature), 'Zur Entwicklung des Imperiums des römischen Oberbeamten' (*Zeitschrift der
Savigny-Stiftung*, 64, 1944, 57 ff.), is directed against the tendency to
emphasize the original unity and universality of the magistral *imperium*,
a tendency represented especially by Wenger and Leifer. See there also
(pp. 104 ff.) basic remarks on the right of *provocatio*; Heuß's theme is
further developed by J. Bleicken in the same *Zeitschrift* (vol. 76, 1959,
pp. 324 ff.); and see too W. Kunkel, 'Untersuchungen zur Entwicklung
des römischen Kriminalverfahrens in vorsullanischer Zeit', 25 ff. A most
instructive contrast between the idealized picture of the Greek historian
Polybius of the Roman constitution in the sixth book of his history with
the constitutional realities of the Roman republic is contained in the
work of K. von Fritz, *The Theory of the Mixed Constitution in Antiquity*
(1954). A list of all the known holders of the Roman magistracies has
been drawn up by T. R. Broughton, *The Magistrates of the Roman Republic* (2 vols. and supplement, 1951–60). The most convenient edition
of the *fasti consulares* is that of A. Degrassi, *Fasti Capitolini* (1954).

On § 2 (*The* ius civile *of early times*)

What has been said of the sources for the early Roman period and of methods of research holds true also for the history of civil law. Between the remains of the Twelve Tables preserved in scattered individual citations in the literary sources and our knowledge about the law of the later Republic there yawns a great gap which can only be filled by inferences from later law and by the methods of comparative law. The research of the last decades has achieved (apart from several not very convincing hypothetical theories) some valuable perspectives and reached some important conclusions. More details can be found in the textbooks on Roman private law; here we may just mention the two important works of M. Kaser, *Eigentum und Besitz im älteren römischen Recht* (2nd edn., 1956) and *Das altrömische Ius* (1949), together with the broadly planned *Introduction to Early Roman Law* (5 vols. up to 1954) by the Danish legal historian C. W. Westrup. Literature on the Twelve Tables will be found in W. Kunkel, *Römisches Recht*, 3rd edn., pp. 3 and 392, and in F. Wieacker's treatise in the *Revue internationale des droits de l'antiquité*, 3, 1956, 459 ff. What is said in the text about the criminal law of the Twelve Tables rests on the author's own essay on pre-Sullan criminal procedure mentioned above, and on the works of K. Latte referred to in notes 117 and 131. The popular statutes known to us are collected and discussed in G. Rotondi's *Leges publicae populi Romani* (1912). On the political backgrounds of the private law statutes see F. Wieacker, *Vom römischen Recht*, 2nd edn., pp. 45 ff.; D. Daube, *Forms of Roman Legislation* (1956) has investigated the forms of speech and thought of Roman statutes. Finally, important insights into the essence of ancient Roman law are provided by Max Weber's legal sociology (*Grundriß der Sozialökonomik*, iii, 1922; improved new edition by J. Winckelmann in *Soziologische Texte*, 2, 1960).

On § 3. 1 (*City state and Empire*)

Nowhere in the literary sources for the Republic and Principate do we find a systematic account of the organization of the Roman Empire. Rome itself and urban Roman politics preoccupied the attention of the ancient authors who dealt with Roman history to such an extent that even the most fundamental measures of imperial organization are often mentioned only in passing, or must be inferred from the context. Abundant material on the administration of a province is found only in the prosecution speeches of Cicero against the governor of Sicily, C. Verres; but even these must be exploited critically, because the selection of material and the style of its presentation are entirely determined by the purposes of the prosecution. Cicero's letters contain a little information about his own governorship in Cilicia. From the Principate we have the correspondence with Trajan of C. Plinius Secundus as governor of Bithynia, together with some modest remains of jurists' writings dealing with provincial government.

Modern research has gathered together the scattered reports from the literary sources and has supplemented them from inscriptions, which admittedly offer no important evidence until towards the end of the Republic, when we have, for example, a large fragment from a municipal regulation for Italy which probably goes back to Julius Caesar—the *Lex Julia municipalis* (Bruns, *Fontes*, 7th edn., pp. 102 ff.)—and parts of the city laws of Tarentum and of Urso—the modern Osuna in Spain (Bruns, ibid., pp. 112 ff.). Then, in the Principate, the documents of imperial administration preserved in inscriptions and on papyri become extremely abundant. But, in general, much is uncertain and disputed, so far as the beginnings of the Roman Imperium are concerned. The present book has attempted only to indicate the main outlines which are more or less definitely established. Of modern literature we may mention: E. Täubler, *Imperium Romanum* (1913); A. Heuß, *Die völkerrechtlichen Grundlagen der römischen Außenpolitik in republikanischer Zeit* (1933); W. Dahlheim, *Struktur und Entwicklung des römischen Völkerrechts im 3. und 2. Jahrhundert vor Christus* (1968); J. Beloch, *Der italische Bund* (1880); A. Afzelius, *Die römische Eroberung Italiens* (1942); A. N. Sherwin-White, *The Roman Citizenship* (1939); H. Rudolph, *Stadt und Staat im römischen Italien* (1935); J. Göhler, *Rom und Italien* (1939); G. H. Stevenson, *Roman Provincial Administration* (1939); M. Gelzer, *Gemeindestaat und Reichsstaat in der römischen Geschichte : Vom römischen Staat*, i. 6 ff. The most recent and very detailed general account of republican imperial government is in the second and third volumes of de Martino's *Storia della costituzione romana*, mentioned above.

On § 3. II *and* III (*Economic, social, and internal political development of Rome at the end of the Republic ; the crisis of the Republic*)

The abundant ancient literature on the history of Rome after the Punic Wars survives only in fragments. But wherever we possess the excellent historical work of the Greek Polybius (c. 200–120 B.C.) or the uncritical but detailed and soundly based account of T. Livy (59 B.C.–A.D. 17) we are very accurately informed. The sources for other periods, particularly for parts of the second century B.C., are less satisfactory, but they are enough to give us a relatively clear understanding even of the internal political development of Rome. For the last century B.C. the sources become much more abundant, thanks to the preservation of important contemporary works (Cicero, Caesar, Sallust); in many respects this period is the best-known of all antiquity.

In the accounts of the ancient historians and in the speeches and theoretical writings of Cicero there is plenty of material for the recon-

struction of the republican political order and for the history of its development. There is also a number of important statutes surviving in
inscriptions (examples given above, p. 32). On the broad basis of these
sources there rests Mommsens's great account of republican constitutional law. Modern research has successfully penetrated beyond the mere
institutions and studied the intellectual, social, and economic motives
in the political developments at the end of the Republic. Important
contributions here are: M. Gelzer, *Die Nobilität der römischen Republik*
(1912; now also printed in his *Kleine Schriften*, i, 1962, 17 ff.); E. Meyer,
Cäsars Monarchie und der Prinzipat des Pompeius (1918); F. Münzer,
Römische Adelsparteien (1910); R. Heinze, *Vom Geist des Römertums*
(1936); Lily Ross Taylor, *Party Politics in the age of Caesar* (1949) (along
with her works on the Roman voting assemblies and districts mentioned
above); the work of K. von Fritz already mentioned, *The Theory of the
Mixed Constitution in Antiquity* (1949). Summaries of conditions at the
end of the Republic are contained (in varying frameworks and at varying length) in: W. Kroll, *Die Kultur der ciceronischen Zeit* (2 vols., 1933);
M. Gelzer, 'Die römische Gesellschaft zur Zeit Ciceros', *Kleine Schriften*,
i. 154 ff. C. Meier, *Res publica amissa* (1966), deals with the peculiar and
hopeless nature of the continuing political crisis from the time of Sulla
onwards. A description of the last crisis of the Roman Republic and of
the emergence of the monarchy, in many respects a book of fundamental
importance, is that of the English historian R. Syme, *The Roman Revolution* (1939; reprinted 1952). Often useful, too, is the work (translated into
German) of the Soviet historian N. A. Mashkin, *Zwischen Republik und
Kaiserreich* (1954).

On § 3. IV (*The Principate*)

Our knowledge of the state formed by Augustus and of its later development comes from the ancient historians of the Empire and from
an extraordinary abundance of inscriptions; to these must be added
the papyri found in Egypt, which admittedly are only occasionally informative on conditions outside Egypt itself. The documentary evidence
is extremely important because the historiography of the imperial period
is, perhaps even more than republican historiography, very tendentious
and restricted in its view to urban Roman politics, indeed to the person
of the princeps himself and his relations with a small upper stratum,
mainly the senatorial nobility. This is true even of the greatest historian
of the Principate, Tacitus, in spite of the brilliance of his expositions and
the truth of his psychological insights. (A more favourable judgement of
him is given by R. Syme in his two-volume book *Tacitus* (1958), an
important work for the history of the early Principate.) But since in fact
the importance of the city of Rome and of its organs (including the Senate)
in the political power-game was steadily dwindling, and since the most

outstanding achievements of the Principate lay in the administration of the Empire, the literary sources give in many respects a quite one-sided picture of conditions and one which can only be corrected from documentary sources.

Some fundamental comments on the political system of Augustus are found in the work of the historian Cassius Dio (who wrote about the beginning of the third century); they are in the form of a fictitious conversation between Augustus and his friends Agrippa and Maecenas about the reform of the State (52. 1–40). There is also the account given of himself by Augustus which is preserved in an inscription called the *Monumentum Ancyranum*. Dio is extremely interesting and instructive, but he is influenced by the conditions of his own time and to some extent distorts the true picture of the Augustan achievement; the *Monumentum Ancyranum*, on the other hand, is authentic in the highest degree (edition with standard commentary by Theodor Mommsen, 1865; supplemented by important fragments of another copy found in Antioch in Pisidia, the so-called 'Monumentum Antiochenum' published by W. Ramsey and A. von Premerstein, *Klio*, Beiheft 19, 1927; these exist in more modern editions by J. Gagé, *Res Gestae Divi Augusti*, 2nd edn., 1950). Here Augustus himself is speaking about his own political system; but, significantly, he represents it with great consistency as a mere restoration of the republican constitution, and leaves as far as possible what was revolutionary and new about it—the concentration of decisive functions and of almost all sources of real power in his own hands—in the background.

The contradiction between its formal shape and reality, the shifting of the notional centre from the legal sphere into the world of ideas and slogans not capable of legal appraisement, made it impossible for historians trained in the constitutionalism of the nineteenth century to penetrate the essence of the Augustan system. Thus even Mommsen's famous theory of the 'dyarchy', i.e. of a division of political power between the princeps and the Senate, misses the point (as is today generally admitted). The modern literature on the nature of the Principate is extraordinarily extensive; only a few works can be mentioned here. One which gave a new impetus to studies of the Principate and determined their direction is the essay by E. Schönbauer, 'Wesen und Ursprung des römischen Prinzipats' (*Zeitschrift der Savigny-Stiftung*, 47, 1927, 264 ff.). The first attempt on a grand scale to penetrate the social and ideological context of the Principate was made by A. von Premerstein 'Vom Werden und Wesen des Prinzipats' (*Abhandlungen der Bayerischen Akademie der Wissenschaften, Philosophisch-historische Abteilung*, Neue Folge 15, 1937). As against this approach, the essays by H. Siber, 'Zur Entwicklung der römischen Prinzipatsverfassung und das Führeramt des Augustus' (*Abhandlungen der Sächsischen Akademie der Wissenschaften, Philologisch-*

historische Klasse, 42. 3, 1933 and 42. 4, 1940) remain strictly within the legal field. The much-discussed notion of *auctoritas principis* was dealt with by the French legal historian A. Magdelain (in a work bearing this title, 1947)—excellently as far as republican times, and especially Cicero, were concerned; his exposition of the development of this notion under the Principate is less felicitous. The most recent special study on the notion of 'princeps' in Cicero is E. Lepore's *Il princeps ciceroniano* (1954). The ideology of the Principate is comprehensively discussed in an ingenious and stimulating book by J. Béranger, *Recherches sur l'aspect idéologique du principat* (1953). Many of its socio-historical and ideological aspects are considered in the long article 'Princeps' by L. Wickert, in Pauly–Wissowa, *Realenzyklopädie der klassischen Altertumswissenschaft*, xxii. 2 (1954). For a discussion of these two authors' views on the Principate see W. Kunkel, *Zeitschrift der Savigny-Stiftung*, 75 (1958), 302 ff. G. Tibiletti *Principe e magistrati repubblicani* (1953) deals with relations between the Principate and the republican magistracy. The present writer's views on Augustus and his creation are set forth in greater detail in an essay entitled 'Über das Wesen des augusteischen Prinzipats', *Gymnasium*, 68 (1961), 353 ff., now also published in the collection of essays, edited by W. Schmitthenner, entitled *Augustus* (*Wege der Forschung*, 128; 1969); the entire collection deserves mention. It contains nineteen essays together with (on pp. 565 ff.) a carefully selected bibliography on Augustus and his political achievements.

The administrative apparatus of the Principate is known to us mainly through inscriptions. Their rich contents are masterfully treated in the work of O. Hirschfeld, *Die kaiserlichen Verwaltungsbeamten bis auf Diokletian* (2nd edn., 1905)—now obsolete in many details, but still the standard book. To this must be added monographic works on individual offices (e.g. those of the *praefectus praetorio* and the *praefectus Aegypti*) and office-categories, especially the important books of H. G. Pflaum, *Les procurateurs équestres sous le Haut-Empire romain*, 1950; and *Les carrières procuratoriennes équestres* (3 vols., 1960–1). On the lower grades of the fiscal and provincial administration—staffed by imperial slaves and by soldiers seconded to this service—see A. H. M. Jones, *Studies in Roman Government and Law* (1960), 153 ff. On the development of the *fiscus*, ibid., 101 ff. On the succession problem and on the joint regency see also, in addition to the general works on the Principate, E. Kornemann, *Doppelprinzipat und Reichsteilung im Imperium Romanum* (1930). Social developments during the Principate, specially amongst the upper classes, have in recent years been more clearly assessed with the help of the inscriptions, for this purpose very instructive. The source-material is collected in the *Prosopographia Imperii Romani* (2nd edn. by E. Groag and A. Stein, vols. i–iv, 2, unfinished, 1933–58; the first edition in three volumes is by H. Dessau and others). The composition of the Senate under the Principate has also been examined in a series of monographs which cannot be listed here. A. Stein threw light on the equestrian order in *Der römische Ritterstand* (1927). Methodological and material contributions to these problems can be found in W. Kunkel, *Herkunft und soziale Stellung der römischen Juristen* (1952) and R. Syme, *Tacitus*, ii (1958), 585 ff. The social and economic development of the Principate period in general is described in a masterly fashion in the work of Rostovtzeff mentioned above. Roman colonization and citizenship policy under Caesar and Augustus are dealt with by F. Vittinghoff (1952); an exhaustive account of the Roman citizenship and its extension is given by A. N. Sherwin-White, *The Roman Citizenship* (1939). The most recent comprehensive treatment of the *constitutio Antoniniana* is the essay by Ch. Sasse, *Die Constitutio Antoniniana* (1958); in this the older literature is comprehensively examined; on Sasse's own additions and interpretation see the objections of H. J. Wolff, *Zeitschrift der Savigny-Stiftung*, 76 (1959), 575 ff.; full references to the literature will be found also in M. Kaser, *Römisches Privatrecht*, i (1955), 193, n. 19. On the question of the so-called double citizenship (closely connected with the problems of the *constitutio Antoniniana*) see below, p. 210. A general history of the Principate is provided by the (unfinished) work of H. Dessau, *Geschichte der römischen Kaiserzeit* (vols. i, ii. 1, 2, 1926-30); recourse should also be had to the *Cambridge Ancient History*. The social conditions of the Principate are dealt with in the celebrated book by L. Friedländer, *Darstellungen aus der Sittengeschichte Roms* (9th edn. by G. Wissowa, 1919-21; a reprint is planned (English translation of the 7th edn. under the title *Roman Life and Manners under the Early Empire*, London, 1908-13).

On § 4 (*Public criminal procedure*)

Section I of this chapter gives the results of the author's own investigations of the development of Roman criminal procedure before Sulla (see above, p. 197). On the jury-court procedure of the late Republic and early Empire (section II) see J. Lengle, *Römisches Strafrecht bei Cicero und den Historikern* (1934) and the author's own article, 'quaestio' in Pauly-Wissowa, *Realenzyklopädie der klassischen Altertumswissenschaft*, xxiv. 720 ff. A number of valuable studies in recent years deal with individual criminal statutes of the late Republic and of Augustus; see in particular J. D. Cloud, in *Zeitschr. der Sav.-Stift.* 80 (1963), 206 ff., and 86 (1969), 258 ff., on the *lex Iulia maiestatis* and the *lex Cornelia de sicariis*; and R. A. Bauman, *The Crimen Maiestatis in the Roman Republic and Augustan Principate* (1967). The most recent discussions on the origin and development of the jurisdiction of the princeps himself and of the Senate are in J. M. Kelly, *Princeps Iudex* (1957); J. Bleicken, 'Senatsgericht und Kaisergericht' (*Abhandlungen der Göttinger Akademie der Wissenschaften, Phil.-hist. Klasse*, Neue Folge 53, 1962); W. Kunkel, on the rise of the Senate's jurisdiction, in the *Sitzungsberichte der Bayerischen Akademie der Wissenschaften*, Phil.-hist. Klasse, 1969, 2; and A. H. M. Jones, *Studies in Roman Government and Law* (1960), 69 ff. On the Roman system of punishment and its development see E. Levy, 'Die römische Kapitalstrafe' (*Sitzungsberichte der Heidelberger Akademie der Wissenschaften*, 1930-1, no. 5); E. Levy, 'Gesetz und Richter im kaiserlichen Strafrecht' in *Bullettino dell'Istituto di diritto romano*, 45 (1938), 57 ff.; U. Brasiello, *La repressione penale nel diritto romano* (1937).

On § 5 (The development of private law in Rome the capital city and in the world empire)

On Roman guest-law see Mommsen, *Römische Forschungen*, i (1864), 326 ff. His interpretation did not, however, remain undisputed; see in particular A. Heuß, *Die völkerrechtlichen Grundlagen der römischen Außenpolitik* (1933) and de Martino, *Storia della costituzione romana*, ii. 1, 11 ff. *Ius gentium* is not studied in isolation by Roman or modern jurists but appears in the context of the private law system embedded in the *ius civile*, which was valid only for Roman citizens. The nature of the *ius gentium* has been discussed in modern times by E. Schönbauer, *Zeitschrift der Savigny-Stiftung*, 49 (1929), 383 ff; Max Kaser in the same *Zeitschrift*, 69 (1939), 67 ff.; W. Kunkel, *Festschrift Paul Koschaker*, ii (1939), 1 ff.; M. Lauria, in the same *Festschrift*, i. 258 ff.; G. Lombardi, *Sul concetto di ius gentium* (1947) and *Ricerche in tema di ius gentium* (1946).

The problem of imperial law and native law was discovered and at the same time largely solved in the epoch-making book of L. Mitteis, *Reichsrecht und Volksrecht in den östlichen Provinzen des römischen Kaiserreichs* (1891). With this work there began a period during which legal history concerned itself closely with the legal life of Greek Egypt and, going further afield, with the pre-Hellenistic law of Greece (i.e. the law in force before the time of Alexander the Great) and with the ancient oriental systems of the Sumerians, Babylonians, Assyrians, Hittites, and Egyptians. A steady supply of newly discovered documents nourished these studies: papyri from Egypt, Greek inscriptions, cuneiform clay tablets, and cylinders from Mesopotamia and other parts of Further Asia, including laws and codes of considerable size, as, for example, the law-code of the Babylonian king Hammurabi (*c.* 1700 B.C.), the antique Greek city law of Gortyn in Crete, and the city law of the Hellenistic metropolis of Alexandria. Jurists now began to study the old oriental languages in order to read these sources in the original. A whole literature arose on the legal world of the ancient East and of the Greco-Hellenistic area. The results of this research were an extraordinary expansion of the perspectives of legal historians, the discovery of numerous parallels between legal systems whose development could not be explained by derivation one from the other, and the consequent recognition of the fact that for certain economic and social situations there is only a limited possible number of legal formulations, which are realized in the individual legal systems according to their environment and the stage of their cultural development. This recognition was of great importance for historical comparative law. In addition, many developmental connections between the Greco-Hellenistic legal world and later Roman legal history were perceived (this was what was chiefly being aimed at in the first place). Yet at the same time it was just the far-reaching independence of Roman legal development, even in later times, that came into relief. It was seen that there could be such a thing as ancient legal history only in the sense of a comparative study of the manifold points of contact of the legal systems which grew up in ancient cultures, but not in the sense of any continuous development from the ancient East up to the threshold of the Middle Ages.

After Mitteis the relation of imperial law and national law was again investigated by E. Schönbauer, *Zeitschrift der Savigny-Stiftung*, 51 (1931), 277 ff.; 57 (1937), 309 ff.; and 62 (1942), 267 ff. See also F. de Visscher, *Nouvelles études de droit romain* (1949), pp. 51 ff. Other works in this field are mentioned by Gaudemet, *La formation du droit séculier et du droit de l'église aux IVe et Ve siècles* (1957), p. 221, n. 2. Much disputed is, in particular, the question raised by Schönbauer as to the importance for the survival of national law of the so-called double citizenship, i.e. the provincials' membership both of the Roman and of their own native citizen bodies. Reference to the literature will be found in Kaser, *Das römische Privatrecht*, i. 193, n. 15, and Gaudemet, op. cit., p. 121, n. 1. See also the essay of D. Nörr, *Tijdschrift voor Rechtsgeschiedenis*, 31 (1953), 525 ff., especially 556 ff.

The standard work on which the section 'Sources of Law and Strata in Law' is based is still that of M. Wlassak, *Kritische Studien zur Theorie der Rechtsquellen im Zeitalter der klassischen römischen Juristen* (1884). On the question of the amalgamation of *ius civile* and *ius honorarium* see below, p. 215.

On § 6 (*Civil jurisdiction and magistral law*)

We know the civil procedure of the republican period and of the Principate mainly from the fourth book of the *Institutes* of Gaius and from the writings of Cicero, especially his forensic speeches; in Justinian, on the other hand, its traces have largely disappeared, because by the time of the codification another kind of procedure (the so-called *cognitio*-procedure) had long been in force. Both the fairly elementary account by Gaius, which is chiefly confined to an introduction to the procedural formula-system, and Cicero's references to procedure presuppose a great deal which was familiar to their contemporaries from seeing it every day in the Forum, but which for us requires a laborious process of rediscovery. For this reason, the accurate exploration of early Roman and classical procedure is one of the most difficult tasks of legal history. Our exposition, which is necessarily restricted to essentials, is based on an interpretation of Roman civil procedure which differs in some important respects from that of M. Wlassak, which, grounded and defended in numerous works, was for long the prevailing one.

Wlassak's view was summarized by L. Wenger in his *Institutionen des römischen Zivilprozeßrechts* (1925). The present position of modern research will be found in M. Kaser's *Das römische Zivilprozeßrecht* (1966; published in the series *Handbuch der klassischen Altertumswissenschaft*). Besides this thorough and exhaustive treatise three Italian works—all of them published lecture-courses—deserve mention: G. I. Luzzatto, *Procedura civile romana* (3 volumes, 1948–50; it goes up only to the rise of the formulary procedure); G. Pugliese, *Il processo civile romano* (so far vol. i, 1961–2, on the *legis actiones*, and vol. ii. 1, 1963, with the beginning of the account of the formulary procedure, have appeared; and A. Biscardi, *Lezioni sul processo civile romano e classico* (n.d.). J. M. Kelly provides in *Roman Litigation* (1966) not a description of the law of procedure, but a series of studies on the realities of Roman judicial practice and, in particular, of its shortcomings (the handicaps of the socially weaker party, the corruption and ineffectiveness of the judicial system, etc.).

Of the German monographs, apart from some critical beginnings in Wenger, an essay by M. Kaser, in the *Festschrift für Leopold Wenger*, i (*Münchener Beiträge zur Papyrusforschung und antiken Rechtsgeschichte*, 34), pp. 106 ff. introduced the break with the basic conceptions of Wlassak. Important advances along these lines were made by the treatises of G. Broggini, *Iudex arbiterve* (1957) and G. Jahr, *Litis contestatio* (1960). Some new points of view on the early Roman judicial system are contained in the author's studies on the development of Roman criminal procedure (see above, p. 197); and these have led to certain changes in the present edition. There is a penetrating monograph on the *legis actiones* by H. Lévy-Bruhl, *Recherches sur les actions de la loi* (1960), a summary of earlier studies by the same author.

For the connection between the rise of the formulary procedure and the beginnings of praetorian creation of law, see especially the above-mentioned work of G. Broggini. On the origin of the *bonae fidei iudicia* see most recently F. Wieacker, *Zeitschrift der Savigny-Stiftung*, 80 (1963), 1 ff.

The difficult task of reconstructing the praetorian edict from the commentaries of the mid and late classical jurists was, after unsuccessful attempts by earlier scholars, accomplished in a masterly fashion by

O. Lenel. His *Edictum perpetuum* (3rd edn., 1927; reprinted 1956) is the starting-point for every investigation in the field of classical private law. A reproduction of the text of the Edict (based on the 2nd edn. of Lenel's book, 1907) is contained also in Bruns, *Fontes* (7th edn.), pp. 211 ff.

We possess some modest remains of older versions of the Edict of the *praetor urbanus*, mainly in the speeches of Cicero, who also gives (in a letter to his friend Atticus, 6. 1. 15) a short account of his own edict for the province of Cilicia. Bits of the provincial edict for Sicily of C. Verres will be found in Cicero's great prosecution speech against this governor. The remains of a commentary on the *edictum provinciale*, composed by Gaius about the middle of the second century and preserved in Justinian (was this a commentary on a uniform edict for all the provinces or merely for the edict of a single province?) show no departures from the edict of the *praetor urbanus*. The edictal style is investigated by M. Kaser in the *Festschrift für F. Schulz*, ii (1951), 21 ff.

On § 7 (*Jurisprudence and jurists' law*)

Roman legal science did not, so far as we can see, concern itself with its own history. For this reason we possess no more than the scanty outline (mentioned above, pp. 104 and 107) of the history of legal science which was included in the Digest (1, 2. 2) of Justinian from the *enchiridium* of Pomponius. We find a certain amount about the history of republican jurisprudence in Cicero also, who, by the way, seems to have been used by Pomponius (or his informant). These sources are supplemented by some scattered remarks in Roman historical and antiquarian literature. Numerous eulogistic inscriptions inform us of the official career of such jurists of the Empire who were also distinguished in the state service (examples are given above, pp. 108 sq.). Finally, we have the remnants of the works of the Roman jurists themselves. They are, admittedly, rather taciturn witnesses so far as the lives and personalities of their authors are concerned: only rarely do we find any biographical hints, and the individuality of the author is more or less obscured by the traditional requirements of his trade as to style and method (see above, about p. 112).

This hardly suffices for a full literary history of Roman legal science, and it is understandable that even the accounts given in the standard manuals of P. Krüger and Theodor Kipp (see above, p. 112) hardly get beyond a mere listing of dates. The first real history of Roman jurisprudence is F. Schulz's *History of Roman Legal Science* (1964; there is a German version entitled *Geschichte der römischen Rechtswissenschaft*), an outstanding work, even though many of its assertions seem to invite contradiction. While for Schulz the inner history of jurisprudence and especially the history of its literary forms occupy the most important place, W. Kunkel has attempted, in his *Herkunft und soziale Stellung der römischen Juristen* (2nd edn., 1967), by the methods of prosopographical research to grasp the social development and stratification of republican and classical jurisprudence. O. Lenel's two-volume work, *Palingenesia iuris civilis* (1889) is a compilation of all the fragments from the works of all the jurists of the republican and classical periods, so far as possible in their original thought-sequence, and is of fundamental importance for the understanding of classical legal literature as well as for a knowledge of the individual jurists. H. Fitting's account of the chronology and sequence of the Roman jurists from Hadrian to Alexander, *Alter und Folge der römischen Juristen von Hadrian bis Alexander* (2nd edn., 1908), remains to a large extent the standard work on the subject. Further details and information about jurists not mentioned in this outline can be found in the works of P. Krüger and T. Kipp. Very informative, too, are the articles on the individual jurists in the great *Realenzyclopädie der klassischen Altertumswissenschaft* of Pauly–Wissowa–Kroll. More recent, special studies on individual jurists and their works are listed in the supplement in the second edition of W. Kunkel's book mentioned above (408 ff.); some more extensive works will be mentioned in succeeding paragraphs. Finally, there is the graphic and stimulating sketch of Roman jurisprudence in F. Wieacker's *Vom römischen Recht* (2nd edn.), pp. 128 ff.

An attempt to give an account of the jurisprudence of the Republic was made by P. Jörs (*Römische Rechtswissenschaft zur Zeit der Republik*, 1888), but he only got as far as Cato and thus did not touch the question of Greek influences. The latter became a topic of central interest with the publication, in 1926, of J. Stroux's *Summum ius summa iniuria* (reprinted, along with a further essay, 'Griechische Einflüsse auf die Entwicklung der römischen Rechtswissenschaft gegen Ende der republikanischen Zeit', in *Römische Rechtswissenschaft und Rhetorik*, 1949). Stroux's idea that the interpretative methods of the Roman jurists were decisively influenced by the so-called doctrine of status in rhetorical theory was accepted by some scholars, rejected by others. In recent times, for instance, B. Vonglis has followed Stroux: *La lettre et l'esprit de la loi dans la jurisprudence classique et la rhétorique* (1968); while J. Himmelschein has denied any strong influence on the part of rhetoric: *Symbolae Friburgenses in honorem O. Lenel*, 373 ff.; and also, more recently, U. Wesel, *Rhetorische Statuslehre und Gesetzesauslegung der römischen Juristen* (1967). The adoption of dialectical method from Greek philosophy is regarded as the essential element by F. Schulz, *History of Roman Legal Science*, 62 ff., and by H. Coing, *Zeitschr. der Sav.-Stift.*, 69 (1952), 24 ff.; *Studi in onore di V. Arangio-Ruiz*, i (1953), 365 ff.; Coing concentrates mainly on the logical system of Aristotle. J. Miquel has demonstrated that several jurists of the Empire (Proculus, Julian,

Cervidius Scaevola) both knew and applied Stoic logical principles: *Zeitschr. der Sav.-Stift.*, 87 (1970), 85 ff. On the Greek origins of the system of the *Institutes* of Gaius, see F. Wieacker, *Zeitschr. der Sav.-Stift.* 70 (1953), 93 ff. In recent years the problem of Greek influences has been somewhat overshadowed by efforts to establish first of all more precisely the methods of the Roman jurists as such, and to study their definitions, their *regulae iuris*, and their justifications of their decisions (bibliography on this will be found in F. Horak, *Rationes decidendi*, i, 1969, p. 1, n. 2; and see also B. Schmidlin, *Die römischen Rechtsregeln*, 1970). A most important contribution to this new direction of research is the noted work of Th. Viehweg, *Topik und Jurisprudenz* (1953, 4th edn., 1965), in which a contrast is drawn between the method of the Roman jurists as a typical example of working by rules and maxims, and the method of conceptual deduction, though legal historians have contradicted this thesis, or treated it with reserve. On this, and generally, see M. Kaser, 'Zur Methode der römischen Rechtsfindung' (*Nachrichten der Göttinger Akademie der Wissenschaften*, Phil.-hist. Klasse, 1962, 2).

In the field of classical jurisprudence the problem of the *ius respondendi* has been frequently dealt with. Arguments on which the view expressed in the text is based, together with further references, will be found in *Zeitschrift der Savigny-Stiftung*, 66 (1948), 423 ff., and in *Herkunft und soziale Stellung der römischen Juristen*, pp. 281 ff. (see the supplement in the second edition, p. 412). With regard to monographs on individual classical jurists the references above must in general suffice; only a few of the more significant works can be specially mentioned here. The extensive work of A. Pernice, *M. Antistius Labeo* (3 vols., 1879-1900, volume two in its second edition) attempts, after a biographical introduction hardly ninety pages long, to set out on the grand scale the entire content of Roman private law at the beginning of our era. Even though in view of the limited sources such an undertaking could not hope to succeed any more than could the attempt at a real biography of Labeo, this work in fact significantly advanced our knowledge of classical law. On a similar scale but of less scientific importance is the Italian E. Costa's monograph on Papinian (*Papiniano*, 4 vols., 1894-9). The literature on Gaius is very abundant. His *Institutes* are the subject of a commentary, unfinished in three volumes, by F. Kniep, who did not, however, succeed in materially advancing our understanding of this work. (For further commentaries, see below in the references to editions of Gaius.) Of the older treatises concerned with the personality of Gaius, only those are noted on which the hypotheses referred to in the text are based. The identification of Gaius with C. Cassius Longinus was first suggested in the Berlin dissertation of the Rumanian S. Longinescu (*Gaius der Rechtsgelehrte*, 1896), and was then improved by W. Kalb (*Jahresberichte für Altertumswissenschaft*, 89, 1896, pp. 231 ff.; 99, 1901, 2, p. 40), who assumed an anonymous version of the writings of Cassius in the second century. The theory of Gaius as a provincial jurist—still thought probable by many—originated with Theodor Mommsen (*Juristische Schriften*, ii. 26 ff.), first published in 1859. The present author's sceptical attitude is argued fully in *Herkunft und soziale Stellung der römischen Juristen*, pp. 186 ff.; and even the ingenious, but in its conclusions often overbold work of A. M. Honoré, *Gaius* (1962), has not persuaded him to change his mind. (On Honoré's book, see Wieacker's review in *Zeitschr. der Sav.-Stift.*, 81 (1964), 401 ff.) On the relation of the *Institutes* of Gaius to the works of the great classical jurists see the essay of M. Kaser, *Zeitschrift der Savigny-Stiftung*, 70 (1953), 127 ff., which provoked a lively discussion; and—with impressive arguments for the quality of the *Institutes*—W. Flume in the same *Zeitschrift*, 79 (1962), 1 ff. Papers devoted to many aspects of the problems surrounding Gaius will be found in *Gaio nel suo tempo* (*Biblioteca di Labeo*, 31, 1966). Editions of the *Institutes* of Gaius: P. Krüger-G. Studemund in *Collectio librorum iuris anteiustiniani*, i (7th edn., 1923); E. Seckel-B. Kübler in *Jurisprudentiae anteiustinianae reliquiae*, i (1908); also a special edition by Seckel-Kübler, whose 7th edn. (1935) includes the fragments found in Egypt. The second and by far the most important of these finds is available, with what has become a standard commentary, in E. Levy, *Zeitschrift der Savigny-Stiftung*, 54 (1934), 258 ff.; also to be found in his *Gesammelte Schriften*, i. 60 ff. After the Second World War several new editions of Gaius appeared: those of J. Reinach (Paris, 1950), F. de Zulueta (2 vols., text and commentary, Oxford, 1946, 1953), M. David (Leiden, 1948, 2nd edn., 1964; a large edition with philological commentary by David and Nelson has been in course of publication since 1954; three parts, text and commentary, have so far appeared, reaching to the end of book ii). The *Institutes* of Gaius are also contained in the collections of Girard and Riccobono-Baviera-Ferrini mentioned above.

On the section on jurists' law: the amalgamation of civil law and magistral law which began in the classical period and continued in post-classical law has been studied and related to Roman legal development, in particular by the Italian scholar S. Riccobono. Of his writings on this subject we need mention here only his essay 'La fusione del *ius civile* e del *ius praetorium*' (*Archiv für Rechts- und Wirtschaftsphilosophie*, 16, 1923, 503 ff.).

On § 8 (*Imperial law*)

Popular statutes and decrees of the Senate in the Principate survive both in the remains of classical legal literature and in inscriptions. The juristic texts give us the more important ones, but, as a rule, fragmented into short quotations and frequently not in the exact original wording. The inscriptions, on the other hand, apart from the accidents of incomplete survival, give as a rule the full and exact text; but fate has preserved for us, at any rate from the Principate, only statutes and *senatusconsulta* that are of little importance for legal history. The Exceptions are the celebrated *lex de imperio Vespasiani* of the year 69 (see above, p. 59, it is doubtful whether this was in fact a *lex* or a *senatusconsultum*) and the *senatusconsultum Calvisianum* on the *repetundae* procedure before the Senate (see above, p. 59). The texts, including those found in the literature, which were then known, are in Bruns, *Fontes* (7th edn.), pp. 111 ff. (popular statutes) and pp. 191 ff. (*senatusconsulta*). More complete, because more recent, is the collection in the Italian edition of the *Fontes iuris anteiustiniani* done by Riccobono and others, vol. i, 1941 (see above, p. 194).

Most of the imperial constitutions preserved in literature date from no earlier than the Dominate. Still, the Justinianic code and the remains of classical legal literature preserved elsewhere contain a mass of constitution-texts and citations of constitutions of the second and third centuries; these are mostly rescripts. (The citations from constitutions found in the fragments of the classical jurists, more than 1,500 in number, have now been collected by G. Gualandi, *Legislazione imperiale e giurisprudenza*, 1963, vol. i; vol. ii uses this material to illuminate the relation between jurisprudence and imperial legislation.) We have in addition the epigraphic sources which are here more informative than in the cases of popular statutes and *senatusconsulta*. In contrast to the usually abridged texts or mere quotations which we find in the literary sources, the constitutions preserved in inscriptions or in papyri are mostly reproduced in their exact and full wording, although of course the preservation may not be complete. They therefore offer a truer picture of the style and formalities of imperial legislation. In addition to the texts collected in Bruns, *Fontes* (7th edn.) there are several new finds, including, for example, five edicts of Augustus discovered during the Italian excavations at Cyrene, which contain important information on jurisdiction and administration in this province and also on the relationship of princeps and Senate (see above, p. 55, n. 2). Of the extensive literature on these edicts the most important works are those of J. Stroux–L. Wenger, 'Die Augustuschrift auf dem Marktplatz von Kyrene' (*Abhandlungen der Bayerischen Akademie der Wissenschaften, Philos.-hist. Klasse*, 24. 2, 1928) and A. von Premerstein, 'Die fünf neugefundenen Edikte des Augustus aus Kyrene' (*Zeitschrift der Savigny-Stiftung*, 48 (1928), 419 ff.); both contain the text of the edicts. The most recent detailed treatment is F. de Visscher's *Les édits d'Auguste découverts à Cyrène* (1940). Not a *liber mandatorum*, but still a service-instruction of similar kind for an inferior government office of the Egyptian financial administration (which was based in part on *mandata*) is the *Gnomon* of the *Idios Logos*, an extensive papyrus of the Berlin collection (*Berliner griechische Urkunden,* vol. 5, with commentary; there is a further very detailed commentary by S. Riccobono, jr., *Il Gnomon dell'Idios Logos* [1950]; and there is a reprint of the text with explanations also in P. M. Meyer, *Juristische Papyri,* pp. 315 ff.); it provides a good deal of information on Roman private law as well, though this material is peculiarly distorted through the incomprehension of lawyers and through the uninhibitedly fiscal outlook of the provincial financial authority. A number of rescripts of Septimus Severus is contained in the Papyrus Columbia 123 (published by W. L. Westermann and A. A. Schiller, *Apokrimata,* 1954; revised text in H. C. Youtie and A. A. Schiller, *Chronique d'Égypte,* 30, 1955, 327 ff.). A collection of all known constitutions of the individual emperors has been long planned in Italy, but has not yet come into being. So far, all that has appeared is the first part of the *Acta Divi Augusti* (Rome, 1945).

On § 9 (*The state and society in the late Empire*)

What we possess of the historiography of the late Roman Empire varies greatly in value. A few authors of standing, like Ammianus Marcellinus (parts of whose work, written about 390, covering more or less the third quarter of the fourth century are preserved) or Procopius, the historian of Justinian's age, are found side by side with the authors of scanty outlines and chronicles. The historical sources for the third century, the period of transition from Principate to Dominate, are the worst; and, since at this point even epigraphic evidence is generally lacking, the third century A.D. is the darkest period of Roman history since the Punic Wars.

However, we are not driven to rely solely on the reports of the ancient historians for our understanding of the political, social, and constitutional developments of the late Empire. In this context the contents of the imperial laws preserved in the *Codex Theodosianus* are much more abundant and important; and research on this *Codex* is probably not yet complete. (A fund of instruction on the conditions underlying the imperial laws of the *Codex Theodosianus* is provided by the commentary of the humanist Jacobus Godofredus, which first appeared in 1583.) A valuable general survey of the structure of the late Roman state at the beginning of the fifth century is the *Notitia dignitatum,* a sort of official handbook, in which the civil offices and the military commands (with the subordinated units) together with information about official insignia and badges are collected (editions by A. Böcking, 2 vols., 1839–53, with commentary, and by O. Seeck, 1876).

As in the case of the Principate period, so too in that of late Roman history the epigraphic sources have brought new realizations and have taught us to understand properly material which was already known. Among the inscriptions there are documents of great importance, above

all the price-edict of Diocletian of the year A.D. 301 by which an unsuccessful attempt was made to cure the currency and economic crisis,
which had been shaking the Empire since the third century, by means
of a comprehensive system of maximum prices (edition by Theodor
Mommsen and H. Blümner, *Edictum Diocletiani de pretiis rerum venalium*,
1893; see also the essays by Mommsen in *Juristische Schriften*, ii. 292 ff.).
The Egyptian papyrus-documents teach us about the economic and
social conditions and the government of a part at least of the late Roman
Empire as these are mirrored in the happenings of daily life.

In the accounts of Roman constitutional law given by Mommsen and
Siber the constitution of the late Empire is scarcely mentioned apart
from a very scanty summary; but we now have the fifth volume of De
Martino's *Storia della costituzione romana*, which is devoted to this
period; and in the three-volume work of the English historian A. H. M.
Jones, *The Later Roman Empire, 284-602* (1964), we have a very accurate
account, derived at all stages directly from the sources, both of social
and economic conditions and of public administration under the Dominate. This work, so far at any rate as the needs of the legal historian are
concerned, overshadows the older historical works of O. Seeck (*Geschichte
des Untergangs der antiken Welt*, 6 vols.; 4th edn. of vol. i and 2nd edn.
of vols. ii–v, 1920-1) and E. Stein (*Geschichte des spätrömischen Reichs*,
vol. i, 1928; vol. ii in French, under the title *Histoire du Bas-Empire*, ii,
1949; the whole work reprinted in French in 1968). Edward Gibbon's
History of the Decline and Fall of the Roman Empire (published 1776-88,
with numerous later editions) retains its place as a classic example of
the older school of historiography. On important individual questions
of political, social, and economic life in the transition period and in the
late Empire we possess excellent monographs; for instance on the half-
free agricultural tenants tied to the soil (*coloni*), M. Rostowzew (=
Rostovtzeff), *Studien zur Geschichte des römischen Kolonates* (1910): compulsory office and obligations of service in the interests of the State
(*munus*, λειτουργία) are dealt with on the basis of the Egyptian papyri by
F. Oertel, *Die Liturgie* (1917). There is a great deal on the fiscal system
of the late Roman Empire; the most important works will be found in
Rostovtzeff, *Gesellschaft und Wirtschaft*, ii. 373, n. 5. On the administration and on social conditions in Egypt in late Roman times see the
relevant sections in Mitteis-Wilcken, *Grundzüge der Papyruskunde*, and
M. Gelzer, *Studien zur byzantinischen Verwaltung Ägyptens* (1909). On
the 'feudalism' of the late Empire see F. de Zulueta, 'De patrociniis
vicorum' (*Oxford Studies in Social and Legal History*, 1919). On the
ideology of the late Roman Empire see W. Enßlin, 'Gottkaiser und
Kaiser von Gottes Gnaden' (*Sitzungsberichte der Bayerischen Akademie
der Wissenschaften, Philos.-hist. Abt.* 1943, 6) and J. A. Straub, *Vom
Herrscherideal in der Spätantike* (1939). The two works of Alföldi

mentioned above (p. 194) show how the external attributes of the monarch which are characteristic of the Dominate, long thought to be direct borrowings from the neo-Persian kingdom of the late third century A.D., in fact gradually developed in the course of the Principate period. The foundations of the crisis in the third century are dealt with by F. Altheim, *Niedergang der alten Welt: eine Untersuchung der Ursachen* (1952).

The basic work on the history of the judicature and of procedure in the late Roman Empire is still the third volume of M. A. von Bethmann-Hollweg's *Der römische Civilprozeß* (1866). The most important of the later contributions to this topic are those of A. Steinwenter; they have been worked over and proved in detail in the excellent account of late Roman procedure in M. Kaser's *Das römische Zivilprozeß*, 410 ff. New insights into the form and essence of late Roman and particularly of Justinianic procedure have been provided by U. Zilletti (*Studi sul processo civile giustinianeo*, 1965) and, above all, by D. Simon in his penetrating book *Untersuchungen zum justinianischen Zivilprozeß* (1969), which appeared too late to be taken into account in Kaser's work. On the dispensation of justice by bishops, see most recently W. Selb, *Zeitschr. der Sav.-Stift.*, 84 (1967), 162 ff., which contains references to the numerous earlier studies on the subject.

On § 10 (Legal development in the late Empire up to Justinian)

We now have a thorough account of the source-history of the fourth and fifth centuries in the work of J. Gaudemet, *La formation du droit séculier et du droit de l'Église aux IVe et Ve siècles* (1957). In addition, the second volume of M. Kaser's *Römisches Privatrecht*, which appeared in 1959, contains in its introduction a general assessment of post-classical legal development, with abundant references to literature. These works may profitably be consulted in connection with the individual questions mentioned below. A summary review of law and society in late antiquity is given by F. Wieacker: *Recht und Gesellschaft in der Spätantike*, Urban-Buch, 74.

The condition of the sources for the history of post-classical jurisprudence has already been indicated. What little we learn from the Justinianic codification and its Greek commentaries, as well as from some non-legal sources like the letters of the Syrian sophist Libanius (314-93), refers to the law-schools of Beirut and Constantinople. For the rest, research has to content itself with comprehending and arranging the post-classical literature, which is either anonymous or has been handed down under classical names. The account given in the text attempts to appraise the main results of research in recent decades. It was already realized shortly after 1920 that most of the anonymous or pseudonymous writings known to us chiefly from West Roman sources belong to the late third or early fourth centuries. The doctrine, however, that the great mass of pre-Justinianic falsifications in the classical fragments in Justinian's Digest also come from this early period of post-classical jurisprudence is of more recent date. Its first convinced proponent was F. Schulz, *Geschichte der römischen Rechtswissenschaft*, pp. 168, 199, 280 ff.; it was then supported and further developed in special studies by F. Wieacker, *Zeitschrift der Savigny-Stiftung*, 67 (1950), 360 ff., and H. J. Wolff, *Seminar*, 7 (1949), 76 ff.; *Festschrift für F. Schulz*, ii. 145 ff., and others. Most recently, F. Wieacker examined the doctrine again and conclusively in an extensive work, 'Textstufen klassischer Juristen' (*Abhandlungen der Göttinger Akademie der Wissenschaften, Philol.-hist. Klasse*, 3. Folge, No. 45, 1960). One must agree with M. Kaser, *Zeitschrift der Savigny-Stiftung*, 69 (1952), 60 ff., that it contains a certain inherent danger of one-sided exaggeration. Still, it seems in the main convincing, even if proof in individual cases must necessarily remain very fragmentary. A second and extremely important advance in the field of post-classical legal history is, as has been indicated in the text, the opening up of 'vulgar law' by E. Levy. See especially 'West Roman Vulgar Law', 'The Law of Property' (*Memoirs of the American Philosophical Society*, 29, 1951); 'Weströmisches Vulgarrecht, Das Obligationenrecht' (*Forschungen zum römischen Recht* 7, 1956). A penetrating and stimulating study on 'vulgarism and classicism in the law of late antiquity', provoked by Levy's research, has been published by F. Wieacker in the *Sitzungsberichte der Heidelberger Akademie der Wissenschaften* (1955, 3); briefer and easier for the general reader is *Vom römischen Recht*, 2nd edn., 222 ff.

The writings mentioned above which have been handed down independently of Justinian will be found, together with the *Institutes* of Gaius and other remains of classical and post-classical legal literature, in the following collections: P. Krüger-Th. Mommsen-G. Studemund, *Collectio librorum iuris anteiustiniani* (3 vols.: vol. i. the *Institutes* of Gaius; vol. ii, 1878, *Regulae Ulpiani, Pauli Sententiae*; vol. iii, 1890, everything else). They will also be found in the collections of Girard and Riccobono-Baviera-Ferrini mentioned above. F. Schulz's 'Die Epitome Ulpiani des Codex Vaticanus Reginae 1128' (*Juristische Texte für Vorlesungen und Übungen*, 3, 1926) is a special edition of the *Regulae Ulpiani* with a critical and analytical commentary. In 1954 there appeared in the United States an exact analysis of the early titles in the *sententiae* of Paulus by E. Levy: *Pauli Sententiae, a Palingenesia of the Opening Titles as a Specimen of Research in West Roman Vulgar Law*; it demonstrates the gradual transformation of this post-classical text from the end of the third up to the fifth century. The extensive literature on the *Collatio legum Mosaicarum et Romanarum*, which is mostly concerned with the chronological origin and purpose of this code, is given most completely in F. Schulz, *Geschichte der römischen Rechtswissenschaft*, 394, n. 1. The Visigothic *interpretatio* on the *Pauli sententiae* was specially published by M. Kaser and F. Schwarz in 1956 under the title *Die Interpretatio zu den Paulussentenzen*.

On the law-school of Beirut we possess a careful and profound monograph by P. Collinet, 'Histoire de l'école de Beyrouth (*Études historiques sur le droit de Justinien*, ii, 1925). The methods of the East Roman lawschools are examined and compared with the mode of work of the medieval glossators by F. Pringsheim, 'Beryt und Bologna' (*Freiburger Festschrift für O. Lenel*, 1921, 204 ff.). The longer known remains of the literary works of these schools, especially the so-called *scholia Sinaitica*, will be found in Seckel-Kübler, ii. 2. On the recently found fragments of such works see F. Schulz, *Geschichte der römischen Rechtswissenschaft*, pp. 411 ff. The sixth-century commentaries on the Justinianic codification, in particular Thalelaeus' commentary on the Codex, also contain quotations from the literature of the pre-Justinianic law-schools; this evidence is analysed by D. Simon, *Zeitschr. der Sav.-Stift.* 87 (1970), 315 ff. The Syrio-Roman code is published by C. G. Bruns and E. Sachau (1880); Syrian recensions discovered later will be found in Sachau, *Syrische Rechtsbücher*, i (1907). The fact that this code contains only Roman law was first recognized by the Semitic scholar C. A. Nallino, *Studi in onore di P. Bonfante*, i (1930), 201 ff. See now W. Selb's essay published in the *Müchener Beiträge zur Papyrusforschung und antiken Rechtsgeschichte* (vol. 49), 'Zur Bedeutung des syrisch-römischen Rechtsbuches', in which it is demonstrated that the assumption of Greek and Oriental elements in the code rested on linguistic and juristic misunderstandings.

The fairly extensive and mostly Italian literature of the last decades on later Imperial legislation is mainly concerned with the question of Greek-Oriental and especially of Christian influences. Detailed references will be found in the notes on literature in Jörs-Kunkel-Wenger, *Römisches Recht* 397. See also the three-volume work of B. Biondi, *Il diritto romano cristiano* (1952-4), and finally J. Gaudemet, *L'église dans l'Empire romain* (1958) with very cautious remarks on the influence of Christian doctrine on Roman law, 507 ff. On the *Codices Gregorianus* and *Hermogenianus* see in particular G. Rotondi, *Scritti giuridici*, i. 111 ff.; a collection of the remains of these codes surviving independently of the *Codex Justinianus* is in Krüger-Mommsen-Studemund, *Collectio* (see above), iii; and a restoration of the *Codex Hermogenianus*, including those *constitutiones* taken over by Justinian, will be found in A. Cenderelli's *Ricerche sul Codex Hermogenianus* (1965). The standard edition of the *Codex Theodosianus* is that of Mommsen: *Theodosiani libri XVI*, vol. i (1905); the second volume, P. M. Meyer, contains the postTheodosian novels. P. Krüger's edition of the *Codex Theodosianus* remained unfinished (book i, 1923). There is an English translation of the

Codex Theodosianus by C. Pharr (1952). As to the commentary of Jacobus Godofredus see above.

The opinion, unchallenged since the time of the humanists, that the *Edictum Theoderici* came from the Ostrogothic king Theoderic the Great has been disproved by P. Rasi, *Archivio giuridico*, 145 (1953), 105 ff. and G. Vismara, *Cuadernos del Instituto Jurídico Español*, Roma, 5 (1956), 49 ff. The idea that it was issued under the Visigothic ruler Theoderic II by the Roman *praefectus praetorio Galliarum* Magnus was suggested by A. d'Ors, 'Estudios Visigóticos', ii 'El Código de Eurico' (1960), 8 (it gained the agreement of E. Levy, *Zeitschrift der Savigny-Stiftung*, 79, 1962, 479 f.). In 'Estudios Visigóticos', ii (published in the volume of the *Cuadernos* mentioned above, pp. 91 ff.), d'Ors defends the theory that all Visigothic law-codes had territorial validity, i.e. one not restricted to Romans or to Goths. The *Edictum Theoderici*, the *Codex Euricianus* and the *Lex Romana Burgundionum* will be found in the great source-collection on the history of medieval Germany, the *Monumenta Germaniae* (*Leges* section, vol. V, i, iii) and in Riccobono–Baviera, *Fontes iuris Romani*, ii. A new edition of the *Codex Euricianus* on the basis of a new reading of the manuscript and a penetrating analysis of this code are provided by d'Ors, 'Estudios Visigóticos', ii (see above); see, on this, the review by Levy cited above. The *Lex Romana Visigotorum* must be consulted in the old edition by G. Hänel (1849); a new printing is planned.

On § 11 (*The codification of Justinian*)

Some of the many works on the Emperor Justinian, his policies, and his code, are: the extensive monograph by C. Diehl, *Justinien et la civilisation byzantine* (1901); the no less grandly planned work of B. Rubin, *Das Zeitalter Justinians*, of which so far we have only the first volume (1960); the *History of the Byzantine State* by G. Ostrogorsky (English version, Oxford, 1956); on Justinian's codification, see B. Biondi, *Giustiniano primo principe e legislatore cattolico* (1936) (a book particularly concerned with the Christian elements in the codification); the essays of F. Pringsheim which are gathered together in his *Gesammelte Abhandlungen*, ii (1961), 9 ff. ('Die archaistische Tendenz Justinians'; 'Die Entstehungszeit des Digestenplanes und die Rechtsschulen'; 'The Character of Justinian's Legislation'; 'Justinian's Prohibition of Commentaries to the Digest'); G. G. Archi's essays 'Giustiniano uomo del suo tempo' and 'La valutazione critica del Corpus Iuris', both in *Giustiniano legislatore* (1970); the work of K.-H. Schindler (based on a large number of specialized studies), *Justinians Haltung zur Klassik* (1966), and the appraisal of the codification to be found in F. Wieacker's book *Vom römischen Recht* (2nd edn., 242 ff.).

As can be seen from the account given above, research into the course taken by the codification has concentrated mainly on the composition of the Digest, and the most important works on this subject have already been noted in this connection. It remains only to mention, as a summing-up of the older studies, H. Krüger's book *Die Herstellung der Digesten* (1922). Basic research on the sources of the *Codex Justinianus* and on the *Quinquaginta decisiones* will be found in the first volume of G. Rotondi's *Scritti giuridici* (1922). The source-analysis of the *Institutes* has been decisively advanced by C. Ferrini (*Opere giuridiche*, ii, 1928, 307 ff.). On the Novels of Justinian: P. Noailles, *Les Collections de novelles* (2 vols., 1912–14). The character and origin of the *Authenticum* and of the *Epitome Iuliani* is discussed by H. J. Scheltema, *Tijdschrift voor Rechtsgeschiedenis*, 31 (1963), 275 ff. The substantive content of the Novels is disclosed by N. van der Wal in his *Manuale Novellarum* (1944).

The philological work of producing what is today the standard text of the Justinianic codification was done by Mommsen and his collaborators. The standard edition of the Digest is the great one of Mommsen (*Digesta Justiniani Augusti*, 2 vols., 1870; reprint planned), that of the *Codex Justinianus* is the edition of P. Krüger (1877). These form the bases for the corresponding parts of the general edition of the *Corpus iuris civilis* by Mommsen, Krüger, Schoell, and Kroll (reprinted 1954). The *Institutes* are there handled by P. Krüger (and there is a separate edition of them), the Novels by Schoell and Kroll. By comparison with this stereotype edition (which offers the same text in all editions) older general editions of the *Corpus iuris* can be used only as auxiliary material. A pocket edition of the Digest, which rests basically on Mommsen's text, is that of P. Bonfante-C. Fadda-C. Ferrini-S. Roccobono-V. Scialoja, *Digesta Justiniani Augusti* (2 vols. on thin paper, 1908–31).

Mommsen's edition of the Digest, one of his great masterpieces, follows the editorial methods which were thought valid by the philologists of his time. It was believed that, if at all possible, one should restore the archetypal source, i.e. the manuscript from which all later ones derived, whether by gathering it from the surviving manuscripts or by reconstructing it with their aid. In fact Mommsen was able to prove that the very numerous manuscripts of the Digest which were made in Italy in the high and late Middle Ages (the so-called vulgate tradition) all went back to a manuscript which was no longer available (the *Codex S*), and that this in its turn came from a manuscript made in the sixth century in Constantinople and now to be found in the Laurentine library in Florence (the *Florentina*). He thus saw in the *Florentina* the archetype of all the Digest versions, and used it to support all his textual restorations, while he gave the 'vulgate' manuscripts very little attention. However, H. U. Kantorowicz showed (in the *Zeitschrift der Savigny-Stiftung*, 30, 1909, 183 ff.) that the writer of the *Codex S* had used, in addition to the *Florentina*, another manuscript independent of the latter, which here and there had given the correct text. Since that time, more-over, philological editorial methods have changed considerably; nowa-days we reckon more than before with the possibility of a mixture of different source-threads, and therefore no longer place so much emphasis as in Mommsen's time on the reconstruction of an archetype. The essay of J. Miquél, *Zeitschrift der Savigny-Stiftung*, 80 (1963), 233 ff., has shown by means of a series of examples how modern methods of source-criticism on the text of the Digest can improve on Mommsen and Kanto-rowicz. One of the most interesting results of this work is the plausible hypothesis that the Justinianic codifiers carried out certain corrections on the text even after the publication of the Digest, that these correc-tions were inserted in the manuscripts already in circulation, but that they did not get as far as the *Florentina* (or its original), while on the other hand they were communicated to the vulgate sources through the other original of the *Codex S*.

In 1916 F. Schulz provided in his *Einführung in das Studium der Digesten* both an account of the problems of the handing-down of the Digest (according to the contemporary position) and a clear and intel-ligible introduction to the methods of interpolation-criticism. The principles developed and exemplified by Schulz are mostly still valid today in the practical handling of source-criticism, although since then opinions on the historical bases of interpolation-research and about its importance for the history of legal doctrines have greatly changed (see pp. 172 sqq., above). Only some supplementary references need now be given. The period of intensive interpolation-research began in Germany in the eighties of the last century. In 1887 O. Gradenwitz published a whole book on interpolations in the Digest (*Interpolationen in den Digesten*), which is mainly devoted to the method and criteria of criti-cism aimed at testing the genuineness of texts. Even in the previous decades, in Italy, I. Alibrandi (d. 1894) had begun to use this form of criticism on the Justinianic sources as a means of recovering the classical law; but he had no successors until interpolation-criticism had asserted itself in Germany also. The zenith of radical interpolation-criticism was marked in Germany by the writings of G. von Beseler (*Beiträge zur Kritik der römischen Rechtsquellen*, i-iv, 1910-20, and essays, mostly in the *Zeitschrift der Savigny-Stiftung*, 43, 1922, onwards) and in Italy by the works of E. Albertario (collected in *Studi di diritto romano*, 6 vols., 1933 ff.). In other countries, e.g. in France, interpolation-research was undertaken with more restraint. In Italy, S. Riccobono produced many works which represented a more conservative approach to the question of genuineness. In the years after 1910 there began the tendency to attri-bute to the Byzantines (i.e. to the work of the pre-Justinianic law-schools) the 'falsifications' of the classical fragments which were supposed to exist whenever any serious variations in juristic thought were identified (see for example J. Partsch, 'Studien über die Lehre vom Scheingeschäft und über das Dogma des Synallagma', in *Zeitschrift der Savigny-Stiftung*, 42, 1922, 227 ff.; and *Aus nachgelassenen und kleineren verstreuten Schriften* (1931), 122 ff. and 3 ff.; F. Pringsheim, 'Animus donandi', in *Zeitschrift der Savigny-Stiftung*, 42, 1922, 273 ff.; W. Kunkel, *Zeitschrift der Savigny-Stiftung*, 45, 1925, 347 ff.). Bibliographical references to the more modern research into 'textual layers', which tends to attribute such changes rather to early post-classical jurisprudence, principally in the west, will be found above. A comprehensive discussion on the limits of the critical search for interpolations will be found in M. Kaser's lecture 'Zur Glaubwürdigkeit der römischen Rechtsquellen' (1968, reprinted from *Atti del II. Congresso internazionale della Società Italiana di Storia del Diritto*); his point of view largely corresponds with that of the present author, but not, for example, in his assessment of the eastern law-schools, to which (in the present writer's opinion) he ascribes too much creative activity, while perhaps underestimating the effect of early post-classical scholastic science. In this respect the present writer is closer to the views of F. Wieacker, although the latter treats with much greater sceptical reserve the whole question of how the classical texts were handed down.

Interpolation-research provided itself with a number of important aids. The *Index Interpolationum quae in Justiniani Digestis inesse dicuntur*, started by L. Mitteis and published by E. Levy and E. Rabel (2 vols., 1929–31, and, up to now, one supplementary volume; in course of continuation) provides a survey of all the allegations of interpolation made in countless books and essays in very various contexts; for the Codex, there is G. Broggini, *Index Interpolationum quae in Iustiniani codice inesse dicuntur* (1969; it goes up to the year 1935). The same thing is done for the juristic writings handed down elsewhere by E. Volterra, 'Indice delle glosse, delle interpolazioni e delle principali ricostruzioni segnalate dalla critica nelle fonti pregiustinianee e occidentali' (i–iii, in *Rivista di storia del diritto italiano*, 8, 1935; 9, 1936). All the words and turns of phrase which have been declared unclassical and therefore signs of non-genuineness are collected by A. Guarneri Citati, *Indice delle parole frasi e costrutti ritenuti indizio di interpolazione* (Fondazione Castelli 4, 1927; supplements in *Studi in onore di S. Riccobono*, i, 1934, 701 ff., and *Festschrift P. Koschaker*, i, 1939, 117 ff.). A complete grasp of the language and of the material content of the Roman legal sources is possible with the help of a system of dictionaries and indexes which in principle list every item found in the relevant source-area. The most comprehensive and important of these works is the *Vocabularium Iurisprudentiae Romanae* (*VIR*) which has been appearing since 1894 and is nearly complete; it takes in the Digest and most of the juristic writings handed down independently of Justinian (namely those that are preserved under the names of classical authors). For the *Codex Justinianus* we possess the

Vocabularium Codicis Justiniani of R. von Mayr and M. San Nicolò (2 vols., 1923 and 1925); for the *Codex Theodosianus* the Heidelberg Index by O. Gradenwitz. All literary legal sources not included in these works are considered by E. Levy, *Ergänzungsindex zu ius und leges* (1930). We also possess exhaustive word-indexes for the *Institutes* of Gaius (though these are also dealt with in the *VIR*): Zanzucchi, *Vocabolario delle Istituzioni di Gaio*; and for the sources collected in Bruns, *Fontes* (7th edn.), in a special volume of this work. For extra-legal sources one must (to the extent to which individual indexes, as, for example, of Cicero, are not available) consult the *Thesaurus linguae latinae*, an all-embracing dictionary which rests on a complete card-indexing of the whole of Roman literature up to the fourth century A.D.; about the (first) half of this *Thesaurus* has by now appeared.

While the works so far mentioned exist for the purposes of research, the *Handwörterbuch zu den Quellen des römischen Rechts* by Heumann, 9th edn. by E. Seckel (1907) serves mainly the needs of students; but this dictionary is also of great scientific value. It includes some important results of Seckel's own research. A. Berger's *Encyclopedic Dictionary of Roman Law* (Transactions of the American Philosophical Society, 1953) is an excellent subject-index of Roman law and contains abundant references to literature.

Epilogue: Roman law after Justinian

1. In the east

The best account of the history of Roman law in the Byzantine area is still C. E. Zachariae von Lingenthal, *Geschichte des griechisch-römischen Rechts* (3rd edn., 1892; reprinted 1955). It still serves as the basis for the most recent detailed summary, in L. Wenger's *Die Quellen des römischen Rechts* (1958), 679 ff. Specialized modern literature on Byzantine legal history and editions of Byzantine legal sources, except for the Basilica, cannot be discussed here; and the Basilica must still be used, in part, in the edition of C. G. E. Heimbach, meritorious enough in its time but, as we now know, by no means free from mistakes (6 vols., 1833–70, with scholia and Latin translation of all texts; also supplements by Zachariae von Lingenthal, 1846; Ferrini and Mercati, 1897). Of a new edition by the Dutch Romanists Scheltema and van der Wal, thirteen volumes (text of books i–lii, scholia to books i–xlviii) have appeared (1953–68). As to the controversy on the existence of the Anonymus-chain see on the one side Scheltma, *Tijdschrift voor Rechtsgeschiedenis*, 25 (1957), 286 ff., on the other Pringsheim, *Zeitschrift der Savigny-Stiftung*, 80 (1963), 286 ff. The judgement which the present author gives on the performance of the Byzantine jurists rests on the penetrating analyses of D. Simon, in his *Untersuchungen zum justinianischen Zivil-*

prozeß (1969), in particular pp. 363 ff.; in *Zeitschrift der Savigny-Stiftung*, 86 (1969), 334 ff., and 87 (1970), 315 ff.; and in *Tijdschrift voor Rechtsgeschiedenis* 16 (1969), 283 ff. D. Nörr had already reached a conclusion not a great deal more favourable in his *Studien über die Fahrlässigkeit im byzantinischen Vertragsrecht* (1960, particularly pp. 110 ff.).

11. *In the west*

Only a few important references may be given in addition to the brief remarks in the text. On the whole section, see the broadly planned, vividly written, and richly perceptive book by P. Koschaker, *Europa und das römische Recht* (1947, new edition in 1953) together with the *Privatrechtsgeschichte der Neuzeit* by F. Wieacker (1952), excellent by reason of its comprehensive perspective and ingenious exposition of the contexts of development. In the special sphere of the history of Roman law in the Middle Ages the great work of F. C. Savigny, *Geschichte des römischen Rechts im Mittelalter* (7 vols., 2nd edn., 1850–1) has not yet been completely replaced, though of course it is in large measure obsolete.

The work of international co-operation—*Ius Romanum Medii Aevi*—intended to fill this lacuna, will, it is to be hoped, continue in spite of the death of the scholar supervising it, E. Genzmer; a considerable number of the contributions are already available, including F. Wieacker's 'Allgemeine Zustände und Rechtszustände gegen Ende des weströmischen Reichs' (1963), and H. Coing's 'Römisches Recht in Deutschland' (1964); but the central portion—a study of medieval Italian jurisprudence—is still missing. A further work, intended to embrace the sources and literature of European legal history from the glossators virtually up to the present day is being prepared under the supervision of H. Coing at the Max-Planck-Institut für europäische Rechtsgeschichte; preliminary studies for it in monographic form are appearing in this Institute's own series of publications, *Ius commune* (3 vols. so far); while the series of treatises entitled *Forschungen zur neueren Privatrechtsgeschichte* contains mainly contributions to 'inner' legal history, i.e. to the history of doctrines of private law. A good but very vrief survey is afforded by P. Vinogradoff, *Roman Law in Medieval Europe* (2nd edn., edited by F. de Zulueta, Oxford, 1929).

An excellent introduction to the work and methods of the glossators can be found in E. Genzmer, 'Die justinianische Kodifikation und die Glossatoren' (in *Atti del Congresso internazionale di diritto romano*, Bologna, 1933, i. 347 ff.). The comprehensive book of W. Engelmann, *Die Wiedergeburt der Rechtskultur in Italien durch die wissenschaftliche Lehre* (1938) deals with the post-glossators and their historical achievement; to supplement this one must use E. Genzmer's article in *Zeitschrift der Savigny-Stiftung*, 61, 276 ff., because Engelmann's work, though good, is not free from mistaken judgements. For about the last three generations the Reception of Roman law has repeatedly been the subject of profound investigations, concerned sometimes with the whole of this historical process, sometimes only with special material or geographical parts of it. The best general account is in Wieacker's book mentioned above. An important contribution to the early history of the Reception was made in 1962 by W. Trusen's *Anfänge des gelehrten Rechts in Deutschland*. Humanistic science still awaits its historian; there exist only monographic works of very varying value on individual humanist jurists. An appraisement of humanistic jurisprudence from the point of view of the history of German legal science will be found in R. von Stintzing, *Geschichte der deutschen Rechtswissenschaft*, i (1880). This main work, together with its even more valuable continuation by E. Landsberg, is still indispensable if one wishes to follow in detail the development of Roman legal science in Germany up to the end of the nineteenth century. Among the portraits of German jurists brought out with admirable skill from the background of intellectual history by Erik Wolf, *Große Rechtsdenker* (4th edn., 1963), Roman law science is represented by Zasius, Jhering, and Windscheid. Savigny, Windscheid, and Jhering are excellently assessed as individuals and in their historical significance by F. Wieacker, *Gründer und Bewahrer* (1959), pp. 107 ff. On Theodor Mommsen we possess the outstanding work of A. Heuß, *Theodor Mommsen und das 19. Jahrhundert* (1956); of the great biography of Mommsen by L. Wickert only the first three volumes have so far appeared (1959–69). Numerous individual contributions by legal historians of all European countries on the survival and the historical mission of Roman law are contained, finally, in the *Gedächtnisschrift für Paul Koschaker* (2 vols., 1954) published under the title *L'Europa e il diritto romano*.

INDEX

law schools (classical), 114 f., 147
— (post-classical), 147 f., 152 ff., 163, 171, 174, 179 f., 221, 225
lectio senatus, 19
legal education, 98, 147 f., 152
legati Augusti pro praetore, 56
leges (laws of *comitia*), 30 ff., 125 f., 203
— (imperial laws), 125, 130 f., 154 ff.
leges edictales, 155
leges generales, 155
leges Iuliae iudiciorum publicorum et privatorum, 90, 125, cf. 69, 70
leges Liciniae Sextiae, 17
leges regiae, 25 n., 27 n.
leges repetundarum, 32, 43, 65, 66
leges Valeriae de provocatione, 16 n.
legis actiones, 26, 85 f., 87
legis actio per condictionem, 88
legis actio per iudicis postulationem, 26, 86, 88
legis actio sacramento, 26
λειτουργία, 136, 218
Leo the Wise, 179
lex Acilia repetundarum, 32
    Aebutia, 90
    Aelia Sentia, 60 n.
    agraria (111 B.C.) 32, 46
    Aquilia de damno, 31, 89
    Calpurnia repetundarum, 65 f.
    Canuleia, 6
    Cornelia de edictis, 92
    curiata de imperio, see *lex de imperio*
    Dei, 150
    de imperio, 10 n., 59, 127
    de imperio Vespasiani, 59, 216
    duodecim tabularum, *see* Twelve Tables
    Fufia Caninia, 60 n.
    Hieronica, 42 n.
    Hortensia de plebiscitis, 22 n., 31
    Iulia de adulteriis coercendis, 60 n.
    Iulia de maritandis ordinibus, 60 n.
    Iulia municipalis, 204
    Papia Poppaea, 60 n.
    Poetelia Papiria de nexis, 31
    provinciae, 42, 85
    Romana Burgundionum, 162, 222
    Romana Visigotorum, 162, 181, 222
    Rupilia (in Sicily), 42 n.
    Sempronia iudiciaria, 66
    Tarentina, 204
    Ursonensis, 204
lexicographical aids, 225 f.
libelli, 128

libellus contradictorius, 144
libri feudorum, 186 n.
libri pontificales, 95, cf. 25 n.
lictors, 13
literary tradition, 192 f.
litis contestatio, 87, 144 n.
Livy, 200, 204

Maecianus (Volusius Maecianus), 109, 118 n.
magic, 14, 29, 95
magister equitum, 17
magister officiorum, 141, 165, 166
magistracy, *magistratus*, 14 ff., 49 ff., 138, 202, 207
maiestas populi Romani, 38
maiestas (*populi Romani imminutae*), crime of, 66 n., 71, 149 n.
malum carmen, 29
mandata principis, 128
Manilius (Manius Manilius), 97
manus iniectio, 25 n.
Marcellus (Ulpius Marcellus), 118
martyrs, trials of Christian, 72 n.
'Massentheorie', see Bluhme
membrum ruptum, 28
militiae (in contrast to *domi*), 15
Modestinus (Herennius Modestinus), 109, 122, 157
Mommsen, 191, 193, 196 f., 205, 223, 228
money, coinage, 8, 137
Monumentum Ancyranum, 49 n., 50, 50 n., 206
Monumentum Antiochenum, 50 n., 206
municipia, 37
munus, 136, 152, 218
murder, 27, 67

native law (in contrast to imperial law), 77 ff., 152, 178 f., 209 f.
natural law, 100
negotiorum gestio, 93 n.
Neratius Priscus, 117
Nerva (M. Cocceius Nerva), 115
new citizens, 37, 112 n., cf. 62
nexum, 26, 31
Niebuhr, 119, 200
nobilitas, 21
nominis delatio, 64, 67
notitia dignitarum, 217
Novel-collection (Greek), 176
Novellae Posttheodosianae, 159, 221
Novels of Justinian, 175 f., 223
Numerius Negidius, 88 n.